FREE YOUR MIND

FREE YOUR MIND

THE NEW WORLD OF MANIPULATION AND HOW TO RESIST IT

LAURA DODSWORTH
& PATRICK FAGAN

HarperCollins*Publishers*

HarperCollins*Publishers*
1 London Bridge Street
London SE1 9GF

www.harpercollins.co.uk

HarperCollins*Publishers*
Macken House, 39/40 Mayor Street Upper
Dublin 1, D01 C9W8, Ireland

First published by HarperCollins*Publishers* 2023
This edition published 2024

1 3 5 7 9 10 8 6 4 2

A catalogue record of this book is available from the British Library

ISBN 978-0-00-860085-3

Printed and bound in the UK using 100% renewable electricity at CPI Group (UK) Ltd

To

Cole
Ethan
Sonny

who inspire our greatest hopes for free minds.

Contents

Introduction

You're manipulated a dozen times before you even put your shoes on. Your phone, your cereal box, your lover, all conspiring to prod, nudge and shove you into compliance.

Persuasion and propaganda are as old as democracy. They are the arts mastered by poets, politicians and priests alike. Aristotle set out the timeless techniques of the persuader – ethos, logos and pathos – in his book *Rhetoric*. Over two thousand years ago, he said you must consider who your audience is, know what to say, be trustworthy – or at least appear to be – and appeal to emotion as well as reason.

Of course, persuasion and propaganda are no doubt older than democracy because they are integral to being human.

We are always trying to persuade one other. To live with each other is to influence each other, from wishing your neighbour a nice day to educating children, from writing a business proposal to punishing criminals. The delusion we need to dispel is that there is such a thing as non-manipulative influence.

We are all mini-propagandists. We craft and publicise edited versions of ourselves online to influence how people see us and treat us. Photographs are edited and flattering filters applied. We make memes to engage or persuade our followers. Modern technology encourages artful choreography above truth.

We need to come clean with you: we want to influence you. We don't want our book to lie forgotten in a dusty corner of a bookshop. Who would write a book without sincerely hoping to influence many readers? The distinction is in the intent: we wish to influence you to resist influence.

Why should you want to resist influence? First, let's be clear, not all influence is problematic. You can't learn to read without influence. Some public health messaging may be good for you. When you curl up with a good book you will inevitably be influenced by it. If a friend tells you to have a nice day, and you walk away with a little spring in your step and actually have a nice day, we don't begrudge it. Please *do* have a nice day. Most marketing and advertising is fairly harmless; there's not much wrong with brand A nudging you into buying it over brand B.

This book, however, argues that we live in an information battlefield. The use of martial language is a technique designed to influence, frighten and encourage compliance, but we don't use the term 'battlefield' lightly. You are being manipulated, constantly. You might think you can resist it. You probably can't. We thought we could too, and we found otherwise while researching this book.

Everywhere you turn, brands, politicians and special interest groups are reaching into your skull and poking around in your brain. They want you to think Coca-Cola will make you happy, that a politician will keep you safe, that a tax will save the planet. Without even leaving the house in the morning, you are nudged by the food packaging in your kitchen, by the news, ads and shows on TV, and by the incessant dings and whirrs of your smartphone. Choice is frightening, and governments and corporations are only too happy to take that fear away from us – for a price.

Empowered by advances in behavioural science, data science and consumer technology, the manipulators know how you think (yes you, personally) and what buttons to push to get you to do what they want, and they have the opportunity to push those buttons 24 hours a day.

Free Your Mind will equip you to recognise, ignore and dispel the myriad efforts to manipulate you. There are many thousands of books that teach the dark arts of the persuader, the propagandist and the pick-up artist. This is the first defence against the dark arts. It is your field manual for surviving the information battlefield.

We all want to be individuals. Making the right choices for *you* – sifting through the news and the fake news, discerning which products to buy, deciding which political party to vote for – all involve knowing your own mind. Knowing your mind is only possible if you retain a level of control over what influences your mind.

Sometimes you may want to let it all wash over you, because it is relaxing, entertaining and easier.

Like that soap opera you've been watching for years. But are you aware that soap operas are used for social engineering purposes? In recent times, script writers have been invited to attend workshops on how to drive up vaccination levels. Or the waft of incense that is burned in church on Sunday. It is not just to smell nice, but also because the fuzzy plumes help your eyes lose focus, just a little, so that you more easily imagine your prayers rising upwards in a contemplative and worshipful frame of mind. Or letting the cereal box with the cutest face on the front catch your child's attention, to shape the decision about which identikit sugary fix is best.

More likely, you want to be able to identify these influences. You may yet want to dispel them.

The essence of the question is the privacy of your mind. When an influencer tries to penetrate and change your mind, by extension they are disrespecting your individual sovereignty. We believe in your right to privacy. It is your mind, and you should control the electronic gates and the passwords to enter.

'The very presumptuousness of molding or affecting the human mind through the techniques we use has created a deep sense of uneasiness in our minds,' warned Howard Chase, president of the Public Relations Society of America, in 1956.[1] Our own uneasiness with the moulding of the human mind caused us to collaborate on *Free Your Mind*.

Patrick is a behavioural scientist with 12 years' experience of emotion sciences and data analytics from inside the industry. You might say he comes from the dark side. He was the lead psychologist at Cambridge Analytica, where he specialised in designing targeted ads to nudge people into doing all sorts of things ranging from buying crypto to voting for politicians.

Covid was Laura's epiphany. She immersed herself in trying to understand the mass evocation of emotion and the government use of behaviour control. SPI-B advisors broke cover when they confessed to Laura that the use of fear was totalitarian, and described psychology as a weapon for her book, *A State of Fear: How the UK Government Weaponised Fear During the Covid-19 Pandemic*.

We have observed the ongoing, large-scale, top-down attempts to nudge people. In the classic book *Propaganda*, Edward Bernays explained:

> The conscious and intelligent manipulation of the organized habits and opinions of the masses is an important element in democratic society. Those who manipulate this unseen mechanism of society constitute an invisible government which is the true ruling power of our country. We are governed, our minds are molded, our tastes formed, and our ideas suggested, largely by men we have never heard of ... It is they who pull the wires that control the public mind.[2]

This invisible government exists to this day, continuing to pull the wires of our minds. Whoever the opinion-makers are, they are relentlessly pushing social engineering agendas from the top down.

There is a gap between what is on our minds, and what we are told should be on our minds. A September 2022 Rasmussen Reports survey found that the top five issues reported by the US media were climate change, the war in Ukraine, the Capitol Riot investigation, Covid-19, and LGBTQ issues.[3] Among American voters, none of these issues made their top ten – they were more concerned about things like crime, gas prices and inflation. It seems there is an agenda, and you will be cajoled, manipulated and nudged until you agree with it.

For instance, there appears to be a determined campaign to switch the human diet to insects.[4] People really don't want to eat insects – there is no clamour: please, please, let us eat insects! – and yet a panoply of persuasive tools, including nudge, propaganda, data insights and public relations, has been deployed. Net Zero is another example of a policy that is accompanied by a widespread and targeted behavioural science campaign.[5] The high-profile and tragic war in Ukraine offers a contemporary insight into propaganda, although this time it comes with a few plot twists: this war is partly fought on social media, your mind is also the battlefield and there is a new degree of transparency about the use of myth.

Sometimes, you may agree with the goals of the influencers. But do you like the means? We at least want you to recognise them. And of course, we are all subject not only to our own government's efforts, but to those of foreign governments. Deliberate disinformation is part of the backdrop to the raft of digital safety laws that are being processed on similar timelines around the world. New technology offers a crucial pivot in how we communicate with each other, and how companies and governments and bad actors communicate with us. It offers unprecedented ways to brainwash us in covert and personalised ways.

We want to show you what is up the magician's sleeve, under his hat and behind his back.

We are not the only ones who care. There is an emerging legion of fact-checkers and disinformation specialists poised to rebut the wrong kind of information, fake news or enemy propaganda. But who is fact-checking the fact-checkers? While experts are important and have their place, we believe that the best person to check your facts, and know your own mind, is you.

Each chapter presents you with a basic principle, expands the idea with interviews, research, cultural references and our own theories, and then concludes with a practical set of rules. Some of our principles may seem extreme to begin with. Take the recommendation to 'turn off your TV'. It might not be necessary to go that far. You will see that where we impose hard demands, there is a middle path too. You can choose to watch less TV and watch it mindfully. The point is to understand how TV exerts influence, from which defence naturally flows.

To prepare for writing this book we interviewed a broad range of experts, from veterans trained in interrogation techniques to magicians, from political scientists to priests. We undertook immersive experiences and tried to be brainwashed. We tried to join secret societies and undertook controversial and intense training courses. Laura went on a short retreat and digital detox in a convent, waded through dating expert videos and experimented with running different accounts on social media. Patrick got naked at a masculinity retreat in the woods, joined a pyramid selling scheme and signed up to transgender forums. These experiences fed into the general body of the book but a few are included as stand-alone case studies, told from our individual perspectives.

We found we were not paragons of unbiased virtue. During immersion in courses we were bedazzled. And we recalled past experiences of being successfully manipulated. It *can* happen to anyone. Yet we have also become much more alert to persuasive attempts and believe we are resilient.

We have contextualised our learnings and principles with the latest theories and research in behavioural insights and psychology. When drawing upon other writers we relied most heavily upon the great body of work that emerged from thinkers and psychologists after the World Wars. Emerging from cataclysmic world events, their writings resounded with gnawing horrors, fragile hope and enduring insights, and so we return to them and reference them throughout, including Carl Jung, Erich Fromm, Aldous Huxley, George Orwell and Hannah Arendt. We also drew on the pioneering thinkers in propaganda and psychological warfare of the last century such as Edward Bernays, 'the father of public relations', and Edward Hunter, who coined the term 'brainwashing'.

Aside from their universal themes, the other reason we return to writers of the last century is that, in this century, we have found ourselves troubled by the deliberate persuasion of the masses, eerily evocative of the past.

The Covid crisis made it painfully clear just how easy it is for people to have their behaviour changed; it illustrated how readily mass movements can take hold and how quickly they can turn dark. In just one example, in the UK, people would wear a face mask to enter a restaurant, walk to the table or head to the toilet, but took it off once they had sat down in the same building. Elsewhere, people wore face masks with holes in to play wind instruments in orchestras; people were banned from seeing dying relatives or going to funerals; parents were denied the care they needed for disabled children; many were isolated and left depressed and suicidal. Now that the dust has settled, most of us can agree that this was not rational behaviour. While natural fear of infection and death provides part of the explanation, a deliberate attempt to persuade the mass of people by leveraging cognitive biases provides the rest.

Anyone is vulnerable to nudging and manipulation. It is not possible to pay attention to everything, to be on your guard all of the time. While you look at one part of the magician's stage, the trick happens elsewhere.

Taken to the extremes, it was the ordinary people of Germany and beyond who inflicted the horrors of the Holocaust.[6] There was nothing particularly special about their character; it happened to them and it could happen to you. As Alexander Solzhenitsyn wrote, the line separating good and evil does not pass through countries or tribes, but 'right through every human heart'.[7]

If you think you're too smart to be brainwashed, if you think you are too savvy to be tricked, you are the most vulnerable of all. To be protected against brainwashing, you must have the humility to know you can be brainwashed. As Carl Jung said, 'Nobody is immune to a nationwide evil unless he is unshakably convinced of the danger of his own character being tainted by the same evil.'[8]

The possibilities of using the insights of psychology, psychiatry and the social sciences to influence our choices and our behaviour are so inviting that it is hopelessly naive to believe we are not constantly being worked on by manipulators. Psychology is no longer just about diagnosing or fixing us, it is now about socially engineering and shaping us. If you don't control your mind, someone else will.

We want you to be able to protect yourself and learn how to free your mind.

1

Realise your brain is a battleground

The world is a battlefield of information. There are many sides, all competing to take control of the disputed territory that is your mind. Amid the many short-term skirmishes, there are forces executing long-range strategic plans to change your mind and behaviour. The first step in protecting yourself is to be aware of the forces conspiring against you, grit your teeth and resolutely prepare for battle. You are a soldier now.

Enhanced interrogation techniques

> When you are being interrogated you think about what is going to happen next. But the interrogator is thinking ahead of you. I know interrogators, I know the way they think. They are evil bastards. They are all about the end game, and the chess moves to get there. They know the moves. I became detached from the interrogation. It became a competition. I focused on how to get ahead of them.

When James was a soldier, he took a five-day course on how to survive interrogation – the most brutal form of brainwashing. It sounds extreme, but the same techniques are used on a smaller scale by the advertisers, politicians and salesmen we encounter every day. If you can understand how to survive interrogation, then you can understand how to resist the most persuasive attempts to influence your thinking. You will be able to free your mind.

James was trained to experience and thereby withstand the techniques an enemy might use to break him down and extract vital information. The crucial first stage – since this was a training operation, and not the real thing – was consent. He agreed to the rigorous and unpleasant experience ahead because he wanted to be better equipped if he was ever captured. He chose to be interrogated.

The next part was his deliberate debilitation. The recruits were sent out on a faux mission and chased across the hills by the 'enemy'. They were given no opportunity to sleep and nothing to eat. How did James cope with being tired and hungry?

'Brute stubbornness. I didn't want to be beaten. I'm not athletic, I'm just mentally competitive. If someone says you are going to be tired and hungry and beat me down in interrogation, I decide I won't be.'

This was just the warm-up act. After three days, the trainers captured the soldiers and brought them in for the 'big guns'. Day and night they were deprived of sleep and had to wear hoods so that they could not see. They were made to adopt stress positions for hours on end. They had to ask permission to go to the toilet, and remained hooded even while relieving themselves. When James dropped his trousers he had no idea where he was or if anyone could see, he could just feel the wind whistling around his legs. It was perturbing, but he managed, while others had 'stage fright' and couldn't go. One time, James found himself naked, with a trainer spitting in his face and verbally humiliating him.

In a diluted form, James was undergoing a process known as 'interrogation in depth', which consists of 'the five techniques': wall standing, hooding, white noise, sleep deprivation, and a reduced and basic diet.[1] These techniques are sadly familiar to prisoners across continents and ages. They have been deployed by the officers and guards in the forced labour camps of the Soviet Union, as recounted in *The Gulag Archipelago* by Alexander Solzhenitsyn,[2] and by British military intelligence officers in the period after the Second World War as part of their counter-insurgency tactics.[3] As we will see throughout this book, confusion, distraction and exhaustion are techniques used even by the fairly harmless manipulators in our lives.

The CIA used 'enhanced interrogation techniques' on terror suspects in the aftermath of 9/11.[4] The five techniques have been brought to vivid, sickening life by the first detainee to suffer them, Abu Zubaydah. He was captured in 2002 and held in secret prisons ('black sites') for years, where he was tortured by the CIA. He is still detained in Guantanamo Bay. In testimony to the ICRC (the International Committee of the Red Cross), he said, 'I was told during this period that I was one of the first to receive these interrogation techniques, so no rules applied. It felt like they were experimenting and trying out techniques to be used later on other people.'[5] Unlike James, there was no consent; this was no training drill.

To begin with, he was subjected to several techniques that were designed to create a sense of helplessness and therefore compliance with the ensuing interrogation. He was kept naked for the first six to eight weeks. Initially, he was kept shackled to a bed and only released to use the toilet. He was not given solid food, only a liquid nutritional drink. These tactics would have combined to infantilise, disorientate and destabilise him before the interrogation began in earnest. A US Senate report found that Zubaydah's interrogations included 83 instances of waterboarding, as well as sleep deprivation and 11 days' confinement in a coffin-like box. He also lost his left eye while in custody.

Zubaydah described the CIA's version of wall standing and stress positions to his lawyers:

> They unchained my hands from the bars and chained them with short chains to the chains that were around my legs, which kept me in a bowing position at all times ... They brutally dragged me to the cement wall ... He started brutally banging my head and my back against the wall. I felt my back was breaking due to the intensity of the banging. He started slapping my face again and again, meanwhile he was yelling. He then pointed to a large black wooden box that looked like a wooden casket. He said: 'From now on this is going to be your home ...' He violently closed the door. I heard the sound of the lock. I found myself in total darkness.

The full details of Zubaydah's torture have not been released in the interests of state security and he is not permitted to speak publicly or to the media, so we don't know how he may have tried to remain mentally resilient and survive these experiences. He did not reveal the information he was tortured for, because he did not have it. But governments continue to employ these brutal techniques in the belief that they will work.

Interrogation, sensory deprivation and brainwashing have been the study of British, American and Canadian governments, and were made famous through the exposé of the notorious MK-Ultra programme and in the book *In Search of the Manchurian Candidate* by John Marks, which exposed CIA-funded mind-control programmes.

British psychiatrist Donald Ewen Cameron was funded by the CIA in his work in Canada to correct mental disorders by erasing memories and programming the psyche – i.e., brainwashing.[6] His patients did not know they were participating in highly experimental programmes, such as being put in drug-induced comas for weeks at a time and listening to repetitive tapes with both positive and negative messaging on loop even while sleeping. Some suffered terrible consequences such as amnesia and urinary incontinence. As recently as the 1980s, his former patients sued the CIA for damages. It's fascinating to note that the Unabomber, Ted Kaczynski, was subject to 200 hours of psychological abuse as part of a Harvard study that some have suggested was part of MK-Ultra research.[7]

A strange cultural amnesia – no doubt encouraged by states – treats these incidents of psychological torture as isolated incidents, but they are not, and they are repeated more than you know or would like.

The information battlefield

Mercifully, life is not an interrogation. You are not being brainwashed in a laboratory or mental asylum. You probably go about your life in a normal fashion and you are not interned in a camp wearing an orange boiler suit. You will almost certainly never be captured by the enemy. So, how does this relate to you?

Although you are not being brainwashed in a lab nor dodging a rain of bullets, you do navigate a storm of advertising, nudges, biased news articles and propaganda. You are not standing in a stress position against a wall, but you are bent under a blitzkrieg of information. Life is a battle for the mind – your mind. Donald Ewen Cameron was inspired by fellow British psychiatrist William Sargant, who wrote a book on it, *Battle for the Mind: A Physiology of Conversion and Brain-Washing – How Evangelists, Psychiatrists, Politicians, and Medicine Men Can Change Your Beliefs and Behaviour*.[8] As you can detect from the title, Sargant identified several categories of people trying to command minds. There are battalions of experts who research, strategise and implement plans to capture your attention, wash your brain and nudge you in different directions. They work in PR and ad agencies, in governments, the media, big data and Big Tech firms. They are trying to sell you products and services, to change how you vote and to change your conduct as a citizen.

A cybersecurity expert recounted a story that highlights just how much we are bombarded with persuasion tactics. He received a dodgy letter in the post claiming to be from the bank. The letter was asking for sensitive information to protect against fraud, and the letter was full of nudges to get it – 'URGENT', 'act today', 'join many others like you', and so on. The expert took the letter into the bank to let them know a scam was afoot.

'Oh no,' they told him, 'that was from us.'

The use of manipulation tactics is so widespread that it's hard to tell who's who. The good guys are using nudges to stop you from falling for the bad guys' nudges. Besides, it's not just advertising or political propaganda where you need to be on the lookout for these kinds of techniques. At the other end of the scale, we experience manipulation even from those who love and know us best. Evolutionary psychologist David Buss found 12 tactics used to influence and manipulate a romantic partner to do something. Different personalities are more susceptible to different tactics, but this handful might be familiar to most people: charm and compliments; reasoning to explain why you want your partner to do it; the silent treatment; pleasure induction, to show them how much fun it is; tell them that everyone is doing it in a form of 'social comparison'; hardball, threaten or use violence; or simply lie.[9]

There is no accurate running total of the number of information bullets you dodge every day. But in 2006, Jay Walker-Smith, president of the marketing firm Yankelovich, claimed that the average American was exposed to five thousand advertising messages per day, ten times as many as in the 1970s.[10] According to Red Crow Marketing Inc., the current figure is somewhere in the range of four to ten thousand.[11] Although these figures have been hotly contested and it's hard to quantify something like this, researchers tend to agree on one thing: it's a lot.[12]

Television, radio, billboards, shop windows, cinemas, direct mail, newspapers, magazines, social media, bus stops, video games, text messages, social media ... There have never been so many opportunities to deliver persuasive messages.

And the pace of the information age is accelerating. According to a study by Dr Martin Hilbert at the University of Southern California, in 2007, Americans consumed information for almost 12 hours per day, corresponding to 100,500 words, or 23 words per second in half a day, and 34 gigabytes.[13] Using the analogy of an 85-page newspaper, a study found that in 1986 we received around 40 newspapers full of information every day, but this had rocketed to 174 in 2007.[14] Is this an information-overload bomb for the human brain?

Human beings – all of us – are what's known as 'cognitive misers'.[15] We have very limited brainpower for paying attention to the world. For example, in *Strangers to Ourselves*, Timothy Wilson estimated that, every second, the brain processes 11 million 'bits' of sensory information (sounds, smells, sights, etc.), with only 40 of these passing through conscious pathways in the brain.[16] By this estimate, only 0.0004 per cent of sensory processing is conscious. You simply can't consciously process all of the information in the world around you. This is why one study found that half of participants walking through a park failed to notice a clown on a unicycle; the figure was even less if they had been talking on the phone during their walk.[17]

Being cognitive misers also makes us vulnerable to manipulation. We don't have the brainpower to think through every decision carefully, so we rely on subconscious rules of thumb that let us make decisions on autopilot. This means that information presented to us in a certain way can often bias – or nudge – our behaviours mindlessly. Take, for example, the Werther effect: a well-publicised suicide can increase the suicide rate.[18] In some cases, all it took was a simple nudge in the media to push people into the most consequential decision of their lives. Perhaps for the same reason, Corona beer's sales increased by 40 per cent in 2020.[19] On the persuasion battlefield, sometimes all it takes is one small whizzing 'bullet', one nudge, to get the better of you.

There is a battle for human attention. More than that, your opponents want to persuade you. They include the all-too-obvious advertisers and marketers, but also big data and predictive analytics, PR and lobbying. Some of the forces of the information battlefield are governments and their agencies. Are they friend or foe? It is not always easy to tell. You would hope your own government is an ally, but would the mental patients 'treated' in the MK-Ultra programme say so? Sometimes the government might be an enemy. In the modern age of behavioural science, it is certainly seeking to 'nudge' you into being a good citizen using subliminal techniques. And governments also command bot and troll armies on social media in addition to the older propaganda techniques. It's open season on delving into and rewiring our brains. World Economic Forum advisor and author Noah Harari thinks that, 'We humans should get used to the idea that we are no longer mysterious souls. We are now hackable animals.'[20]

The military is the classic example of treating humans as hackable. The soldier James told us, 'Everything in the military is about changing how people think. That is what they do. Hearts and minds.'

Content and information are abundant, but your attention is a scarce resource, and advertisers can only capture so much of it. You can only notice so many ads per day – for example, Media Dynamics reported that people are exposed to 362 ads a day via the media but only 153 (24 per cent) were attended to for a few seconds or more,[21] while marketing guru Byron Sharp found that brands are explicitly recalled from watched ads only 16 per cent of the time.[22] With all this noise and our limited abilities to process it, you will appreciate how hard advertisers are working to gain your attention. They mean business.

It isn't possible to estimate how much money governments spend on political communications around the world, when you consider some of the units and departments engaged in that work are secret and not obliged to publicly disclose it. If one considers political communication in its broadest sense, including central and local government, state-run media, military and police forces, then it is not unreasonable to suggest that spending amounts to trillions of dollars globally each year. For example, in 2020, acknowledged UK government advertising alone surpassed £160 million, making the government the biggest advertiser that year (albeit due to special circumstances prompted by the pandemic).[23]

To put all this in the language of war might seem extreme – but it is how our leaders are thinking about us. King Charles has called for 'a vast military-style campaign' to influence behaviours around climate change.[24]

With these military campaigns comes psychological manipulation. 'War is deception,' so the Islamic proverb goes. Sometimes it is an illusion – so much so that some Japanese soldiers famously hid in the jungle for decades after the Second World War had ended, believing the war was still being waged.[25] How much of your own conception of current affairs, of the world, is the result of illusions from the screen?

En masse, we are exposed to an unprecedented volume of information. No human beings in the history of the world have faced this. The volume is one matter, but the intent is another. Make no mistake, like the interrogators James faced, your opponents are playing a game of chess with you, and sometimes it is a long game. The ad men, the behavioural scientists, the social media troll farms, the government propagandists, they are not playing for fun – there is a strategy. They want to capture your attention and influence your behaviour. Right now, they are one step ahead of you.

Brainwashing, or coercive persuasion, is a slow, repeated, covert process of undue influence. The first step in surviving, and keeping your mind free, is to recognise there is a process, even though it is not the singular strategy of a singular enemy.

Fighting back

How did James survive interrogation? First of all, it was a training programme, survival was guaranteed, so he had an intrinsic advantage. But he still needed resilience. He realised early on that his 'captors' were one step ahead of him. It was a game, and the uncomfortable, humiliating and mind-bending moves were as orchestrated as a series of chess moves. He decided to steel his brain, even to adopt an arrogant attitude. He simply decided he could do it and he would beat them if he put his mind to it. Indeed, there is a lot of research on the power of the conscious mind and positive thinking, and that psychological concepts like self-esteem, self-regard and self-affirmation can improve productivity, performance and life outcomes.[26] As the saying goes, whether you think you can or you can't, you're right.

James knew there were only so many types of interrogation that would be applied to him. He was in a fortunate position. In a real capture scenario, endless, cruel permutations would be possible. During the two days of interrogation, he observed what they were doing and counted down the tactics, one by one. He was 50 per cent of the way there. Then 75 per cent of the way there. Then he was nearly done.

To survive the daily barrage of real-life brainwashing you do not need to be prepared for endless cruelties, but you do need to prepare. You need to understand your psychological weaknesses, and how people seek to exploit them. As the famous Chinese military strategist Sun Tzu said, 'If you know the enemy and know yourself, you need not fear the result of a hundred battles.'[27]

The key to resisting is what's known as psychological resilience. As we've seen in this chapter – and as you'll see throughout this book – you can build resilience by shoring up your defences and knowing what you're up against. One study, for example, found that people who had experienced traumatic life events were less likely to have their memories manipulated by misinformation or leading questions.[28] Other research has found that persuasion is resisted via tactics like attitude-bolstering, counter-arguing, and asserting confidence that nothing could change one's mind.[29] Meanwhile, openness to experience has been identified as a trait linked to suggestibility:[30] to avoid being persuaded, it is better to put up the defences and not be so open-minded that your brain falls out, as G. K. Chesterton put it. Those who can resist persuasion also tend to feel that they are in control of their own lives.[31] If you are to free your mind, you must first take responsibility for yourself.

As for James, he remained mentally resilient by counting the seconds while enduring a new stress position or episode of interrogation. He occupied his brain. As he said,

> You have to think about something and keep track of time. If you lose track of time you have lost control of everything. That's why they put you in solitary confinement and turn lights on and off and give people meals at weird times. It is all about information and control.

Martin, another soldier, underwent the same training. He went further and took special forces training, and became a trainer in interrogation techniques. He learnt to build up an 'intolerance to pain, and basically torture'.

Like James, Martin busied his brain to remain resilient:

> Interrogation training is an experience. It's not one for the faint-hearted. When you are interrogated and thrown back in your cell you can't dwell on what's happened to you. It would drive you nuts. You have to build defences in your mind. In my mind I would imagine building a car. The other one I would do is build a house. You have to think about the logistics and do it brick by brick. If a

> civilian gets themselves into trouble, they panic. In the military, we don't. We look at the situation. We stay calm, we assess, we have a mental checklist.

A 2009 paper by researchers at the Aberdeen Centre for Trauma Research concurred, concluding that methods for surviving and coping with extended capture included distraction (for example, reading and fantasising), discipline (such as exercise and personal hygiene) and looking for a positive spin on the situation.[32] Terry Waite, for instance, prepared his autobiography in his mind, while a study on victims of a hijacked plane reported they viewed the experience as an exciting adventure. Ultimately, it's all about taking control of what you can – your own thoughts, emotions and perception of the situation. In the words of Holocaust survivor Viktor E. Frankl, 'Everything can be taken from a man but one thing: the last of the human freedoms – to choose one's attitude in any given set of circumstances, to choose one's own way.'[33]

The idea of battling through information warfare on a daily basis might seem exhausting. You can't spend the entirety of your days imagining building a car, or writing your autobiography, in order to deflect billboards and salesmen. To go through life paranoid that each interaction with the media is an attempt to unduly influence us, or that everyone we encounter seeks to harm us, would rob us of worthwhile experiences.

Perhaps it would be easier to let it just roll over you. Just allow each of those 174 metaphorical newspapers to give you a gentle rap on the skull every eight minutes. After all, some of the information is valuable. Some of it is true. Some of it is entertaining. You might learn something new. It's not all bad. But how do you tell?

Only you can decide what is valuable, and what is not. This book is not in the business of brainwashing, censoring or suggesting, but rather of equipping you to apply your own discretion.

You need to be one step ahead, and this book is your field manual. The first step is to recognise that you are a soldier, and you must prepare for battle. You can get out of this one with your mind intact and under your own control. You might come home with honours. You might even have fun.

Let the training commence.

The rules:

- Acknowledge that all forms of communication are designed to persuade you in some way.
- Make an effort to note persuasion attempts throughout the day, and the techniques that are being used to do so – and make the deliberate choice to defeat them.
- Most importantly, read every page of this book – your field manual for surviving the information battlefield.

2

Stand your ground

The road to brainwashing is a slippery slope that starts with but a single nudge. To keep your psychological integrity, you mustn't cede any ground to the brainwashers. Give them an inch, and they'll take a mile. Even interacting with them in the first place allows them to set the rules of engagement and puts you on the back foot. The best thing is not to engage – not even to argue with them – but to instead totally switch off.

The slippery slope

Wild hogs are one of the most destructive invasive species in the United States. They decimate crops and wolf down newborn lambs, they strip fields of grass and tear up the earth, and they even terrorise tourists. The country is besieged, wrote *Smithsonian Magazine*, by a 'plague of pigs' who 'evade the best efforts to trap or kill them'.[1]

The problem is, pigs are rather intelligent – more intelligent than dogs, so they say[2] – and yet their greatest talent, according to the California Potbellied Pig Association, is for stubbornness.[3] This downright pig-headedness can be annoying for those finding their farms decimated by wild hogs.

So, what's the solution to these pesky pigs?

Fortunately for the farmers (not so much for the pigs), a company called Jager Pro Hog Control Systems ('Army trained. Combat tested. Farmer approved') has developed a systematic solution for capturing entire drifts of wild hogs, which it calls the Capture Success Matrix®.[4] There are three steps: first, condition the pigs to trust the bait site; then condition them to trust the corral enclosure; and finally flip the switch to trap them in.

One of the company's YouTube videos tells of a herd of wild hogs that had destroyed an acre of peanuts.[5] While this was costly for the farmer, it was also costly for the pigs, for it had revealed their single greatest weakness: a taste for peanuts. Armed with this knowledge, Jager Pro strategically scattered peanuts across a field. There was no attempt to trap the hogs yet – the goal was to lull them into a false sense of security.

An enclosure was built in the same field. Half of the peanuts were baited in front of its entrance, and half inside. Initially, the pigs were wary and wouldn't enter the enclosure; it took them some time to feel comfortable. However, eating the peanuts outside the corral's entrance made them trust it. The first to snuffle their way in were the foolhardy younger pigs, and where the kids went the adults would follow. Over the next few days, the pigs learnt that nothing bad would happen to them inside the corral, and they began to feel safe there.

Whereas the peanuts were once baited both inside and outside the enclosure, now the hogs would have to shuffle their trotters all the way inside to find them. By day four, they showed little hesitation jogging into the corral to gobble up the peanuts.

Little did they know they were being watched on camera by the farmers, who manually triggered the gate closed with a snap. The hogs, in a panic, charged at all sides of the enclosure, looking for an escape – but it was too late.

Little by little, the patient farmers were able to lure even the most pig-headed of pigs. What chance would a human have?

The principle here is an old one. In the 1940s, the Stalinist dictator of Hungary, Mátyás Rákosi, coined the term 'salami slicing' to describe his step-by-step approach to dismantling the political opposition.[6] Even if you cut very thin slices off a salami, eventually you'll have eaten it all. The technique is reminiscent of the ancient Chinese torture of death by a thousand cuts.

When it comes to brainwashing, think of it like boiling a frog. If you try to drop a frog into a boiling vat of water, so the analogy goes, it will jump out. However, if you put it in a cold pot of water and slowly turn up the heat, you'll be able to cook it without resistance.

Consider how the biggest social changes rarely, if ever, occur overnight. They are the culmination of many small increments.

For example, income tax was first introduced as a temporary emergency measure in 1799 to finance Britain's role in the Napoleonic War.[7] It was just 10 per cent at that time. The unpopular tax was repealed and reintroduced several times over the following century, and it wasn't until 1909 that Lloyd George officially made it permanent. Today, British income tax rates sit at 20 per cent, 40 per cent, and 45 per cent, among a deluge of corporation tax, value added tax, road tax, council tax, inheritance tax, fuel duty, import duty, stamp duty and so on.

A paper in the *Journal of Applied Psychology* was based on four experiments to support what it referred to as the 'slippery slope'.[8] The researchers referred to corporate scandals such as Enron (which 'grew out of a steady accumulation of habits and values and actions that began years before and finally spiraled out of control'), much like Bernie Madoff's Ponzi scheme, rogue trading at UBS and the *News of the World* phone-hacking scandal. The paper cited past studies that demonstrated that people are more accepting of moral discretions when they are small – for example, they were more likely to cheat on a task to win ten cents per problem solved than they were for five dollars per problem solved, and stealing pens from work was deemed more acceptable than stealing money from the cash drawer. Importantly, the researchers themselves showed that smaller transgressions lead to larger ones.

A clear example from modern history of this gradation effect is the government's responses to Covid-19. In the UK, the lockdowns were sold as temporary measures. You must stay indoors and close your businesses for three weeks to stop the spread, said Prime Minister Boris Johnson in March 2020.[9] Yet they persisted in one form or another for two years. Throughout the pandemic, the British government appeared to follow a three-step process to soften people up for the measures they inevitably introduced. This dance comprised deny, debate, demand. First, the government would deny they were introducing a measure (often as a result of plans being leaked). This denial would sow the seed of possibility purely through mention of it (even in the negative) and make a policy palatable; although it wouldn't be popular, it would go from the realm of unthinkable to thinkable, while at the same time putting people's fears at bay through the denial. Psychological research shows people are more amenable to something if they have merely been exposed to it. From this first denial, the government would then debate the policy in order to reduce resistance: the effect is to take the idea from thinkable but unacceptable to thinkable and acceptable. By the time the government demands the policy, the public has been softened up enough that they are ready to accept it with little protest.

In January 2021, then Secretary of State for Health and Social Care Nadhim Zahawi tweeted that the government had 'no plans to introduce vaccine passports' – in fact, the government denied plans to introduce them at least eleven separate times.[10] In April 2021, gears had shifted to debate: Zahawi said it would be 'completely remiss and irresponsible' not to consider trialling vaccine passports as a way of re-opening the country.[11] The demand came by December, when Covid passes became mandatory for nightclubs and other large venues.[12]

While vaccine passports have since been ditched in the UK, it is important to remember the gradual nature of these social changes. It is two steps forward, one step back. Income tax was repealed and reintroduced several times before it became permanent. The foundations for mandatory digital ID have now been laid, and the public has been conditioned to accept it.

It isn't possible to prove this process was deliberate, but there was a consistent pattern of this form of psychological softening up. An alternative explanation – although by no means kinder, since it indicates a level of incompetence – is that the government flip-flopped uncertainly throughout the pandemic response.

What vaccine passports have done is put a 'foot-in-the-door' for mandatory digital ID. This is a well-established principle of persuasion. One study, for example, found that people were at least 25 per cent more likely to agree to put a large safe-driving sign in their front garden if they had agreed to a smaller request beforehand, such as signing a petition or accepting a bumper sticker.[13] If you want people to do something, it's better to make a smaller, more reasonable request of them first; once committed, they'll follow through on the larger ask later. This is perhaps why, for example, car dealerships encourage prospective customers to take a test drive, which is much less intimidating than buying a car but which nudges them along the journey to do so.

The influential behavioural insights expert and Chief Executive of the Nudge Unit David Halpern calls this 'radical incrementalism'.[14] It is the very essence of nudging: tiny changes can have an enormous cumulative impact. A thousand nudges make a shove. The Nudge Unit is the colloquial name for an organisation called the Behavioural Insights Team, which was set up with the UK government's Cabinet Office and is still 'at the heart of the UK government', according to the unit's own website, reflecting how much techniques such as radical incrementalism have become standard government tactics, unbeknownst to most people.[15]

Psychologists have even developed scripts using something called 'the mere agreement effect'.[16] If you can get people to say yes to two questions, they are more likely to then say yes to your target question. For example, 'Do you want the best for your family? Are you concerned about what might happen in the future? Do you want to buy our insurance?'

You may have experienced this foot-in-the-door technique from 'chuggers' (charity muggers) on the street. With a disarming smile and official-looking vest, they try to stop you with a compliment or a question about your day. While this seems harmless, once you've taken that first step into the engagement you are more likely to sign that direct debit to the Donkey Sanctuary.

Expert salesman Mike Herberts explains it like this:

> A large part of success in selling is to create a sense of obligation in the person you are selling to.
>
> A classic example – I'm wandering around a town in Turkey with my wife. We walked past a shop, there's some lace, we walk in, there's an old guy who gets a ladder and climbs up and pulls out a big box, snips the string, pulls out some lace, some more lace, some more, and so on, until it comes to the piece she's interested in.
>
> At that point you are gonna be buying some lace.
>
> A local company had a recruitment drive on the streets of Scotland. The recruiters were dressed in the company's uniform and were approaching people to recruit them literally on the street. Things were not going so well. I suggested the opening lines, 'Excuse me, are you local?'
>
> The minute you're asked that question, the brain immediately does an analysis – 'This person is lost, they need help, so I'm going to engage.'

Ex-multi-level marketing scheme member, Denise, likewise described how recruits would always wear stripes of lipstick on their hands to generate conversations in public with strangers. These schemes draw people in gradually before it becomes all-encompassing.

The process is not always linear – it can be a bit of a dance. This is what hypnotists call 'fractionation' (a deeper trance can be reached by bringing people in and out repeatedly), and what pick-up artists call 'two steps forward, one step back'. As self-professed dating coach Corey Waynee put it on his blog:

> Maybe you're kissing or maybe you're making out. Your hands are wandering and then they go a little too far, and then she stops you. Now, most guys that don't know any better, they think, 'Well, that's it, I'm not getting laid,' and they just give up. All it really means is you're going a little too fast and you need to slow down, back up a little bit. Hence the two steps forward. In other words, you keep moving forward until you encounter resistance. Then you take a step back. You refocus on conversation and talking, getting her to talk. And then a little while later, you start making out, heavy petting, start removing items of clothing, things of that nature.[17]

There is a related principle of persuasion called the 'door-in-the-face' technique: by making two unreasonable steps forward, and getting rejected, people are more likely to accept the one step forward that was your goal in the first place. In one experiment, some people were asked if they'd chaperone youths from the County Juvenile Detention Center to the zoo for two hours one day; 17 per cent agreed.[18] However, if people were presented with an extreme request beforehand (volunteering to be a counsellor to them for two hours a week, every week, for two years), compliance with the zoo request then increased to 50 per cent. When decadent rockers Mötley Crüe made their strip club music video for 'Girls, Girls, Girls', they knew MTV would be unlikely to accept it.[19] So, they made two versions: an uber-raunchy cut, which was sent first, and duly rejected; and a toned-down compromise, which was what they actually wanted to be aired all along.

These techniques can of course be used by people more sinister than charity chuggers and Eighties rockers.

Totalitarian regimes also don't get there overnight. They are the result of many tiny steps. In *They Thought They Were Free: The Germans, 1933–45*, journalist Milton S. Mayer painted a vivid picture:

> To live in this process is absolutely not to be able to notice it ... Each step was so small, so inconsequential, so well explained or, on occasion, 'regretted,' that, unless one were detached from the whole process from the beginning, unless one understood what the whole thing was in principle, what all these 'little measures' that no 'patriotic German' could resent must some day lead to, one no more saw it developing from day to day than a farmer in his field sees the corn growing. One day it is over his head.[20]

In the wake of the Second World War, psychologist Stanley Milgram conducted his famous experiments on authority, showing that people would give what they thought was a deadly electric shock to someone else simply because a scientist in a white lab coat told them to.[21] However, it wasn't just the authority cues that had this effect. Participants were asked to start with a harmless buzz of voltage and gradually increase it. The incremental nature of the task contributed to its literally shocking results. Another psychologist, Philip Zimbardo, once said that 'all evil starts with 15 volts'.[22]

Avoidant resistance

Given that this insidious technique is so effective it can cajole even the most pig-headed of pigs, what can we do to resist it?

Broadly speaking, there are two methods for resisting persuasion.[23] The first is active resistance: deliberately challenging the information and its source. For example, the aforementioned slippery slope researchers found that the slope could be avoided by adopting a prevention-focused mentality: that is, being more pessimistic.

The issue with active resistance is that we are not hardwired to be so cynical. The 'truth bias' refers to our tendency to believe people tell the truth more often than they really do, for example.[24] What's more, we simply don't have the time or attention spans to do battle with every bit of information we meet.

Engaging with persuasive information can also generate what's known as 'ironic processes': even if you disagree with the message, the simple act of consuming it will influence your thoughts and behaviours in some way.[25] If you were told not to think of a pink elephant, the first thing you'd do is think of a pink elephant. You could be a cynical, critical consumer of news content, social media feeds and adverts – but the very act of consuming them at all would have a psychological impact on you, in one way or another.

What we see becomes familiar and normal in our minds, even if we disagree with it. The 'mere exposure effect' is a psychological principle in which simply being exposed to something makes us like it more. In experiments, Western participants showed a preference for letters of the Chinese alphabet (which were completely meaningless to them) if they had been exposed to them previously.[26] In China itself, influencer marketing is known as *seeding* – it is about planting, or incepting, an idea in people's minds so it can grow organically there. So, even if you consume information sceptically, it is still being implanted in your mind. The mere exposure to something makes it seem normal and familiar. Likewise, research on the 'illusory truth effect' shows how we are more likely to believe something is true the more often we hear it.[27]

Let's imagine a propaganda campaign that tells you to eat insects. You might find it disgusting, you might complain – but that is not the point. It's less about whether you agree with what you saw, and more about whether you saw what you saw. Like it or not, the idea will enter your mind and change your perception of reality. The people who think it's disgusting that people eat insects, and the people who think it's great that people eat insects, are both united in thinking that people eat insects.

Perhaps the answer lies not in active resistance, but in the second type: avoidant resistance. This means staying away from manipulators rather than trying to fight them.

Alcoholics Anonymous, for example, are experts at resisting things – every day is a war with their addiction – and they have a saying: that if you hang around in a barber's, sooner or later you're going to get your hair cut. But there is so much power in leaving the barber's shop, or stepping away. Often, political resistance is not about fighting the system, but about leaving it entirely to create something new. Czech political dissident Václav Havel called it the *parallel polis*.[28] In *The Discourse on Voluntary Servitude*, French political theorist Étienne de La Boétie wrote: 'I do not ask that you place hands upon the tyrant to topple him over, but simply that you support him no longer; then you will behold him, like a great Colossus whose pedestal has been pulled away, fall of his own weight and break into pieces.'[29]

The classic brainwashing book *Battle for the Mind* has just a few pages at the end on how to resist brainwashing – but they are powerful.[30] The author, William Sargant, makes the case that the most difficult animals to condition are those that will not engage with the experimenter. 'When a dog sullenly refuses to pay any attention to the flashing lights and other food signals intended for his conditioning,' wrote Sargant, 'his brain remains unaffected.'

Like dogs, people will not break down and give in to brainwashing if they simply refuse to engage with it in the first place. For example, prisoners of war can survive interrogations if they refuse to cooperate with their captors or answer any questions at all, and criminal suspects would be less likely to be convicted if they simply refused all questions except those answered in writing via their lawyer. As American law professor James Duane put it, 'Anybody who understands what goes on during a police interrogation asks for a lawyer and shuts up.'[31]

Even fighting with brainwashers can be counterproductive. If an angry bull charges again and again at a matador, it is still eventually worn down so that it may be slain with a sword. Only the bull that remains calm and refuses to engage with the matador at all has a chance of survival. While you might think you ought to get riled up and fight against the brainwashers, it can leave you exhausted and vulnerable. More effective is a strategy of total avoidance.

Gary Noesner worked as a hostage negotiator for 30 years, including seven years as the FBI's Chief Negotiator. His technique to bring people round was to move slowly and carefully, drawing them in like pigs with peanuts, albeit for a much nobler cause. He was asked if there were ever any people he couldn't negotiate with:

> I can't negotiate with people who refuse to talk to me. They'll put a hostage on and say, 'You speak for me.' That's tough on someone like me. I have to convince the hostage to get you to talk to me. In order to have a positive influence on another's thinking and behavior, we must first engage them in a genuine, sincere, and impactful dialogue. Without such engagement it is difficult to achieve positive outcomes.

You can't be negotiated with if you don't pick up the phone; and you can't be brainwashed if you don't pay attention to the brainwashing.

Likewise, we asked magician and psychology professor Gustav Kuhn how people can avoid being tricked by magic.

He said, 'Don't go to the show!'

The rules:

- Notice the gradual changes and stubbornly stand your ground; don't be afraid to say no even to seemingly reasonable requests.
- Take a more cynical and negative approach in situations with a high likelihood of manipulation, and focus on potential losses rather than gains.
- If something has the potential to manipulate you, consider not engaging with it at all, even in a critical or combative way.

3

Get immunity

You are better at resisting manipulation when you know what to look for. Inoculate yourself against brainwashing by educating yourself on common tactics, putting your guard up and exposing yourself to nudges in small doses.

Once bitten, twice shy

Paris. With its moonlit cobbled streets, with revolution and romance lying in its bones, it is perhaps the one city that is most likely to steal your heart. But also, your purse, passport and phone. A study of TripAdvisor reviews found that, among the places to get pickpocketed worldwide, the Eiffel Tower, the Sacré Cœur, the Louvre and Notre-Dame were all in the list of the top ten locations.[1]

Writing for travel website Fodor's Travel, for example, Katie Jackson recounted a Parisian paramour's picturesque Tinder date that left her $4,000 poorer.[2] While she was smooching her Frenchman – 'the six-foot-something French banker' – beneath the glittering lights of the Eiffel Tower, a nearby couple of wayward youths made off with her purse. Katie had to foot the bill for a new iPhone and another six days in Paris while she jumped through all the hoops to replace her passport.

This was a painful learning experience for Katie. While she won't stoop to wearing a money belt in future ('they're ugly'), she has pledged to carry a copy of her passport instead of the real thing from now on.

Kim Kardashian was also robbed in Paris, of $10m in jewels, by masked gunmen who may have used her Instagram feed for intel. Kardashian has since toned down her social media posts as well as her clothing: 'As far as jewellery, if I'm wearing something, it's borrowed. It's fake.'[3]

What these two Parisian plots have in common is that the ladies learnt from their experiences, and likely won't get fooled again.

Even manipulation experts can be tricked if they don't know what to look for. Simon Horton, who has been teaching persuasion techniques to people such as hostage negotiators and CEOs for a decade, was scammed not in Paris but in London:

> Knowledge protects you from scams. When I first moved to London as a fairly naïve 21-year-old, I fell for a scam where a chap in impressive clothes said he worked for the West African version of *The Economist* as a journalist. He needed to go back to Heathrow but his stuff had been stolen out of his locker, so could I lend him some money. So I gave him a tenner. I've since met someone very similar asking me exactly the same thing. I told him to get stuffed.

That is the key principle here: fool me once, shame on you; fool me twice, shame on me. An insider from the cybersecurity industry put it this way: 'If you stop someone getting scammed for £10, that's a good thing. Or is it? Actually, it can be a good learning experience to get scammed for £10 if it stops you getting scammed for £10,000 in the future. If you can give people hands-on experience, they can recognise the patterns and circumstances, they will be ready for it.'

Of course, you don't have to get robbed – or scammed, manipulated or nudged – before you can learn how to avoid it. Small inoculations can help you recognise, and avoid, manipulation techniques in real life. The social psychologist Solomon Asch once said, 'The greater man's ignorance of the principles of his social surroundings, the more subject is he to their control; and the greater his knowledge of their operations and of their necessary consequences, the freer he can become with regard to them.'[4]

In marketing psychology there is even a name for this principle: the 'persuasion knowledge model'.[5] It argues that people learn about persuasion tactics, use this knowledge to spot when someone is trying to influence them, and deploy psychological countermeasures accordingly. For example, if you were to shop for a new car, and notice that the salesman is pushing you to buy the car today or lose out on a discount, you might recognise this as a sales technique, become more suspicious and decide to shop elsewhere.

In a different model, researchers at the University of Amsterdam identified three such techniques that people use to resist advertising once aware of it: they can simply avoid it, for instance by leaving the room or looking at their phone instead; they can actively argue against it in their heads; and they can bolster their own identity, by, for example, asserting that they can't be persuaded.[6]

The researchers, in their paper 'A typology of consumer strategies for resisting advertising, and a review of mechanisms for countering them', also identified ways for advertisers to overcome these resistance techniques. To overcome avoidance, the paper recommends forcing people to watch adverts (for example, an unskippable ad at the start of a YouTube video), hiding the advert in other content through techniques like product placement, using attention-grabbing and memorable viral advertising, using surrogates such as celebrities and influencers, or enlisting customers to spread word-of-mouth through schemes like referrals. To overcome contesting strategies, the paper recommends that an advert present two sides of the argument, advertise to people when they are tired or distracted, bamboozle them with confusing information or include reassurances like warranties. Finally, empowerment strategies can be overcome by reminding the audience of prior successes to boost their self-esteem, or by using 'reverse psychology'. Ultimately, it seems there is an arms race between manipulators and their targets – emphasising how important it is to stay informed.

The key is to keep all this front-of-mind – not only the mechanisms of persuasion but also the possibility of it.

This is why British banks recently introduced new measures for online banking. Try and make a transfer and you will be asked if you're sure, and given some fraud clues to watch out for. When behavioural science agency The Behaviouralist tested these in-app warnings, they reduced the frequency of falling for fraud from 22 per cent to 10 per cent.[7] By bringing attention to fraudsters' tricks, their power is deflated. Sunlight, as the saying goes, is the best disinfectant.

This may explain manipulators' obsessions with secrecy: if you were to recognise their techniques, they would probably stop working. Which could be why secret societies like the Skull and Bones Club are in fact so secret, why con-men pretend to be secret agents and why totalitarian regimes crack down so hard on freedom of speech. As Thomas Jefferson once noted, 'Enlighten the people generally, and tyranny and oppressions of body and mind will vanish like evil spirits at the dawn of the day.'[8]

Magicians have known about all this for a long time. Members of the Magic Circle are sworn to secrecy, on pain of expulsion. Gustav Kuhn, a professor of psychology and member of the Magic Circle, confessed:

> Magic relies on you not knowing how the tricks are done. If you knew how they were done, the magic wouldn't work any more – so magicians work hard to

protect their secrets. In fact, it's not just about seeing deception, it's also about suspecting deception. It doesn't matter if the suspicion is right or not – if you think the magician pulled the rabbit out of his sleeve, even if he didn't, the magic disappears.

Magicians have developed a whole host of techniques of distraction and misdirection to make sure this doesn't happen. The goal is, as pioneering magician Arturo de Ascanio put it, to 'ensure that the secrets are not shown, not known to exist, not even suspected'.[9] The audience's eye is drawn elsewhere, so that an invisible and unsuspected action can drive the magic trick. Where the audience looks is known as the 'illuminated' area, while the secret remains in the low-attention blind spot known as the 'shadowy' area. Magicians often use a cognitive bias known as 'the illusion of absence', for example: when a magician palms a cigarette, hiding it in his hand, we tend to assume the hand is empty and so the cigarette appears to disappear.[10]

The beauty is that once you've seen how a trick is done, it it loses its power. Once you see it, you can't unsee it. For example, the word 'it' was just repeated in the first sentence; you probably didn't see it the first time, but now you're aware of it, you can't help but notice it.

Psychologists once conducted what is famously known as the invisible gorilla experiment.[11] Participants watched a video in which two teams (one wearing white and the other wearing black) passed a ball to one another. Viewers had to accurately count the number of times the white team passed the ball. At some point in the video, a man in a gorilla costume walked across the screen. About half of respondents didn't even notice it. A similar study had 24 experienced radiologists review medical scans looking at lung nodules for abnormalities; in the final scan was inserted the image of a gorilla, 48 times the size of an average nodule. A massive 83 per cent of them didn't notice it.[12]

Importantly, however, when people are told about the gorilla, and shown the video again, almost all of them can see it. Once it's seen, it can't be unseen.

This can result in a sort of awakening to a whole new reality. Dr Rachel Lawes, an expert in semiotics, explained, 'If you are consciously aware of symbols, that's where the fun really starts – you see it [the use of symbols] everywhere. It's every single thing all the time. It's a switch in the head.'

More broadly, lifetime exposure to manipulation might predict resistance to it. One study, for example, found that people who had experienced negative life events scored lower on compliance and were less susceptible to giving false confessions in police interviews.[13]

Cult recovery educator Gerette Buglion described the process she went through herself, and how it impacted on her perception of the US government.

> There are a lot of people who are waking up to what power abuse looks like. One can harness that experience from four decades ago and see how it applies to what the government is doing. I'm going to stand up and share that with people. Another one can see how that politician is hoodwinking people in the same way I was hoodwinked by a multilevel marketing scheme. It was shady then and it's shady now.
>
> If someone goes through a traumatic experience and has been in an environment where they're able to truly heal, my guess is that those who've weathered trauma well are more likely to not be drawn into a controlling group.

Lifting the veil

So, what are the tricksters' tactics to watch out for? There are various models developed by behavioural scientists, often with overlapping ideas and catchy acronyms.

Robert Cialdini's book *Influence* is, fittingly, one of the most influential frameworks when it comes to changing someone's behaviour.[14] Cialdini originally outlined six nudges.

The first is 'social proof'. Human beings are very social animals, having evolved in tribes; as a result, we tend to follow the crowd. It makes evolutionary sense to do this: we don't have the time or the energy to think through every decision in detail, and if everyone else is doing something, it's probably correct. If everyone is screaming and running away, you probably ought to as well. To dither and analyse could be fatal. This was hilariously illustrated in a piece of CCTV footage that went viral in September 2022: as some marathon runners passed by the terrace of the Cervejaria Alphaiate Bar in Brazil, some diners panicked and ran away too, leaving their belongings behind.[15] Psychologist Stanley Milgram ran an experiment in which researchers stopped in a busy New York street and stared up at a fixed point where absolutely nothing was happening.[16] Many passers-by stopped and looked too, following the herd instinct. It is this instinct that drives the 'bandwagon effect' on election days (when favourable early exit polls give a candidate's vote share a boost, in places where this is legal)[17] and in the financial markets (where cryptocurrencies live or die on the perception of popularity).[18] This is the principle behind McDonald's 1994 slogan 'Over 99 Billion Served', and Amazon's use of 'Customers who bought this item also bought ...'

'Scarcity' refers to the fact that we value something more if it's scarce. Again, there is a good evolutionary reason for this: in the dead of winter, we'd need to hoard food in order to survive. This is why, as one study found, people savour a cookie more when it's the last one in the jar.[19] In practical terms, another study found that the rate of opting into a 'quit smoking' course increased from 7 to 10 per cent simply by saying there were only 300 places left.[20] It is the scarcity instinct that makes Americans go bananas for Black Friday deals, even though the discounts are not great (*Which?* found that 99.5 per cent of Black Friday deals are the same or cheaper at other times of the year).[21] The perception of a limited number of discounts for a limited time has resulted in stampedes, arrests and shootings in the past.[22] The scarcity instinct is why children can spend hours looking for rare Pokémon, while adults can spend tens of thousands of dollars on a handbag that cost Gucci only a couple of hundred dollars to make.

The 'liking' principle alludes to our tendency to be persuaded by people we like; we like people who are attractive, familiar to us or similar to us. For example, research shows that attractive people are judged less harshly by jurors,[23] and that the most handsome people at work earn 5 per cent more on average while the ugliest earn 7 to 9 per cent less.[24] Liking is why Beyoncé got paid $50 million to promote Pepsi: advertising messages are more palatable to us when they come from someone we know and trust.[25] One study had people rate their likelihood of buying from a pictured salesman, not knowing that he was a photoshopped blend of two faces: 65 per cent a stock model, and 35 per cent Tiger Woods.[26] Although they didn't consciously recognise that Tiger Woods had been blended into the face, they trusted this salesperson more (that is, until Woods's famous infidelities hit the headlines, when a repeat of the experiment found the effect was reversed). The liking principle may explain why the US government paid influencers up to one thousand dollars a month to promote the Covid vaccines, and perhaps why influencers' vaccine selfies ('vaxxies') were so prevalent.[27]

'Reciprocity' is about our tendency to comply with someone to whom we feel indebted. Being social animals, we risk ostracism if we take from the herd without giving back. In fact, this principle is so hardwired that it is even observable in monkeys, where 'I'll scratch your back if you scratch mine' explains 30 per cent of nit-picking behaviour.[28] There is even a species of fruit fly whose male secures sex with the female by giving her a gift of food.[29] Researchers intercepted the female-bound male fly and used tweezers to replace the food with useless fluff – the female still gave up the goods, showing that it really is the thought that counts. This may explain why men spent almost a billion pounds on Valentine's Day in 2021.[30] Reciprocity is why brands will give away free gifts, and governments give benefits to voters – it makes us more likely to comply with their requests.

The next principle is 'commitment and consistency', which refers to our tendency to comply with a request if we already feel committed to it. There are a couple of reasons for this. The first is that, being social animals, we face ostracism if we don't do what we say we'll do. The British political party the Liberal Democrats have never quite recovered in terms of their vote share since they formed a coalition government in 2010: one of their election promises was to abolish university tuition fees, but they actually tripled them.[31] The second reason is that we don't like to lose our investments. One study gave car-wash customers a loyalty card with eight spaces to fill in order to redeem a free car wash; half of the customers got a card with just eight empty spaces, while the other half got a card with ten spaces, but two of them were already stamped to begin with.[32] In the first group, 19 per cent of customers bought enough car washes to fill in the card – compared with 34 per cent when the commitment nudge was used.

Finally, there is the 'authority' principle. The world is a confusing, chaotic place; there is an infinite amount of information in the universe, and we have very tiny brains for making sense of it. We do not have the time or the brainpower to think everything through rationally, so we have to trust other people to tell us what's what. You presumably do not believe the earth is flat, for example – but how do you know? There are experiments with pendula and so forth, but you probably haven't done them; there are photos from space, but these are often computer-edited composites. Most of us believe the earth is not flat simply because our parents, newsreaders and people in white lab coats have told us so. Stanley Milgram demonstrated the principle in his famous electroshock experiments.[33] People were sat at a booth with a radio console and instructed to talk to a participant in a different room. They were to quiz the other participant with a set of trivia questions and, for every wrong answer, give an electric shock of increasing voltage. The other participant was not, of course, actually being shocked; they were an actor trained to complain, then scream, then beg, then cry, then go completely silent. Milgram found that, under normal-ish conditions, around half of the subjects complied and gave what was a fatal electric shock just because they had been asked to by an authority figure. When this figure had the additional authoritative trappings of a university location and a white lab coat, this deadly compliance increased to 65 per cent. This principle of authority explains why one study found a letter from a dentist's office got a 54 per cent return rate when it was signed by the dentist him- or herself, but only 18 per cent when it was the dentist's secretary: the dentist's title was an authoritative cue that made people comply.[34] Authority explains why testimonials, certifications and awards are so effective.

In summary, all of these techniques can be fashioned into 'nudges': small, environmental changes that can have a big behavioural effect. In the book *Nudge*, Richard Thaler and Cass Sunstein define them as:

> any aspect of the choice architecture that alters people's behavior in a predictable way without forbidding any options or significantly changing their economic incentives. To count as a mere nudge, the intervention must be easy and cheap to avoid. Nudges are not mandates. Putting fruit at eye level counts as a nudge. Banning junk food does not.[35]

Let's imagine, for example, that you're booking a holiday, and you've found a hotel room that you like. The website tells you that three people have booked this hotel recently (social proof) and there's only one room left available at this rate (scarcity). The hotel has a really good user rating and has even won an award (authority), and there are lots of positive reviews from real people just like you, with names and profile pictures (liking). If you book now, they'll throw in a complimentary breakfast (reciprocity), and you just have to put your card details down – you won't pay any money until you get there (commitment and consistency).

A discussion paper prepared by the Competition and Markets Authority outlined several ways in which websites can nudge people into acting against their best interests.[36] For instance, 'roach motel' tactics add behavioural friction to cancelling a subscription (where, like a pest control trap, it is made enticing to enter but difficult to leave, familiar to anyone who has tried to cancel Amazon Prime), while search engines can rank information in a particular order to influence user perception and choice.

Moving to the world of governance, consider the following text message sent during the British government's Covid vaccination drive: 'You have reached the top of the queue and are a priority for getting a free NHS COVID-19 vaccine.'

By saying there is a queue, the message is using social proof to imply the vaccines are popular, and by calling you a priority they are implying that supply does not meet demand, using scarcity to drive a sense of urgency. Having reached the top of the queue, you feel invested, like you have been waiting and don't want to lose your place thanks to the principle of commitment and consistency (and being at the top is likely to activate ego concerns and make people feel superior to those below them). The vaccine being free is probably using reciprocity to make people feel obligated, while having the message come from the NHS, a likeable and authoritative institution, makes it more likely to be accepted.

A mandible in the door

Similarly, as we've already seen, a concerted campaign to make us eat creepy crawlies is being pushed by celebrities and supranational organisations. The United Nations and the World Economic Forum are keen advocates of edible insects, because of the claimed environmental benefits. And the UK's Food Standard's Agency is currently consulting on edible insects. The EU has already approved crushed cricket flour to be added as an ingredient to bread and other foods. It is claimed that insect farming has a lower carbon footprint than livestock, and that insects will be able to eat human waste, compost and animal slurry.

Despite these alleged benefits, people are not clamouring to eat insects, which is why the efforts to nudge and manipulate are coming at us hard and fast. There is a battle for your dinner plate and the edible insects agenda has behavioural scientists' fingerprints all over it. The campaign to make us eat insects is an excellent illustration of the deliberate manipulation of your mind.

The insects offered tend to have some connection to food, where mealworms remind us of meals and crickets are phonetically similar to chicken. Both are inoffensive: the propagandists don't try to get us to eat cockroaches, spiders or wasps, though all three are equally as fit (or not) for consumption as crickets. Despite this, mealworms and crickets don't yet fit into our cultural nutritional lexicon. While some cultures may traditionally eat insects (or at least resort to them in the absence of other protein sources), we consider them revolting. Food is part of our social and cultural identity and, short of starvation, we're not likely to change overnight.

Our revulsion towards insects has a biological basis: we're supposed to be put off foods that can be harmful. Insects can sting you, they can be poisonous or carry diseases. Some insects eat dung, or swarm around rubbish, rotting carcasses and food, and therefore remind us of decay, as well as carrying bacteria. Insects can ruin crops, debilitate animals and infest us. We normally think of them as uninvited guests on our bodies and in our homes. We have set up industries to control and exterminate them. They have lots of legs, a strange appearance and jerky, unpredictable movements.

Hence, when propagandists talk about edible insects, they nudge our perceptions of social norms. Two billion people already eat bugs, wrote *The Economist*.[37] A paper in the *Journal of Insects as Food and Feed* concluded that, actually, 'It is difficult to establish an exact figure of how many people eat insects globally and that the much cited two billion figure … must be an overestimation.'[38] At any rate, the figure has been nudged. Presented as a proportion (25 per cent) it would be less impressive. It is also a reframing of the fact that the vast majority of people (six billion; 75 per cent) do *not* eat insects.

The propagandists also use 'messenger effects' by having celebrities like Nicole Kidman, Robert Downey Jr and James Corden endorse them.[39] Once we see someone else doing something (particularly if we like them), we are more likely to follow, sheep-like. Similarly, including edible insects on popular TV programmes such as *The Great British Bake Off* changes our perception of what is normal and familiar.[40]

A Finnish baker launched the world's first insect-based bread. If it's something you normally eat, and it only contains a small percentage of insects, well, does it even matter? One loaf contains about seventy crickets – who's counting? Getting you to try a product you are used to and that you can't see bugs in is one way to gently acclimatise you to the new ingredient. Will you notice when the flour is more cricket than wheat? How will you next feel about eating a bag of crickets instead of a ham and cheese sandwich? Watch that plague of locusts flying through the Overton window.

A 2022 paper titled 'How to convince people to eat insects' emphasised the importance of this sneaky mandible-in-the-door technique.[41] The paper cited a psychologist who said, 'We repeatedly find that if you don't see the insects, people are much more open to eating it,' and a food tech entrepreneur who said, 'Having the grasshoppers on the front of the package is not a good thing for us.'

Once people have eaten the obfuscated insects as powder, they are more likely to go for the real thing. The paper quoted a chef who said, 'They're like, "I ate that cricket gougères [sic; cheese puff made with cricket powder]. That was easy. I could eat that all day. Alright, give me something else."'

Meanwhile, if you ask Google, 'Should we eat insects?' there are about 75 million results. Crucially, the first page of results are all positive. If you ask the same question about any meat you will find negative results on the first page and in the top position in some cases. That's a strange inversion of what you would expect, and implies that reputational management has been employed on behalf of edible insects. The top non-sponsored link is an article by the BBC, entitled 'Insects are good for you'. Further articles suggest you drink up your cockroach milk and replace beef with grasshoppers to save the planet.

The media plays an important role in changing perceptions. Journalists are hungry for content, even if they're not hungry for insects yet, and they'll be fed research reports and press releases. Repetition leads to acceptance and belief. Psychologists call this the 'illusory truth effect'.[42] Multiple exposures make something more palatable.

A trial in Wales planned to invite children from several schools (to start with) to participate in workshops and discussions about 'the environmental and nutritional benefits of alternative proteins'.[43] This project is all about influencing children. A spokesperson for a business called Bug Farm in Wales commented that, 'Children, in particular, are very open minded, so we believe that working with them is how we can change attitudes in the long term: they are the shoppers of the future.'

Once children are influenced it can create a multi-generational spillover. As a report published by the Nudge Unit in October 2021 said:

> Education also plays a key role in establishing new norms. Indeed, schools have often been a vector for building national identity. Children can then in turn have profound impacts on their parents, or through other means by making new behaviours observable.
>
> How might this apply to Net Zero? School canteens should lead the way in being Net Zero. The UK government spends £2.4 billion buying food for public hospitals, schools, prisons, courts, offices, military facilities and more. This is a powerful lever through which the government can begin to normalise plant-based food, and signal the legitimacy of a healthy and sustainable food system.[44]

So watch out for further insect studies and trials in prisons, military facilities and other government buildings, although probably not in the Houses of Parliament.

As the edible insects case study shows, there are many other nudges besides Cialdini's six. Academics have tried to collect them into simple frameworks and models. One of these frameworks is known by the acronym MINDSPACE, developed for the Cabinet Office in the UK.[45] The nine principles are: 'Messenger' (we are influenced by authority figures and by people we like); 'Incentives' (we tend to do something if it will bring us pleasure or avoid pain); 'Norms' (we are more likely to comply with a request if the action appears popular); 'Defaults' (we tend to do the easiest thing and stick with the status quo); 'Salience' (we will act on whatever is visible and front-of-mind); 'Priming' (our behaviour can be influenced by subtle cues); 'Affect' (we tend to act on emotion); 'Commitments' (we try to keep our obligations and be consistent with our habits); and 'Ego' (we do things that will improve our social status and foster an identity).

The National Health Service used the MINDSPACE model to increase uptake of the Covid-19 vaccines, as discovered via a December 2020 internal document titled 'Optimising Vaccination Roll Out – Dos and Don'ts for All Messaging, Documents and "Communications" in the Widest Sense'.[46] The guidelines, for example, used the 'incentives' principle in advising that young people be told the vaccine would help them towards 'getting their life back'; it used 'affect' in advising 'focusing on the potential regret one might feel if they were not vaccinated and were to subsequently infect [loved ones]'; and it advised using 'champions within the system (CEOs, Medical and Nursing Directors, etc.)' to exploit 'messenger' effects.

Elsewhere, the pandemic response involved using a coterie of black celebrities, such as comedian Lenny Henry, as messengers to persuade minority ethnic Brits to get vaccinated.[47] An NHS document advised immunisers to 'use figures that are perceived to have authority or expertise to deliver vaccine communications, such as faith leaders'. An anonymous member of the government's behavioural science pandemic response group SPI-B admitted that face masks 'conveyed a message of solidarity', using the principle of social norms to make pandemic compliance visible on faces on the street.[48] Of course, incentives were used in the form of vaccine passports allowing or denying access to venues and flights, a follow-on from the Behavioural Insights Team's recommendation to implement paper wristbands for those with a vaccine or negative test result.[49]

Puncturing the propaganda

On the point of government messaging, there are also well-defined propaganda tactics to watch out for. In *War and Anti-War*, Alvin and Heidi Toffler outlined six of them.[50]

The key principle, from which the others follow, is 'polarisation'. This involves the creation of an out-group and contrasting its behaviour and beliefs with those of the in-group; the in-group's leaders are heroes, the out-group's are villains. What Freud called 'the narcissism of small differences' is emphasised – small details in dress, food, worship, and so on.[51] As Christopher Hitchens said: 'In numerous cases of apparently ethno-nationalist conflict, the deepest hatreds are manifested between people who – to most outward appearances – exhibit very few significant distinctions.'[52] What, really, is the difference between an Irish Catholic nationalist and an Irish Protestant unionist to, say, an Indian man? And how much difference would an Irishman see between a Kashmiri Hindu and a Kashmiri Muslim?

Following polarisation, the first tactic is 'atrocity accusations', where the other side is accused of gross violations of basic values (such as bombing a hospital or killing innocent victims). These shock the target audience and make them perceive the enemy as subhuman. For example, a headline in the *Sun* in February 2022 read, 'SICK & TWISTED: Russia accused of bombing NURSERY as pictures show it "surrounded by bodies" in strikes that killed child & four others'.[53] While bombing a nursery is of course abhorrent, it should be noted that such incidents are not uncommon on both sides in wartime, that apparent school bombings on both sides in the conflict have been alleged to be 'false flags',[54] and that in any case a genuine nursery bombing would not call for smearing all of Russia as 'sick and twisted'. This headline also has other propaganda tells: it builds a clear mental image of a nursery with bodies strewn around and its language lies in the grey zone between truth and falsehood (rather than explicitly claiming Russia bombed a nursery, the newspaper says Russia is 'accused' of bombing a nursery – an important distinction). This is not to condone Russia's actions, of course, but to point out the propagandistic techniques that exist on both sides of the conflict.

This story also uses a second principle – 'demonisation and dehumanisation' – which is about portraying the enemy as entirely corrupt and without hope of redemption. While the Nazis compared the Jews to rats, the modern equivalent is, ironically, to compare one's enemy to the Nazis. In September 2022, for example, failed presidential candidate Hillary Clinton said that Trump conventions put her in mind of Nazi rallies.[55] After the 2020 election, Nancy Pelosi said that Trump would be 'fumigated' out of the White House, recalling the common trope of likening enemies to disgusting vermin.[56]

The third principle is 'hyperbolic inflations', where the enemy's actions are cherry-picked and exaggerated to seem particularly bad. A common tactic here is generalisation, where one instance is used to smear an entire group. In politics, for example, pundits on the right might use rare instances of drag queens gyrating in front of toddlers to attack the left, while pundits on the left might use equally rare instances of tiki torch-carrying protestors chanting 'Jews will not replace us' to attack the right.

'Divine sanction' involves claiming that the in-group is doing something with a higher purpose, and that they are more holy and righteous. During the Covid lockdowns, for example, Queen Elizabeth II said the unvaccinated should 'think about others', implying they were selfish,[57] and the Archbishop of Canterbury said that getting vaccinated was a 'moral issue', implying that the unvaccinated were immoral.[58]

Finally, the principle of 'meta-propaganda' refers to propaganda about propaganda: it shows how the other side distorts and deceives, while the in-group only tells the truth and uses evidence-based communication. This is manifested both in the right-wing pejorative about unthinking 'non-playable characters' (NPCs) brainwashed by the 'mainstream media', and in the left wing's claim that only they 'follow the science' in opposition to right-wing 'science-deniers'.

Whether you're vaccinated or not, whether you support Republicans or Democrats, this is not really the point. The point is that all sides use propaganda to propagate their ideas – that's where the word comes from. The only difference between propaganda and education, said Edward Bernays, is whether or not you agree with its message.

This book, in fact, is a piece of meta-propaganda in its own way, teaching you to dissect manipulation attempts, so that they lose their power.

Inoculation

How, then, can we resist these techniques?

First, it can be helpful to simply put your psychological defences up when entering a high-stakes decision-making context. Research discussed in this book shows that effective strategies to resist persuasion include avoidance, counter-arguing, derogating the source of the argument, and being in a negative mood – in other words, being a bit disagreeable. In information security, for instance, where it's particularly crucial to resist scammers, there is the notion of being a 'justified know-it-all' – someone who trusts no one and asks every visitor what they're doing and where their identification is.[59]

The key is to question more; to overcome lazy thinking patterns and do a bit more critical thinking. Will Moy, fact-checker from Full Fact, outlined three important questions to ask when it comes to news, for example:

> Where is it from, what's missing, and how do you feel?
>
> What's the source and do you have a reason to trust the source? Have you looked beyond the headline, and at other sources? Does it get you angry, or worked up or getting a reaction from you? If so, is it worth looking at, is it worth sharing? Misinformation tries to play on people's emotions. You can't perfectly research every topic but these are pragmatic rules of thumb which help you spot the risks.

While online fact-checkers are far from perfect, the ideal of questioning more is something to which we all ought to aspire. American philosopher John Dewey was one of the first to formalise the study of critical thinking; he essentially defined it as engaging deeply with a problem.[60] Since then, psychologists have pinpointed specific skills such as applying set standards when judging and deciding, deliberately analysing information and making logical deductions, and seeking information and looking for the patterns within it.[61]

However, aside from being disagreeable and critical, there are three techniques that can protect you from persuasion.

The first is being forewarned. Essentially, if you know a persuasion attempt is imminent, you are generally better at resisting it. A study published in the *Journal of Experimental Social Psychology* in 2010 is a good example.[62] The researchers gave the students a task to do and then asked them how much time they would be willing to volunteer to clean up the campus. For some of the students, the task involved typing out a dense paragraph about statistics. This exhausted them and made them volunteer an average of 59 minutes compared with the non-bamboozled controls, who only volunteered 40 minutes on average. However, some of the participants were warned in advance that the clean-up charity would try and persuade them to volunteer. Among the bamboozled students who typed out the dense paragraph, those given a warning volunteered around 28 minutes, while those who weren't warned volunteered around 99 minutes – over three times as much. The researchers ultimately found that, if you know someone is going to try and persuade you, you can do a better job at saving your energy to keep your guard up.

The second principle of persuasion protection is something known as pre-bunking. If you know what manipulation attempts look like, and how to refute them, you'll be better at recognising and resisting them when you encounter them in real life.

The idea first originated with psychologist William McGuire in the 1960s, in response to thought control in the Far East.[63]

He wanted to develop what he called a 'vaccine for brainwash', a way of inoculating people against the enemy's ideas. Vaccines originally contained weakened versions of a pathogen, which trigger the body into making antibodies that can later be activated in the presence of the real virus. In the same way, McGuire demonstrated that pre-emptively exposing someone to a weakened version of an argument makes them more immune to it later. For example, if you did not want the masses to believe something, you would get ahead of the information and publicise it in a way that makes it look ridiculous. This kind of messaging can create 'mental antibodies'.

Since McGuire's time, a lot of scientific research has supported the idea of his 'vaccine for brainwash'. Meta-analyses have confirmed how effective they are.[64] One paper entitled 'When it strikes, are we ready?' even advocated for pre-bunking misinformation about asteroid strikes now so that people accept it, should the worst happen.[65] The paper advises pre-bunking the false equivalency technique ('to say the views of one person equal the findings of thousands of scientists and engineers'), reminiscent of the Netflix movie *Don't Look Up*. If we are to be prepared for every possible disaster, perhaps we should simultaneously consider preparation for an epidemic of anxiety.

Sander van der Linden, a professor at the University of Cambridge and the Director of the Cambridge Social Decision-Making Lab and author of *Foolproof*, says the pre-bunking technique works on two levels.

First, you can have a pre-bunk to tackle a specific falsehood. In one experiment his team of researchers challenged the reactions to the Oregon Global Warming Petition Project, with and without pre-bunking.[66] This website claims to hold a petition signed by over thirty-one thousand American scientists, stating there is no evidence that humans cause climate change. A general inoculation warned that 'some politically-motivated groups use misleading tactics to try and convince the public that there is a lot of disagreement among scientists'. A detailed inoculation pointed out that some signatures were bogus and that the template mimicked the National Academy of Sciences. The general inoculation saw an average opinion shift of 6.5 percentage points towards acceptance of the climate science consensus, and the detailed inoculation of almost 13 percentage points.

The detailed inoculation is obviously more effective but there are risks. Pre-bunking requires confidence in what is misinformation, and what is factual. Fact-checking can be prone to errors, especially as information evolves. Van der Linden says he would defer to 'mainstream scientific consensus as fact'. It is important to note that this can also be prone to error. Facts are said to have a 'half-life', in recognition of the fact that knowledge in a particular area is superseded or shown to be untrue – in the field of psychology, for example, it is estimated that a fact is only true for about seven years.[67]

Pre-bunking is also subject to ideological and political bias, hinted at in the titles of studies, 'Countering Science Denial', 'Inoculating against Fake News about COVID-19' and 'Inoculating the Public against Misinformation about Climate Change'. There appear to be no studies, for example, about how to inoculate people against the reality-denying misinformation that men can get pregnant. Social scientists do tend to be left wing and share similar 'progressive' outlooks.[68]

In this way, these studies may ironically constitute a form of meta-propaganda, implying that their political opponents are biased and misinformed. One, for example, concluded that 'one's likelihood of not getting the vaccine was associated with retweeting and favoriting low-quality news websites on Twitter', yet the paper relied for its definition of 'quality' on NewsGuard, which, among other things, gives a 'real news' endorsement to Vice.com (where previous headlines have included 'This Guy Served His Friends Tacos Made from His Own Amputated Leg').[69]

The second type of pre-bunking is general and therefore benefits from avoiding bias, hot button topics or arbitration of the truth. In his work in partnership with Meta, Van der Linden says he strongly advises 'to focus on the techniques not the claims', such as fake experts, fear-mongering and cherry-picking data. This evades the issues of uncertainty and changing facts but still trains people to be more open-minded and sceptical of manipulation.

In a 2022 study, researchers from the University of Cambridge crafted YouTube videos outlining common manipulation tactics found online.[70] Participants who watched the videos were significantly less likely to trust or share tweets that contained the techniques, although not in all cases.

While the academics might be biased, the principle is universal. In the aforementioned YouTube study, the videos were entirely politically neutral, using pop culture references to make the point rather than topical issues. The video on scapegoating, for example, used *South Park*'s 'Blame Canada' song as an illustration, and the video on false dichotomies quoted *Star Wars*: 'Only a Sith deals in absolutes.'

The final technique for persuasion protection is debiasing interventions. In this case, someone is given a reality check that they are in fact susceptible to cognitive biases. One game, for example, had people respond to emails where they would lose points if they fell for a phishing scam (an email designed to collect sensitive information).[71] Studies have consistently shown that these kinds of interventions can have long-lasting effects in real life.[72]

Whether it's forewarning, pre-bunking or debiasing, experts are unanimous concerning the importance of educating people about manipulation.

'The ability to differentiate between truth in the news and propaganda is a skill in and of itself that you must commit to developing,' says Professor Colin Alexander, a Senior Lecturer in Political Communications at Nottingham Trent University, who specialises in propaganda and communications. 'If I think back to myself as seventeen or eighteen, my critical faculties were not what they are now. Even as an academic I have to spend time doing this.'

Denise, who has escaped both cults and multi-level marketing schemes, pondered, 'After twenty years, I'm still reading books about this and wondering what the hell happened. There's layers and layers. How did they influence me? It's perplexing. We have school education, sex education, drug education. But there's no training for kids on undue influence. Kids should be taught.'

Author, mental health counsellor, and cult survivor Steven Hassan agreed:

> We are in a period of authoritarianism which is so sophisticated and unless people realise what is happening to them we will have fewer and fewer human rights. Brainwashing is a public health crisis. We need epidemiological studies to document the harms. We need to educate people that there are many psyops out there all the time.

'It's about naming it and claiming it,' explained Hassan, 'Name the technique that can be used on you – then it loses its power.'

In other words, bring the magician's tricks out of the shadows and into the light, where you rob them of their power.

The rules:

- Be on your guard and know when you're going into a manipulative situation: don't be afraid to be cynical and sceptical, and engage your critical-thinking faculties.
- Educate yourself, by reading classic books on persuasion and propaganda.
- Look out for common techniques in your day-to-day life, including social proof, scarcity, authority, liking, reciprocity, and commitment and consistency.

4

Don't overthink it

Intellectualism is not necessarily a defence against brainwashing. In fact, it can be a weakness. It makes people good at justifying their beliefs (even if wrong) and therefore more likely to spiral into rabbit holes disconnected from reality. The lesson for us all is that intellectual thought should be balanced with intuition, wisdom and humility.

Away with the fairies

The European winter of 1917 was bitterly cold, one of the harshest of the twentieth century. England was smothered by heavy snowfall and battered by high tides and severe gales. Amid this chaos, the country was at war. On 25 May, the first ever daylight bombing raid killed 95 people in Folkestone, the bombs loosening the earth with what one poem called 'the broken thunder of the German death'.[1]

It was a seismic winter, in which the great tectonic plates of the collective psyche were shifting, allowing repressed thoughts and fantasies to bubble to the surface. It was under these conditions that two young girls managed to convince the world that fairies were real.

Sixteen-year-old Elsie Wright and her nine-year-old cousin Frances Griffiths loved to explore the stream at the end of their garden, called Cottingley Beck. To this day, the stream runs over a rocky staircase shadowed by trees. Elsie and Frances would often get into trouble for coming home muddy from their adventures. They would explain to their parents that they had been there 'to see the fairies'. Scolded for lying, the girls borrowed their father's camera to bring back proof.

The first photograph would become infamous. It showed Frances frolicking with fairies.

It was fake, of course. The pixies had been copied from images in *Princess Mary's Gift Book*, with wings added, and held upright by hatpins. Elsie confessed to the hoax in 1983, and admitted astonishment at just how easily she had fooled seemingly intelligent adults.

Sir Arthur Conan Doyle, the medical doctor turned acclaimed creator of Sherlock Holmes, soon became aware of the photos. While Conan Doyle's legendary detective was famed for logical deduction, it seems that the author himself was more amenable to fantasy. Not only did he fail to deduce that the photos were cut-outs (taken from a book that featured some of his own writing, no less), but, using his undoubtedly superior intellect, he went to extraordinary lengths to explain and justify the fairies' existence. Where some people could see the hatpin holding a fairy upright, Conan Doyle saw a belly button. He even borrowed from modern science for his rationalisations, explaining that fairies were typically invisible to humans because they were 'constructed in material which threw out shorter or longer vibrations'.[2]

One psychology professor has since explained: 'Conan Doyle used his intelligence and cleverness to dismiss all counterarguments ... [He] was able to use his smartness to outsmart himself.'[3]

Dysrationalia

Conan Doyle is not alone. Many extremely intelligent people, it seems, can believe things that are simply unbelievable to the majority. Researchers have even coined a phenomenon called 'Nobel Disease', referring to the tendency for some Nobel Prize winners to embrace unconventional beliefs.[4] Charles Richet, for example, won the 1913 Nobel Prize in Physiology or Medicine for his work on anaphylaxis, and he also believed in dowsing, ghosts and extrasensory perception; and Nobel Prize-winning physicist Brian Josephson believed in homoeopathy, where water can 'remember' the chemical properties of substances passed through it.

Steve Jobs, though not a Nobel Prize winner, was undoubtedly a genius. With this great intellect he could, according to Walter Isaacson's official biography, create a 'reality distortion field'.[5] While this revolutionised technology, it may also have killed him: diagnosed with pancreatic cancer in 2003, Jobs ignored his doctor's advice, and opted instead for herbal remedies and a juice diet. He used his intellect to convince himself he could cure his illness and to dismiss any doubts from naysayers. Sadly he was wrong.

It can be perilous to afford geniuses too much power without checks and balances. Some of history's greatest geniuses, like industrialist Henry Ford and chess prodigy Bobby Fischer, have been outspoken anti-Semites.

And it seems there could be a darker side to this principle than believing in winged fairies dancing in a babbling brook. The danger of unchecked intellectualism – of purely following 'the Science' – is encoded in our culture, from Frankenstein's monster to *Jurassic Park*. As the French philosopher Denis Diderot once said, 'Evil always turns up in this world through some genius or other.'[6]

Taken to the extreme, the Nazis were fixated on science too. Their technical prowess allowed them to blitzkrieg Europe and design the V2 rockets that would lay the foundations for NASA. They were also obsessed with race and eugenics, of course, to which they took the same scientific approach. The 1937 book *Volk und Rasse*, for example, used a line graph to plot the prevalence of German–Jewish intermarriage over time, titling it 'The Trend in Racial Pollution'; a visual in Nazi newspaper *Der Stürmer* in 1943 showed a drop of blood under a microscope, with Stars of David seen floating in the blood ('With his poison, the Jew destroys / The sluggish blood of weaker peoples'). What's more, Hitler was described in *Die Volksgesundheitswacht* ('public health service') as the doctor of the German people.[7]

In fact, during the Weimar Republic, almost half of all German doctors joined the Nazi Party early – more than any other profession.[8] Compared with the average employed German, doctors were overrepresented within the SS by a factor of more than seven. They also played a significant role in some of the worst scientific atrocities ever documented, subjecting people to deadly experiments involving freezing temperatures, high altitudes, infectious diseases, poisons and transplants, not to mention forced sterilisation and euthanasia.

Of course, this is not to disparage doctors. They are highly valuable members of society, and the majority, just over half, did *not* join the Nazi Party early. But the point is that intellectualism does not necessarily protect you from brainwashing.

A study led by researchers at Carnegie Mellon University examined something called 'the bias blind spot' – that is, the belief that other people are more biased than you are, something that has detrimental consequences for decision making.[9] For example, doctors might believe that gifts from pharmaceutical companies affect other doctors' prescribing choices, but not their own. The researchers found that, out of over six hundred participants, only one said that they were more biased than the average person. People tended not to know just how biased they are. Importantly, this blind spot was not mitigated by intelligence. Similarly, another paper looked at 'the myside bias', the tendency to process information in a way that's biased towards your own prior beliefs, and found 'very little relation to intelligence'.[10]

One study on children illustrates the point nicely: even though children are less likely to believe in Santa as they get older, 'strong belief in Santa was found among several children who exhibited mature causal reasoning'.[11] Even smart kids can believe in Santa Claus.

It's a phenomenon psychology professor Keith Stanovich called 'dysrationalia' – even with adequate intelligence, people are sometimes irrational.[12]

However, what's really interesting about one Stanovich study is that it found intellectuals were actually *more* likely to be biased.[13] He co-published it in the *Journal of Personality and Social Psychology* in 2012. Participants completed all sorts of tests of the 'blind side bias', as well as intelligence tests, across five experiments. Stanovich discovered some slight positive correlations. 'None of these bias blind spot effects displayed a negative correlation with measures of cognitive ability … If anything, the correlations went in the other direction.'

Motivated reasoning

In conversation with Sir Arthur Conan Doyle, the illusionist Harry Houdini once said, 'As a rule, I have found that the greater brain a man has, and the better educated, the easier it has been to mystify him.'[14]

Eventually, Houdini and Conan Doyle had a public falling out. They had attended a séance together, where a psychic had claimed to transmit messages from Houdini's recently deceased Hungarian mother. The messages were communicated in perfect English, a language she had never learnt. Houdini was frustrated that such a great mind as Conan Doyle's could fall prey to an obvious scam.

For his part, Conan Doyle, like much of Europe, was suffering. He had lost his son during the Great War. Among the carnage, is it any wonder that he might have been searching for something more? Until his death, Conan Doyle was convinced of the legitimacy of séances, and of the existence of fairies thanks, in no small part, to the young girls' photographs.

In an interview in 1985, Frances Griffiths was amazed about people's response to the fairies: 'It was just Elsie and I having a bit of fun and I can't understand to this day why they were taken in. They wanted to be taken in.'[15]

With a deep psychological need to fill, Conan Doyle had wanted to be fooled. His remarkable intellect simply provided the justification. This is what the rational brain does: it rationalises. Whereas people generally used to believe that the conscious brain was like the Oval Office, making all of our important decisions for us, the psychological consensus these days (as advertising guru Rory Sutherland put it) is that the emotional brain is the decision-making Oval Office, while the conscious brain is more like the Press Office, coming up with explanations after the fact.[16]

In a nice illustration of this point, psychologists Lars Hall and Petter Johansson had participants fill in a survey indicating their agreement with moral issues of the day.[17] Participants completed the survey on a piece of paper attached to a clipboard. Little did they know that one set of statements was written on detachable paper, which, when the page was turned, stuck to the back of the clipboard, replacing the statements with their polar opposite beneath; for example, 'It is morally defensible to purchase sexual services' became 'It is morally reprehensible to purchase sexual services.' The participant's written answer remained unchanged. They were then asked to explain the answer they had seemingly given.

About half of participants gave justifications for answers they hadn't provided. Their intellectual minds came up with post-rationalisations.

In *Delusion and Mass Delusion*, psychoanalyst Joost Meerloo wrote in the aftermath of the Second World War:

> One supposes what one has to prove, and reasoning moves in a circle. It is like the story of the accused dishonest borrower, who attempted to prove before the court, first, that he had never borrowed anything, second, that he had received it in bad shape, and finally, that he had returned it long ago and did not owe anything.[18]

This is what's known as 'motivated reasoning', where intellect is used to produce logic that satisfies an emotional motivation, like Conan Doyle taking a scientific approach to séances perhaps motivated by the death of his son.[19]

He probably wouldn't have listened to any kind of debunking fact-check. When people are presented with information, they filter it through their existing beliefs. When there is a conflict between them, two areas of the brain light up, one part related to stress and threat response, and the other to their sense of self-identity.[20] Thus, when people are presented with painful information, the rational brain often goes into overdrive to discount it. They are more likely to accept information that is consistent with their worldview, and more likely to reject information that isn't.[21] For example, in the book *When Prophecy Fails*, psychologists infiltrated a doomsday cult; when the leader's predictions didn't come to pass, the cult members didn't all leave; instead many of them rationalised excuses and became even more committed.[22]

This may explain why American Democrats can fall for unfounded conspiracy theories such as Trump–Russia collusion, while Republicans can fall for those like QAnon. In fact, research has consistently shown that people with the highest level of political knowledge are more likely to engage in this kind of biased information processing.[23] People who are politically sophisticated have stronger beliefs they are motivated to protect, they are better at assessing whether information aligns with it, and they are better at rationalising why they should accept or reject this information.

One study found that scientific messaging around man-made climate change is more likely to be accepted by liberals if they have better numeracy and scientific knowledge, whereas these cognitive skills made free-market capitalists more likely to reject the message and say it was an exaggeration.[24] Whether or not climate change is real is not the point – people accepted or rejected it depending on their pre-existing worldview, and intelligence simply made them better at doing so. Elsewhere, another experiment found that the smartest participants were about 45 per cent more likely to read the data correctly if it fitted their worldview.[25]

This is a very important point: smart people are better at deceiving themselves. Academic studies have variously found that intelligence is linked to 'bullshitting' ability,[26] that smarter people are more likely to tell lies[27] and that creative thinkers are more likely to cheat in a task since they can better come up with justifications for doing so.[28] In life, people reach the conclusions they want to reach, but smarter people are better at coming up with justifications for them.

The scientific brain trusters

Hannah Arendt was a political philosopher, Holocaust survivor and author of *The Origins of Totalitarianism*, and she distrusted intellectuals. During the Holocaust, she was shocked by how many of her intelligent friends were able to rationalise their involvement; she became aware of the intellectual ability to massage facts to fit theories, and to therefore live divorced from reality. 'There are,' she once wrote, 'few things that are more frightening than the steadily increasing prestige of scientifically minded brain trusters in the councils of government.'

About the Vietnam War, Arendt lamented what she called the professional problem-solvers who took pride in their rationality, theorising and lack of sentimentality. They were 'eager to find formulas, preferably expressed in a pseudo-mathematical language', while 'the hard and stubborn facts, which so many intelligence analysts were paid so much to collect, were ignored'. 'No reality and no common sense,' Arendt wrote, 'could penetrate the minds of the problem-solvers.'[29]

So, while rationalising can help us achieve great things, it can also cause us to build castles in the sky, to spiral into a world of fantastical gibberish, disconnected from reality. To paraphrase George Orwell, there are some ideas so absurd that only an intellectual could believe them.[30]

It seems the spectre of intellectualism looms particularly large today, among the eddy of the so-called Fourth Industrial Revolution – the new technological age of robotics, AI and genetic engineering. This is an era in which we are all chided to follow 'the Science', and in which something cannot be true unless it is supported by a statistically significant finding in a high-powered study, and has been pre-bunked, fact-checked and reality-checked. While it might sound like a science fiction film, or a conspiracy theory, governments and international bodies have drafted papers proposing how societies and economies will adapt to this industrial revolution.

In America, the General Social Survey found that the percentage of Democrats who have a great deal of confidence in the scientific community leapt from 51 per cent to 64 per cent between 2018 and 2021.[31] Meanwhile, the percentage of Americans who believe in God has dropped from almost everyone in the 1970s to 81 per cent today, according to Gallup.[32] Some have pointed to a rising philosophy of 'Dataism' – where information and algorithms light a path for us in the darkness.[33] Science, we are told, is our salvation.

This makes us ripe for brainwashing. As noted psychoanalyst Carl Jung wrote in the wake of the Third Industrial

Revolution and the mechanised slaughter it had wrought upon Europe: 'one of the chief factors responsible for psychological mass-mindedness is scientific rationalism, which robs the individual of his foundations and his dignity. As a social unit he has lost his individuality and become a mere abstract number in the bureau of statistics.'[34]

A purely intellectual approach to life often neglects what it means to be human. It can cause people to 'miss the trees for the wood' – that is, to focus on abstract patterns at the cost of subjectivity, nuance and reality.

The American historian Richard M. Weaver argued in his 1948 book *Ideas Have Consequences* that modern man has fallen prey to technical specialism to the point of obsession, and that this reflects a disconnect from the whole picture of reality.[35] As the Second World War went on, for example, the Germans put an increasing amount of faith into the technology of rocket bombs at a time when they could serve no practical purpose.

Weaver makes the analogy that the modern thinker is like a drunk who, losing his balance in an increasingly technological and abstract world, tries to save himself by grasping at certain details. 'So the scientist,' wrote Weaver, 'having lost hold upon organic reality, clings the more firmly to his discovered facts, hoping that salvation lies in what can be objectively verified ... Having been told by the relativists that he cannot have truth, he now has "facts".'

The result of this type of obsession is mental instability, since people become detached from the centre of reality that keeps them stable. It is like the stability of the investor with a diversified portfolio, compared with the sensitivity of the investor who puts all of his money into one fund. Weaver argued that this volatility 'shows itself in fits of fickle admiration, in excitation over slight causes, in hyper-suggestibility and proneness to panic ...'

Today, getting lost in the intellectual weeds of cryptocurrencies, vaccine efficacy or Harry Potter fan fiction can be so tempting because it provides a refuge from an increasingly frightening reality. Psychologists have long recognised that intellectualisation is a defence mechanism against trauma. Instead of engaging with a fear, we retreat to the world of abstract thought. As Weaver wrote: 'Let us not question the genuineness of the sigh of relief when people are allowed to go back to their test tubes and their facts.'

In *Delusion and Mass Delusion*, Meerloo succinctly explained how this kind of obsessive thinking 'exercises a narcotic influence':

> People with too many arguments should always be approached with suspicion. Dialectic and endless reasoning are usually used as resistance against disagreeable truths ... People lose themselves in the great problems of life to avoid facing problems of their own; they become pseudo-philosophers in order to escape the activities at home ...

Luxury beliefs

Could all this explain why, today, everyone has to have an opinion on everything? In a world of deafening echo chambers, people may be cocooning themselves within fantastical logic spirals to protect against the existential terror that is modern life.

In *Fear of Freedom*, Erich Fromm (following the Second World War) provides the memorable example of the fisherman and his two summer guests from the city.[36]

Imagine that all three have listened to the weather forecast on the radio and are asked what the weather will be like tomorrow. The fisherman has had a lifetime of experience with the weather. Knowing the direction of the wind, the humidity and so on, he will weigh up all of the information and come to an informed conclusion from his own thinking.

One of the city guests admits that he does not know much about the weather. He repeats what he heard on the radio but says he cannot judge if it's true.

The other city guest is different. He believes he knows a lot about the weather, even though he actually knows almost nothing. He feels that he must be able to answer every question, and gives his opinion, which is, of course, not his – it is identical to the radio forecast. Feeling compelled to have an opinion, he repeats the forecast as if it were his own.

> He has the illusion of having arrived at an opinion of his own, but in reality he has merely adopted an authority's opinion without being aware of this process.
>
> Ask an average newspaper reader what he thinks about a certain political question. He will give you as 'his' opinion a more or less exact account of what he has read, and yet – and this is the essential point – he believes that what he is saying is the result of his own thinking.

The 'cultural mediation hypothesis' suggests that intelligent people are more likely to get swept up in these kinds of manufactured opinions.[37] They are more likely to be liberal today, so the theory goes, for the same reason that so many doctors joined the very illiberal Nazi Party in the 1930s: smart people are better at sussing out what the dominant cultural norms are, and therefore what to think and say in order to get ahead.

Rob Henderson received a PhD in psychology from Cambridge University. He knows about getting ahead: he grew up in foster homes and worked as a dishwasher, bus boy and supermarket bagger before enlisting in the US Air Force and subsequently attending Yale on the GI Bill in 2015 and then getting a scholarship to Cambridge. His working-class background gave him a unique perspective on the upper crust by which he found himself surrounded. He coined the term 'luxury beliefs':

At Yale there are more students from the top 1 per cent than the entire bottom 60 per cent. At Cambridge this disparity is probably even more pronounced. There are people from very upper crust backgrounds who have beliefs completely at odds with people from the working and middle classes. In the past people used to display their position with material goods. As material wealth and abundance proliferated, you can't tell status just from looking at the size of a bank account anymore – so now, their position is communicated through vocabulary, beliefs, the 'current thing'. Only people who have white collar jobs who can read Twitter and articles all day can keep up with these beliefs.

It's not conscious. It's a social positioning game. If they express a view, it'll bolster their status. They don't really think through the consequences. Like the 'Defund the Police' idea. There were a lot of people who didn't want to upset or hurt anyone – if they saw an op ed in the *New York Times*, they assumed it was a good idea. They are generally affluent people who live in gated communities and have private security. They say one thing but the practices they implement in their own lives are different.

A luxury belief confers status on the upper class while the lower classes bear more burden from it. A luxury belief does not have to reflect reality, and often the measure of a luxury belief is how it is at odds with reality. The 'Defund the Police' idea – we're still seeing the effects of rising crime and murder and so forth. The idea is at odds with what's good in reality.

Expressing a belief that is harmful to the lower classes is how some signal their social status. This might explain why posh students want to Just Stop Oil: it's a signal of success to interfere with the energy market when daddy doesn't mind paying a few thousand more for your electric bills; and it's a signal of success to sit in the road blocking traffic when you don't have to drive to work.

An article from, ironically, the *New York Times* summed it up this way: 'To feel at home in opportunity-rich areas, you've got to ... possess the right attitudes about David Foster Wallace, child-rearing, gender norms and intersectionality.'[38]

Curse of the midwit

There's another reason why smart people can fall for this kind of gobbledegook: they assume that, being smart, they couldn't possibly be wrong. In psychology, this is known as the 'Dunning–Kruger effect': people who know a bit about a subject overestimate how much they really do know.[39] True experts, meanwhile, concur with Socrates: 'The more I know, the more I realise I know nothing.'

Before he was sentenced to death, Socrates explained the origin of his reputation for wisdom. Being declared by the Oracle of Delphi as the wisest person in Athens, he scoured the city for the greatest poets, politicians and artists for someone wiser than himself, to no avail.

> Because they were accomplished in practising their skill, each one of them claimed to be wisest about other things too: the most important ones at that – and this error of theirs seemed to obscure the wisdom they did possess ... Those with the greatest reputations seemed to me practically the most deficient, while others who were supposedly inferior seemed better endowed when it came to good sense.[40]

A study published in the *Bulletin of Economic Research* did indeed find that, in relative terms, cognitive ability has a significant, positive effect on the overconfidence bias.[41] Other studies have demonstrated something called the 'illusion of expertise': subject matter experts are more likely to guess at an answer, and get it wrong, than admit their ignorance.[42] A different experiment found that, when people were primed to feel knowledgeable, they were less likely to listen to the opinions of people who disagreed.[43]

Those who have a little bit of knowledge, but not too much, are what controversial academic Edward Dutton would call 'the midwit' (someone with above-average, but not genius, intelligence). Dutton is Professor of Evolutionary Psychology at Asbiro University and Honorary Professor in the Institute of Psychology at the Russian Academy of Science in Moscow. In an interview, he told us:

> What the data indicate is within the normal range, above-average intelligence correlates with social conformity. They are better at norm mapping and looking around the world and correctly discerning the way the wind is blowing and doing the mental gymnastics to convince themselves of the current thing and to competitively signal it. Less intelligent people are less able to norm map, less able to force themselves to believe the current thing, so they just don't.

Editor-in-Chief of the journal *Medical Hypotheses* Bruce Charlton wrote a 2009 article, 'Clever Sillies: Why High IQ People Tend to be Deficient in Common Sense'.[44] Charlton described 'the absent-minded and socially-inept "nutty professor" stereotype in science' who 'is brilliant at his job while at the same time being fatuous and incompetent in terms of his everyday life'. Clever sillies exist because 'IQ brings with it a tendency differentially to over-use general intelligence in problem-solving, and to override those instinctive and spontaneous forms of evolved behaviour which could be termed common sense'.

It's not just about intelligence, but also character. Edward Dutton explored the personality of clever sillies in a study published in the journal *Intelligence*. He explained:

> The people with middling high intelligence will get brainwashed. The people who won't get sucked in are low IQ or outlier high IQ which correlates with aspects of autism. It is these traits which distinguish between the genius and the clever silly. The genius has outlier IQ and autistic traits and moderate psychopathic traits. A paper by Felix Post on 291 eminent men shows they are significantly overrepresented in subclinical psychopaths. If you are low in conscientiousness, you will be able to think outside the box, you will come up with things that are unthinkable to most people – like Darwin. If you're low in agreeableness, you don't understand you'll offend people or you just don't care. Isaac Newton was horrible.
>
> On the other hand you have what I call the 'head girls' – the 'Karens' who demand you wear a mask. They have normal-range high IQ plus high conscientiousness and high agreeableness. They are very rule-following and don't like offending people and have high anxiety. They want to fit in and not upset people.

Dutton seems to have fallen foul of what he might call these 'head girls'. He is described by RationalWiki as a terrorist-sympathiser, anti-feminist, race and intelligence pseudoscientist, homophobe, Islamophobe, sexist, transphobe, anti-Semite, white supremacist and even *anti-vegan*. RationalWiki is a leftist website that purports to refute 'anti-science' and was set up specifically to oppose an online encyclopaedia run by conservatives.[45]

Although some of Dutton's conclusions are certainly objectionable, he would perhaps argue that his case illustrates the point. Although he presents his arguments with supporting evidence, they fall outside of the bounds of acceptable discourse for the 'current thing', and the people whose high conscientiousness and agreeableness make them sensitive to norm-breaking and offence, and whose above-average intelligence allows them to comprehend and debate his points, go into overdrive to put him back in his box.

In the aforementioned paper 'Why did so many German doctors join the Nazi party early?', one of the hypotheses is that doctors often have an authoritarian personality typified by a strong adherence to the rules (and for good reason – you probably wouldn't want a wacky doctor to give you off-the-wall suggestions about how to mend your broken leg). In *Delusion and Mass Delusion*, Joost Meerloo wrote that, 'Knowledge and insight can be dangerous … In scientific circles, students who try to free themselves from scientific tradition are treated with much aggression.'

Dutton suggests this kind of suppression can be counterproductive.

> We can talk online because of innovative people. Those are the people who should be supported – those autistic weirdos. The flip side is those people are also questioning everything else. Hans Eysenck produced massive innovations in psychology but he also believed in eugenics and astrology. There are people who get their self-esteem from mocking people who are different. For every person looking for Atlantis, there's someone working on something important.

There is a powerful example in the book *The Intelligence Trap*.[46] The author, David Robson, has written a fantastic book but does not seem to have taken his own advice on intellectual humility. He writes about Kary Mullis, who, being the Nobel Prize-winning inventor of the PCR test, would probably qualify as a true genius. He also has some out-there beliefs about the existence of aliens, the value of astrology, and the validity (or lack thereof) of claims around HIV and climate change. Robson, who is not a Nobel Prize winner, makes it clear what are the reasonable bounds for discussion: 'I hope I don't have to tell you that Kary is wrong.'

Elsewhere in the book, the author adds a parenthesis lest the reader start coming to the wrong conclusions: 'To be absolutely clear, overwhelming evidence shows that vaccines are safe and effective, carbon emissions are changing the climate, and evolution is true.'

Rational thought is great, of course. However, the lesson from this chapter is that it can also lead us astray. Smart people are great at believing their beliefs, even if those beliefs are twisted from reality, or have been implanted from elsewhere. While most of us are not Nobel Prize winners, we do rely on logical justifications for our thoughts and behaviours. We can use our intellect to rationalise bizarre thoughts and harmful behaviours. Our intellectual ability to infer the done thing, to justify our compliance with it and to have confidence in our conclusions makes us vulnerable to brainwashing.

This is used by manipulators when they provide a rationalisation for behaviour – what is known as 'placebic information'. A psychology study found that people are more likely to let someone cut in line for a photocopier if the request includes a meaningless justification such as, 'Can I cut in line because I need to make some copies?'[47]

Listen to your heart

So, besides a lobotomy, what's the answer?

First, trust your gut. Former FBI hostage negotiator Gary Noesner described how people's gut feeling in the teeth of a crisis can serve them best. 'It made me realise how many times that fight or flight radar is ignored, how critical it is, and how we should learn to listen to it,' he says. 'The human mind has this incredible unconscious way of telling us when things are not going well or the relationship is sour and you have to realise that. Take it head on. Listen to your gut.'

Our instinct has developed over millions of years of evolution and, though we may call it irrational or biased, it has actually served us very well. Without our emotional intuition, we would actually be rather bad at decision making, even for what we might consider to be rational decisions. Famed neuroscientist and author of *Descartes' Error* Antonio Damasio found that many patients who had lost the ability to feel certain emotions also had major impairments in their decision-making abilities.[48] When a particular part of the frontal lobe is damaged, people retain their intellect but experience difficulties in planning their behaviour and learning from past mistakes – and they also have trouble expressing and experiencing emotion. Damasio argued that this part of the brain uses emotions to direct behaviour based on past experience. If you were once bitten by a snake, for example, that would cause your heart to race; the next time you see a snake, your heart would race again, and that fear response would be used by the brain to make sure you stay away from it. Without this use of emotion, decision making becomes completely intellectual – and thus slow and inefficient.

Damasio wrote: 'Rather than being a luxury, emotions are a very intelligent way of driving an organism toward certain outcomes.'

There is, accordingly, experimental research that using your gut can be good for decision making. In a month-long study of stock market investors, the best performers were those who reported the most intense feelings when they made their investments. Importantly, they also used more precise vocabulary to describe these feelings.[49] They were better able to differentiate between their emotions (for instance, between anger and anxiety). They were more consciously in tune with their instincts.

The recommendation, then, is to listen to your heart and to become consciously aware of exactly what it is saying. One route to this could be meditation, which improves 'interoceptive awareness': one study found that a 15-minute mindfulness session reduced the incidence of a particular cognitive bias by 34 per cent.[50] Another route could be physically noting your emotions: doctors in one piece of research jotted down their immediate gut instinct and then consciously interpreted it, resulting in diagnostic accuracy increasing by up to 40 per cent.[51]

It is our gut instinct that helps to keep us grounded. Referencing the Second World War, psychoanalyst and author Joost Meerloo explained in *Delusion and Mass Delusion*:

> Intellect becomes vulnerable when no personality is developed to fortify it. The cultural acquisition of intellectuals is easily paralysed by terror and fear when character falters. Character, its potency, and the stable personality it provides for mental functioning is more important in society than a purely analytical intellect. This we could observe among the people who formed the resistance movement [under Nazi occupation]. The pure intelligentsia stayed away. In a full-grown personality feeling and thinking harmonize with each other.

Similarly, a good protection against brainwashing is good old common sense.

Psychologist Igor Grossman set about putting a formalised structure to common sense in his research on wisdom, by breaking down classic philosophy into four principles of 'thinking about thinking' (known as metacognition).[52] The first is seeking other people's perspectives, which considers information from all sides even if it conflicts with your own, and thinking about how things might affect other people; the second is integrating different opinions into an overall resolution, finding a balance and compromise; the third is the ability to recognise that things can change (including your own beliefs); and the fourth is having a sense of intellectual humility and realising that your own perspective is limited and imperfect.

Benjamin Franklin, after reading an account of Socrates' trial, determined to always question his own judgement and to respect other people's. He made a deliberate effort to avoid words like 'certainly, undoubtedly, or any others that give the air of positiveness to an opinion'.[53]

'Those who affect to be thought to know everything,' he said, 'and so undertake to explain everything, often remain long ignorant of many things that others could and would instruct them in, if they appeared less conceited.'[54]

Psychological research has indeed shown that giving people humbling feedback can reduce biases like overconfidence,[55] while deliberately taking time to consider a conflicting perspective and argue against yourself can reduce a range of biases.[56]

With a little practice, putting more faith in your gut instinct and less faith in the certainty of your rational conclusions could prevent your brain from taking you, like Conan Doyle, away with the fairies.

The rules:

- Be aware that your mind is flawed and have the humility to stay unattached to your beliefs.
- Listen to your heart and gut, and become consciously aware of what they are trying to tell you; meditate.
- Be wary of experts who claim with certainty that they hold all the answers to complex problems.

5

Be aware of your sensations

You make sense of the world through your senses. Would-be manipulators will use yours to influence you, by drawing you in, seducing you, and moulding the thoughts and emotions at the front of your mind. Beware of beguiling environments if you want to keep your mind free.

Jingles and jackpots

'Ker-ching, ker-ching, ker-ching! When you won, the machine mechanism spat out the coins and you'd hear the sound of the coins landing. There were loud punchy noises. It would attract attention, kids would come running over to see what you had won. It was a good feeling.'

Simon's recollections of his early childhood experiences of arcades were drenched in sensory experience. The sound of coins landing, the 'fairground-style music' and 'flashing lights, bright red and orange' featured large in his memories. Sound, sight and touch were indivisible from emotion, wonder and excitement.

Fruit machines, coin pushers and arcade games were a fun hobby for a child with a few pounds of pocket money burning a hole in his pocket. But they 'massively programmed me to be a gambler', he confessed. As an adult he went on to become heavily addicted to roulette. 'Some people see it as a bit of fun and they can spend £5 or £10 and that's it,' he said.

> There's a difference between being a gambler and a compulsive gambler. No matter how much a compulsive gambler wins, they will continue. If they lose, they still want to gamble. You think you can beat the system but it's deeper than that. A compulsive gambler thinks they can change the world. I'd spend £50, then it went up to £100, then it went up to thousands.

As an adult, he found that the roulette table in a casino offered an equally compelling sensory experience. 'It's a simple concept, and it's the worst game you could possibly play. But it's the most exciting – there's movement, spinning, randomness, the board is cool, you're waiting for red and black.' Simon would feel anxiety and excitement while he was playing, until 'the dull feeling when everything just drops when you have no chips left at the end'.

Arcades and casinos are environments designed to play with your senses, to persuade you to stay and, at the same time, help you forget about the outside world. For instance you don't see clocks in casinos, because they would remind you of your schedule and obligations. There are often no windows, so you don't think about the outside world, or how many hours you have been there. Doors are deliberately positioned away from natural light, so there is no chance it will leak in.

There is an urban myth that casinos pump extra oxygen in to keep people awake longer. That is disputed by the industry, but casinos do use high-tech purification systems to improve the air quality, which could give the effect of more oxygen. And, of course, pleasant scents are circulated in the ventilation systems to make the surroundings as enticing as possible. Staff bring food and drink to where you are gaming so you have no need to leave your machine or table in order to satisfy your hunger, thirst or cravings. The chairs are very comfortable. Good luck messages dazzle and lucky symbols flash, creating a sense of you and your good fortune being pitted against the gods. Pictures of beautiful women shine from gaming machine screens. One modern London casino has vertical screens poised by each table to announce the play, and these screens are in the same dimensions as our addictive smartphones. They ooze a siren lure and form alpha waves in receptive brains before bets are even placed.

As an anonymous CEO of a gambling and entertainment company said: 'We want to give our customers an encapsulating experience, we want to take care of every need. We try and make it feel relaxed, to make it feel safer. And we use flattering lighting so people look good. We think about the whole sensory experience, the sounds, the smell.' Some of the attention to detail is quite subtle. Feng Shui experts are hired to ensure that the environments are primed for Asian customers who have 'a stronger inclination to wager'. Gold colours are popular choices for the interior design, to evoke the idea of actual gold and luxury. The high-end casinos do allow windows now – that trick is old and everyone knows about it.

Echoing Simon's memories, the CEO confirmed that sound is an important element:

> We like the sounds of winning. Even in a cashless society there are the sounds of coins falling. We like the machines to announce that we have a winner. There is signage announcing the jackpot. We make sure it's noisy when people win, but the slot machines have noises even if no one is playing them.

He points out that there is no lying: people do win. It's just that by the end of the year the casino is the real winner. It is a business, after all.

Pleasure Island

Our senses – sight, sound, touch, taste, smell – help us to create an objective perception of reality. They help us to make sense of the world. They influence our feelings about ourselves, other people, our environment and our behaviour. That means our senses can be used by others to attract us, influence us and extract more money from us. In the time of Shakespeare the five senses were also known as 'wits'. This chapter encourages you to open your eyes, follow your nose, listen intently and keep your wits about you.

Children's stories lay bare the dangers of becoming lost in our surroundings. In *The Wonderful Wizard of Oz*, the Wicked Witch of the West used flowers to ensnare Dorothy, 'with poison in it … attractive to the eye and soothing to the smell … poppies, poppies, poppies will put them to sleep'. Poppies are not deadly, so Dorothy thought it was safe to fall asleep in the alluringly pretty red field. Of course, at the time the author L. Frank Baum wrote the book, the opium from poppies was a common medicine, but the US was to pass legislation to control its distribution. Baum may have intended a caution.

In Hans Christian Andersen's 'The Snow Queen', all of Gerda's senses are lulled by an enchanted garden. When she arrives she is struck by the warm sunshine, wondrous light shining through red, blue and green glass in the sorceress's cottage, she eats exquisite cherries and her hair is combed out. Then she sees the garden and 'Oh, what odour and what loveliness was there! Every flower that one could think of, and of every season, stood there in fullest bloom; no picture-book could be gayer or more beautiful.' This is one of multiple environments that bewitch the heroine and hero of the story. Each time, they must overcome their senses to come to their senses.

Pinocchio falls for the superficial amusements of Toy Island. In the Disney film of the story, Pleasure Island is presented with dark undertones, but he chooses an environment of toys and games above the harder discipline and study of school. The kids trapped on Pleasure Island turned eventually into donkeys, unthinking beasts of burden toiling for their manipulative masters.

In fairy tales, the heroes and heroines enter enchanted forests that symbolise the realm of the subconscious. And under the canopy of the tall, forbidding trees, one way or another, they must defeat their secret shadow selves and penetrate the darkness to find meaning. The everyday threat for us today is not as dangerous, or as obvious, as a gingerbread house, or a path of breadcrumbs, or spellbound flowers, but the lesson remains: to be aware of where our powerful senses may lead us.

Simon told the story of his addiction through sensations he remembered. A familiar song or a fragrance can conjure long-distant memories and emotions. Walking past hay bales as an adult could recall a pony ride as a child. A whiff of perfume can bring back memories of a former lover. Odour appears from research to be the sense most strongly linked to memories, but they all work together to jolt other memories of sensations, resulting in a stronger impression.[1] The rush of memories from sensory experience has its own name: the Proustian moment. Just a morsel of tea and cake caused this reaction in Marcel Proust's *À la Recherche du Temps Perdu*: 'I carried to my lips a spoonful of the tea in which I had let soften a bit of madeleine. But at the very instant when the mouthful of tea mixed with cake crumbs touched my palate, I quivered, attentive to the extraordinary thing that was happening inside me.'

The combined tea and cake relied upon taste but also, crucially, smell. If you hold your nose while eating vanilla ice cream you will taste sweetness but not the flavours.

'I can control your emotions and influence your behavior without showing you anything, without touching you, and without saying a single word to you,' said Dawn Goldworm, founder of marketing company 12.29, in a talk.[2] Olfactory branding is the new frontier of emotional communication in marketing. 12.29 integrates scent into brand identity, and is run by two sisters who have smell–colour synaesthesia, an unusual condition that means they experience odours as having colours and textures too.

For Cadillac, the scent they manufactured is a combination of nutty coffee, dark leather and resinous amber, with fresh sage, woody cedar wood and clean musk. This scent is pumped through air-conditioning systems in the New York headquarters and dealerships around the world. For Nike they created a scent identity informed by the smell of the skid of a basketball sneaker on the court with the mix of oil and rubber from handling a basketball and a new pair of Air Force Ones when you open the box.

When a retail space diffuses the right scent it creates an emotional link between us and the brand. It's hard to begrudge this pleasant marketing technique that makes our surroundings more enjoyable. Would you rather smell the fresh subtle scent of new rubber trainers in the Nike store, or the stench of dog poo that might grace your trainers once you step on the pavement outside? Only one of those will induce you to spend time in the store and buy the trainers. And you walked in there to spend money, after all. At the same time, it's important to be aware your nose has effectively been hijacked to make you spend more money. Nike reported that adding scent to an environment made 84 per cent of customers more likely to purchase shoes and to be willing to pay 10 to 15 per cent more for the same product.[3] A London nightclub found that sales of the drink Malibu more than doubled when there was a coconut fragrance diffused. Novotel increased breakfast, coffee and pastry sales by diffusing a coffee scent in the morning.

Marketers know that sensory, emotional and social experiences combine to produce the most memorable experiences. And they neglect the senses at their peril. Starbucks is a case in point. Back in 2007, Starbucks Chairman, Howard Schultz, realised that sales were slipping because of the loss of the powerful coffee aroma in the stores due to a shift towards sealed packaged coffee and automated espresso machines. In a memo to the CEO he wrote that aroma was the most powerful non-verbal signal in the store, and ceasing to grind coffee in front of customers had stripped the stores of 'tradition' and 'the soul of the past'.

The bakery smell in the supermarket creates the impression of freshness, as well as arousing your taste buds. Likewise, fresh flowers and fruit and vegetables near the entrance are supposed to convince you of the 'freshness' of all the produce in the store. People are known to buy what grabs their attention, so point-of-sale displays at the start of the journey boost the sales of selected products.

Christmas is an ideal time to witness the multi-sensory revolution in retail, with seasonal scents pumped into shops, yuletide décor and festive tunes playing. Studies have unsurprisingly shown that Christmas music and a pine-needle scent increase sales at the right time of year.[4] At the other end of the spectrum, sometimes the sensory environment is pared back, to achieve a different end. Think of Apple: the white, minimal, clean environment signals you are in the hands of a modern, high-tech company.

The temperature of the environment affects your mood and purchasing decisions. Warmth increases feelings of social closeness. One interesting effect of this was confirmed in an analysis of betting behaviour at a racetrack over a three-year period.[5] It was found that bets were more likely to converge on the favourite (the majority-endorsed option) when the temperature at the track was warm. This field study was backed up by laboratory studies that also demonstrated that warm temperatures increased the participants' preferences for products endorsed by the majority – in summary, physical warmth engenders 'social warmth' and conformity. Music can prime purchases too. One study found that people bought more expensive wine when the store played classical music rather than pop, because the classical music put people in a sophisticated frame of mind.[6]

Mesmerising music

The impact of sound on the mind has been written about for thousands of years. Plato wrote in *Laws* that music is a useful instrument for education 'because more than anything else rhythm and harmony find their way into the inmost soul and take strongest hold upon it'.[7] And in *Republic*, he said that music can be used to deliberately evoke different emotional responses, such as 'soberness, courage, liberality, and high-mindedness, and all their kindred and their opposites, too, in all the combinations that contain and convey them'.[8] Babies can be crooned to sleep and Bacchants put into a hedonistic frenzy, depending on the tune.

The 'Mozart effect' refers to the (contested) claim that listening to Mozart's music can increase your general intelligence.[9] The original research by Frances Rauscher found that people enjoy brief (10–15 minute) improvements in visual–spatial reasoning after listening to short excerpts of Mozart's music. The term has also been used to describe the apparent health benefits of listening to music – including benefits for people suffering from anxiety, hypertension and epilepsy. The research gripped the public imagination, fuelled clickbait headlines and, ultimately, was somewhat misunderstood. Playing a woman's pregnant bump music will make the baby move, but it won't make the baby a genius, despite the implied claims of products sold on the back of the 'Mozart effect'. Conversely, there is also some evidence for what might be called a 'Cardi B effect', where loud, aggressive and percussive music can reduce cognitive function.[10]

Since the days of the German physician Franz Anton Mesmer (from whom we get the word 'mesmerise'), some have argued that behaviour can be manipulated through vibrations.[11]

Mesmer used a glass harmonica during his hypnosis procedures. He was also friends with Haydn and Mozart. The neurologist Jean-Martin Charcot hypnotised Parisians in the nineteenth century using gongs and tuning forks – as did respected psychologists like Alfred Binet.

Psychoanalyst Joost Meerloo called rock 'n' roll 'a form of rhythmic mass hypnosis', and William Sargant wrote that, 'From the Stone Age to Hitler, from the Beatles to the modern "pop" culture, the brain of man has been constantly swayed by the same physiological techniques. Reason is dethroned, the normal brain computer is temporarily put out of action, and new ideas and beliefs are uncritically accepted.'[12]

There is an archetype of the musician hypnotising people and leading them astray, which traces itself back to stories like the Greek Sirens who would lure sailors to their death, and the Greek goat-footed Pan, the god of shepherds and the allegorical origin of pan-pipes.

There is a more scientific basis to the power of music to brainwash. Two principles are supported by empirical research: first, music has the power to get stuck in our heads, in particular thanks to what are known as 'earworms';[13] and second, the more often we hear something, the more we believe it to be true.[14] Catchy songs will have you playing a message on repeat in your own mind, whether you want to or not.

The powers-that-be seem to recognise this persuasive power of music. In April 2022, a German musician known as Mr Bond was sentenced to ten years in prison for making neo-Nazi music (with lyrics like, 'Lying press, banks, sick Hollywood shows, behind all these crimes, a Satanic hooknose').[15] His songs were unquestionably hateful. Yet the airwaves are polluted with distasteful songs including violent and misogynistic rap. Eminem (one of the highest-selling recording artists of all time) has written multiple songs about abducting and murdering his ex-wife in explicit detail. If we are to recognise and inhibit the hypnotic potential of Mr Bond's bile, why not the insidious earworms that make their way into our brains from the pop charts?

The implicit messages of these songs can be pernicious. Ke$ha advised her young fans to 'make the most of the night like we're gonna die young' and to live 'dancing like we're dumb, our bodies going numb'; Lady Gaga sang both, 'I don't wanna think anymore, I got my head and my heart on the dance floor,' and 'I love this record, baby, but I can't see straight anymore … Just dance, gonna be okay'; while Britney Spears instructed listeners to 'keep on dancin' 'till the world ends'. The message is clear: don't think, just gratify. It is hardly conducive to a healthy society.

By contrast, composers of the past wanted to create the most delightful and imaginative recitals possible, but modern-day concerts go further. Coachella, for example, echoes the peace and love vibes of forerunner Woodstock, but is a spectacle of controlled mass stimulation. As one writer put it, 'upon entering the festival, you're blasted with fireworks sponsored by Coca-Cola, Ferris wheels slathered with the Nike logo, and other, equally branded sensory overloads. The crowd is transported into the consumerist city of Coachella. The audience no longer wants reality, they want Coachella's reproduction of it.'[16]

Once upon a time, Coachella banned brand names in the grounds; now it is known as the 'Super Bowl of Branding'. Believe it or not, one of the most popular spots at the 2022 Coachella was the American Express lounge, according to *Forbes* magazine.[17] Amex's Shizuka Suzuki explains that the company is there to reach Millennials and Gen Zs in an experiential and holistic environment. In other words, go for the music, stay for the sensory experience and leave with great memories, some merchandise and Amex burned into your brain.

Modern-day festivals are commercial beasts of manipulation, controlling your clock time and imposing a sensory overload, all with the ultimate aim of giving sponsors a prime emotional connection to your brain and your wallet. Naturally, a memorable experience means you are more likely to return next year.

Music is a powerful way to communicate and manipulate. Experimental research has indeed shown that rhythmic percussion can have peculiar impacts on the brain – there is, for example, activity in the supplementary motor area and left premotor area such that body movements synchronise with the beat of the drum.[18] Other studies have shown that people match their pace of exercise to the tempo of music they are listening to.[19]

None of this is to say you should not enjoy musical concerts, casinos, or shopping, or luxuriating in sensation. Organisations use senses artfully to improve our frame of mind; the key is to distinguish whether it benefits us, or them.

Harnessing the senses for good

Religion uses the environment and senses to create a worshipful frame of mind. It is easier to contemplate and pray in the right setting. Father Daniel, an Anglican vicar, pointed out that 'the physicality of church is really important and underplayed. The architecture of a church is trying to talk to the human heart and imagination, rather than propose a series of logical arguments.' The design of traditional churches is supposed to connect you with the transcendent, to 'unbalance you in some ways'. The space asks you to look upwards, as does the incense, which works for smell and sight senses. It creates a 'fog and it takes things out of focus, it's an appeal to the imagination. The visions of heaven are full of smoke. The visions of the other place are full of smoke too. It's ethereal.' Even some charismatic evangelicals use smoke machines.

Some people find churches spooky, which Father Daniel says is because they are 'thin' places, to use the Celtic term. People have prayed in churches for hundreds of years, which creates an unprovable 'sense that the place is touching heaven'. More materially, the church inspires you to 'switch off your left brain' by using 'gargoyles, incense, and seeing light in different ways through the glass'.

Some worship involves physical movement of the body. A first-time visitor to a Catholic or Anglo-Catholic service, repetitively asked to stand, sit and kneel, might feel like they are unwittingly in a game of 'Simon Says'. 'From the Anglo-Catholic point of view, at our best we worship using all our physical senses,' says Father Daniel. 'Posture in religious worship is important. It invites us to worship by using our body rather than our mind.'

What we do from the neck down impacts on how we feel from the neck up. You can use your body to change your state of mind. It is believed that standing in a power pose increases feelings of confidence. Smiling and frowning create different emotions and attitudes. There is early research to investigate the use of Botox in improving mood by blocking frowning muscles.[20]

Andrew Huberman, a neuroscientist at Stanford University, says that vision and breathing are the fastest ways to regulate the autonomic nervous system, a component of the peripheral nervous system that regulates involuntary physiologic processes including heart rate, blood pressure, respiration, digestion and sexual arousal.[21] This is not just about what we look at, but how we *use* our eyes.

In the modern world, we use tunnel vision a lot, such as watching TV, or using a computer or smartphone. When we talk to people, we often look mainly at the face and eyes. But for millions of years human beings evolved in the natural environment, and our physiological functions and senses respond to it.

'When [you] look at a horizon or at a broad vista, you don't look at one thing for very long. If you keep your head still, you can dilate your gaze so you can see far into the periphery –

above, below and to the sides of you,' says Huberman.[22] 'That mode of vision releases a mechanism in the brain stem involved in vigilance and arousal. One can actually turn off the stress response by changing the way that we are viewing our environment, regardless of what's in that environment.'

In other words, just getting outside into nature and looking at a panoramic view is good for you. You can ease your own state of mind and reduce stress by putting down your phone, going for a walk and looking at the horizon.

The natural world is an important environment for human health. The term 'forest bathing' emerged in Japan in the 1980s to describe the physiological and psychological benefit of getting into nature among trees.

And if you want to go more woo-woo than that, you can also try out a sound bath produced by Tibetan singing bowls. Research shows that the therapy has a positive impact, reducing tension, anger, fatigue and depressed mood by propelling the brain into states of deep relaxation, such as beta waves and theta waves.[23]

If you can't easily access broad vistas, forests or sound baths, then you could at least tidy your room and 'make your bed', as Jordan Peterson advises in *12 Rules for Life: An Antidote to Chaos*. This simple daily routine creates an organised environment within your control. Visual clutter has also been shown to cause errors in decision making.[24]

In many small ways you can take steps to improve your own environment and how you stimulate your senses for healthful benefits. Importantly, you can't free your mind without being aware of your body and environment.

Sensations should be enjoyed. They add to how we experience emotions and the environment, and create memories. The saying 'Stop and smell the roses' invites you to pause and take pleasure in your senses.

Smell the roses, but don't be enchanted by them.

The rules:

- Stay alert to how your senses are influenced in your surroundings.
- Have clear goals in mind when you go to enticing environments, and don't allow your senses to overrule your mind.
- Adapt your own surroundings and use your senses to have a happier, more ordered mind.

6

Practise social media distancing

Social media has given us the power to shape and share our identities and political movements. It also creates global crowds (and crowds can be dangerous), exposes us to manipulation, offers a sophisticated vehicle for propaganda, affects our mental health and can turn us into mini-propagandists. You need to be aware of the multiple risks and learn how to keep a safe social media distance.

The Fourth Industrial Revolution

'Don't be evil,' proclaimed the founders of Google. They didn't exactly set the bar high, but at least they didn't say, '*Do* be evil.' Since then, the Silicon Valley techno-optimists have transmogrified into Big Tech oligarchs. Google and other search and social media giants wield political power similar to nation states over vast global userships.

It's estimated that 83 per cent of the entire global population owns smartphones.[1] The fastest-growing social media platform, TikTok, claims to have over one billion active users.[2] In the UK, over 91 per cent of the population use social media.[3] We are in a unique time – the confluence of algorithms and nudges have made human beings' brains and behaviours more hackable than ever before.

The proliferation of smartphones has ushered in an era of unprecedented connectivity. Access to the world and each other is packed into small devices that fit in our hands. We have the world at our fingertips.

Where will this new technology lead?

According to historian, philosopher and author Yuval Noah Harari, 'Humans will no longer be autonomous entities directed by the stories the narrating self invents. Instead they will be integral parts of a huge global network.'[4] This is a far-reaching hypothesis, but aspects of it are appreciable today. And perhaps it's why Harari does not even own a smartphone, for all his apparent enthusiasm for a transhumanist chipped-brain future.[5]

Imagine a world where algorithms and data make the decisions, and in which robots and artificial intelligence undertake most jobs. It has begun. 'Do you need any help?' queries the AI customer support on a website pop-up. Primary healthcare apps already use AI. Roles from accountant to travel agent to oncologist could risk replacement in the not too distant future. A 2013 study into the future of employment predicted that over the next decade or two, up to 47 per cent of US jobs were at risk of computerisation.[6] It's easy to see how generative AI platforms like ChatGPT and Midjourney will make humans redundant in various industries. This will lead to the rise of the 'useless class', as Harari terms the future unemployed, destined, he says, to be pacified with video games and drugs.

The velocity, scale and fusion of new technologies with the physical and biological worlds has been termed the 'Fourth Industrial Revolution'. Some speculate that these societal and economic changes will be mirrored in the emergence of a new philosophy, or 'religion' of sorts: Dataism. According to Harari, 'proponents of the Dataist worldview perceive the entire universe as a flow of data, see organisms as little more than biochemical algorithms and believe that humanity's cosmic vocation is to create an all-encompassing data-processing system – and then merge into it'. Bleakly, he sees humans as losing free will and authority, and democratic elections becoming meaningless.

He may not be wrong. In 2015 a study was published in which magnets applied judiciously to the threat-processing centres in people's brains could make them less politically conservative and weaken their faith in God.[7] Since then, Elon Musk has announced that his human–internet brain interface, Neuralink, would be moving to human trials.[8] The implications for political influence are clear. In 2019, Facebook acquired a neural interface start-up. Its name? CTRL.[9]

The Fourth Industrial Revolution is a new paradigm that requires a new moral code. In this modern digital world, when we flounder to determine good and evil, algorithms are the angels. As angels intermediate between people and the ultimate authority, observe human behaviour, deliver messages, convey judgement and carry us to heaven, so algorithms observe our every digital footprint and decision, uphold the rules and boot us off social media platforms for transgressions. They also predict, personalise and persuade.

Even while we were writing this chapter, algorithms made themselves known. As we edited on Google Docs and replied to each other's comments, the software suggested responses: 'That would be awesome' and 'Great idea'. There are still questions about whether algorithms reduce or embed bias – after all, the human authors are not bias free. An algorithm is by its very nature a bias, having learnt patterns from positive and negative feedback in much the same way a once-bitten human would be biased against dogs. You'll notice that the authors of Google Docs' algorithms tend towards agreeableness, rather than encourage lively critique and debate that might feel conflictual.

Harari goes so far as to claim that human beings are themselves nothing but a form of organic algorithm, shaped by natural selection. By extension, algorithmic biology makes the philosophical case for the absence of free will, not to mention the absence of the superstitious notion of a soul. This does make it easier to position humans as equal to algorithms, or possibly even lower down the decision-making food chain. Could algorithms one day own property and businesses and make laws? In this unsettling future, individualism could collapse, and authority could shift from humans to networked algorithms.

Well, we are not there yet. This future imagined by intellectuals and beloved of technocrats is still just a prediction, a hypothesis, a dream or a nightmare, as you will. Innovation is not entirely predictable, as Nobel Prize-winning economist Paul Krugman proved, when he predicted in 1998 that, 'By 2005 or so, it will become clear that the internet's impact on the economy will have been no greater than the fax machine's.'[10]

Digital footprints

The futurist cheerleaders believe that algorithms may come to know us better than we know ourselves. To be fair, they already know a lot. Our behaviour is driven by latent psychological constructs that predict how we'll act across different contexts in fairly consistent ways. Someone who votes for liberal political candidates is also more likely to be open to a threesome,[11] as well as to read philosophy[12] and listen to jazz[13] because there is an underlying trait driving all of those behaviours – in this case, openness to experience.

In psychology, this relates to a principle known as thin slicing.[14] If you were given a very thin slice of cake, you could look at it and accurately predict what the rest of the cake looks like; likewise, given a very thin slice of a person, it's possible to make quite accurate predictions about them based on inferred underlying characteristics.

There are several implications for all this, as well as practical actions you can take.

People can be read rather well from their digital footprints. A review, 'Human and Computer Personality Prediction from

Digital Footprints', summarised how data points like social media posts, smartphone logs and linguistic features have been used by algorithms to predict personality, and concluded that the computer is generally more accurate than human judgements.[15]

Spotify can assess your personality according to your genre preferences and how you use the app. For instance, conscientiousness was related to country, soul and funk, as well as to having a premium account and being less likely to skip tracks.[16]

Can you remember all the books you have read? Amazon knows your browsing and buying behaviour, which means it can suggest books, and other products, based upon your previous purchases. In time, its recommendations could become far more accurate. Kindle can monitor which parts of a book you read fast, or slowly, where you bookmark for a break, and if you abandon the book before finishing it. Imagine if Kindle were also to observe your reactions to the book with biometric sensors and a camera. It would know when you laughed or cried, when your heart raced or your blood pressure spiked. Amazon could then make preternaturally accurate predictions for your next political polemic or racy romance.

Mark Zuckerberg knows what you like in the bedroom. Metaphorically, of course, but also, perhaps, literally. In 2013, a Cambridge University study found that not only could Facebook likes predict personality, but they could also predict intimate traits such as depression, drug use and sexuality.[17] Research since then has similarly suggested, for example, that even profile pictures can predict personality[18] as well as sexuality.[19] This is to say nothing of the fact that MindGeek – the parent company of porn sites like Brazzers and Pornhub – boasts on its website, 'Every action taken by a user on a web property generates dozens of data points. When carefully analyzed, these data points reveal important information about products and the way they are used by clients.'[20]

All this shouldn't come as a surprise. Since the Cambridge Analytica affair, it is well understood that innocuous social media data can predict political preferences. For example, Democrats tweeting more about feelings and Republicans about group membership.[21]

Personality-targeted adverts can increase clicks by up to 40 per cent and sales by up to 50 per cent according to one academic study.[22] Their power in politics is proven. An early randomised controlled trial of political mobilisation messages delivered to 61 million Facebook users during the 2010 US congressional elections was found to directly influence political self-expression, information seeking and real-world voting behaviour.[23] Another study found that micro-targeted political ads outperformed random or blanket strategies by up to 70 per cent.[24] This should surprise no one, as the revenue model of social media platforms follows the assumption that sponsored posts and advertisements can change the buying behaviour of their users. The danger for governments and for us all is that AI becomes a 'black box' for democracy and transparency.

Mandatory digital identities, 'vaccine passports' and central bank digital currencies (CBDCs) are looming. The IMF has recommended that search histories be used to calculate credit scores.[25] This kind of personal data has already been used to freeze protestors' bank accounts in Canada, and to exclude the unvaccinated from flights, restaurants and venues worldwide. How easy would it be for governments to switch from using the technology to suppress viral diseases, to using it to suppress viral ideas?

Hiding your tracks

Of course, you may want the social media platforms to know you as well as possible, so you can benefit from accurate book, album and even friend suggestions, plus useful career connections and articles about subjects you enjoy. But if you do want to maintain your privacy and anonymity, you will need to tread with a light digital footprint. What can you do?

Futurist and author Tracey Follows has worked with Big Tech companies for years. Her research with young people has uncovered that they don't always provide the right information to platforms. She doesn't advise providing platforms with falsehoods if it goes against their terms of service, but the younger generation have told her that having multiple accounts with different profile information does open up new information: 'They tell me that they aren't truthful all the time. They don't give their real birthdays. They want to make it hard for the platforms to put them in a box.'

When social engineering expert Jenny Radcliffe was asked how people could protect themselves from manipulation, she was unequivocal: 'Stop sharing everything about your life online! Choose the audience that can see the post online. Scammers can even use what's reflected off someone's glasses, off their wine glass. Every September people post pics of their kids in their uniform outside the school. Now I know your kid's school and where you live. I know the shops nearby. Every piece of information makes an approach familiar and personal, which you're much more likely to fall for.'

Following the advice to create multiple accounts is an interesting exercise in its own right, but practising social media hygiene between personal and professional accounts means you stay one step ahead of the platforms' predictive powers.

While researching this book, one of us followed a dating expert on Instagram – purely for research, we hasten to add. The platform took note of this and proceeded to suggest other dating expert accounts. Cue many more reels from similar men in their thirties with stubble and a penchant for romantic and emotional development advice than we ever bargained for. We learnt to be cautious about clicking 'like' or 'follow', or slowing down on content. The more aggressive platforms readily misconstrue a little curiosity for insatiability. Creating 'sandbox' research accounts allows you to pursue different interests without cross-contamination.

Excluding the more subtle algorithmic inferences about your personality, just changing sex also makes a difference. In our own mini personal experiment, a female Facebook account was served ads for cosmetic surgery, makeup and shape-wear. (It's all too easy to see why girls' self-esteem is dented on social media.) When the sex of the account was changed to male, the advertising changed overnight to sheds, cars and finance apps. Despite the plethora of choices of self-identified gender in Facebook's 'About You' form, it seems sexual stereotypes are alive and well when it comes to advertising. Presumably, this is driven by algorithms, because men tend to buy more sheds and so forth, but it is a blunt tool that may not suit you personally.

Aside from creating multiple accounts, you might want to consider how often you 'like' content. It's satisfying to signify enthusiasm and support for the content you like, but it also gives the tech companies a window into your brain. One study showed that giving just ten likes on Facebook allowed a computer model to more accurately predict a subject's personality than a work colleague could.[26] The more liberally you 'like', the better Facebook will know you. If you click the like button 300 times, Facebook will know you better than your spouse does. Facebook may even become aware of your sexuality before you do. Imagine a scenario where Facebook detects that a 13-year-old is gay from their likes and behaviour before they have worked it out themselves. Should Facebook be able to out you, to *you*?

But perhaps the question we should really ask is, should social media algorithms be outed? Governments are scrambling to legislate social media, but not to force transparency. As we've seen, algorithms get to know us very well, but we do not know them well.

The gods of the algorithm

Platform design is central to what people see and experience on social media, and platforms do not neutrally present content. For most user-to-user platforms, algorithms are used to curate a unique personalised environment for each person. This offers commercial opportunities, but can also lead to artificial amplification of content, 'rabbit holes', feeding people's natural biases and obsessions, and also potentially to suppression of content.

Algorithms are also the secret editors the online world doesn't want you to understand – they influence how news companies choose to publish and prioritise stories. 'Before you decide whether to publish, you have to think whether it will please the algorithm,' says an anonymous social media editor who works at a 24-hour news channel. (He won't share his identity as his job depends upon his relationship with the tech platforms.) 'If it doesn't, it won't perform well. Unfortunately, the algorithms can be at odds with the end user, who feels like their concerns are not being met by the content publisher.'

Rather than serve content chronologically to the end user, social media companies deploy algorithms that prioritise or suppress content based on various factors. How many comments, shares and 'likes' a post receives can determine how well something is promoted on Twitter, Facebook or Instagram. But there are concerns that the political and ideological preferences of the platforms may also be shaping what we see online. While the platforms themselves insist this is not the case, there is no way of knowing for sure, because the algorithms remain a closely guarded secret.

'It's only when you publish content every day that you notice which content does well and which doesn't,' the social media editor explains. 'I pick it up almost subconsciously, because I'm not just on there 9-to-5, I'm always looking, in a constant feedback loop. The performance of posts is not completely organic, there is something else at play: algorithms.'

Environmental protesting is 'pushed upwards' on Twitter timelines – 'XR [Extinction Rebellion] content takes off like a rocket' – while immigration and race are pushed down, in his opinion. Across platforms, news reporting about child abuse is pushed down because the algorithm might be confusing it with paedophilia, in a misguided attempt to protect users. Ideological, political and safety-driven decisions are determining which content you are exposed to.

The social media editor says that, in his experience, Twitter is very unwilling to discuss how algorithms work. Facebook is more open, and a representative told him that algorithms have evolved and they didn't know why, 'a bit like the rise of the machines in *Terminator*'.

Facebook's desire for meaningful interaction has resulted in content that courts controversy and division. 'If you know how algorithms work then you can exploit them,' says a social media guru employed by high-profile media, political campaigns and FMCG brands. 'Content is designed to be divisive, and create an emotional response and confrontation. My job is to get the best results for my clients. I am judged by metrics and data. I am not there to make people feel better. My clients are interested in reach and sales. They don't care whether people have a good day at the end of it.' Emotional content will impact on your rational thinking and you are more likely to fall into the trap of interaction. Make no mistake that social media platforms want you to feel extreme swings of emotion and react based upon that.

The UK government appears to have missed an opportunity to address one of the most pressing problems on social media platforms: the secrecy behind how algorithms work. The draft Online Safety Bill suggested in one iteration that regulators might be given oversight to audit, review and regulate algorithms. Does this go far enough? If the internet is so harmful – and this is the premise of the Bill – perhaps algorithms should be declared on home pages like health warnings on cigarette packets. Instead of us second-guessing the algorithms and trying to please them, let the algorithms try and please us.

Imagine this hypothetical solution: you land on a social media platform and there, in the top menu, or presented as a pop-up, is a prominent declaration that algorithms are used. There is an option to read a user-friendly explanation about how the algorithms affect your interaction with the platform and content. This explanation could fully disclose all functionality, and the regulator would ensure that disclosure is complete. The use and functionality of algorithms could be declared like a list of ingredients on packaged food. The impact of these ingredients should be honestly described, just as packaged foods list nutritional composition, or restaurants disclose the calorie count of meals.

This is as yet an unreleased hypothetical solution, although it could come to pass. A court ruling in Japan could force Big Tech to reveal their algorithms in a precedent-setting case. Hanryumura, a Korean-style BBQ restaurant chain, successfully argued that a change in how user reviews are calculated in Tabelog harmed the scores of its outlets.

Once upon a time you went to a news-stand and picked up your usual newspaper, or you perused the front pages and picked up the most enticing option. The key point is that all the newspapers were there in plain sight. The power to choose which news to read was yours and, of course, Fleet Street's. 'The people cannot be safe without information,' said Founding Father Thomas Jefferson. 'Where the press is free, and every man able to read, all is safe.'[27]

These days the social media and search companies are far more sophisticated versions of news-stands, pushing some content up and other content down on your timeline according to their predictions of your interests as well as corporate and political bias. This matters. A recent study found that over half of US adults get their news often or sometimes from social media, with over a third relying on Facebook for their news regularly.[28] In the UK, the picture is similar, with half of adults using social media for news, and 35 per cent of adults saying Facebook is their most commonly used news source.[29]

When Aldous Huxley asserted in *Brave New World Revisited* that 'technological progress has hurt the Little Man and helped the Big Man' he was referring to a vast communications industry, which, at that time, did not yet include the internet.[30] He predicted that modern methods of communication would result in deprivation of independent thought and more uncritical recipients of orders. We should be trying to avoid that at all costs, and we must take responsibility for our own critical thinking.

For now, you do have a limited ability to turn algorithms off, which returns your timeline to a chronological list on both Twitter and Facebook. (At least, so far we know, since the deployment of algorithms is not declared.) But it might be useful to consciously balance your news sources on social media from opposite ends of the political spectrum, as well as continuing to access other sources such as the TV, radio and the good old-fashioned news-stand. While it still exists.

Human intervention and bias creep into automated systems. Twitter says, 'We believe real change starts with conversation. Here, your voice matters. Come as you are and together we'll do what's right (not what's easy) to serve the public conversation.' Sadly, we don't know enough about how Twitter 'serves' the public conversation. Twitter has claimed it does not manipulate timelines or shadow ban (deprioritising accounts and content), but leaked videos featuring Twitter employees published by Project Veritas contradict their promises.[31] At the time of writing, Elon Musk, new CEO of Twitter, is releasing dossiers (known as 'The Twitter Files') revealing that senior Twitter staff were pushing down content and accounts they did not like, via shadow banning, search blacklists and 'visibility filtering'. There is a suggestion that Twitter staff were at least unofficially collaborating with the White House on a secret blacklist.

Governments may not be truly invested in requiring Big Tech to come clean about their algorithmic methodology to the public, because they work closely with these companies. In just one example, Google has also piloted programmes to ensure counter-narrative videos produced by agencies that work with the government are more discoverable. This quote from openDemocracy illustrates the implications:

> To be clear about what this means in practice, imagine an internet user fitting the profile of 'impressionable young Muslim' (as defined by Prevent), searching Google for 'Syria war' (or clicking on a Facebook link about it) and being referred to Breakthrough's 'Open Your Eyes: Isis Lies' campaign, among others. And as we know from the Snowden revelations, these searches will be logged and investigated by the intelligence services.
>
> The symbolism of all of this cannot be understated. Removing one kind of 'propaganda' and promoting another at the request of governments – or via government-backed NGOs or contractors – is a far cry from the free speech-cum-great leveller Silicon Valley told us to believe in.[32]

Tracey Follows says that human intervention on social media is exacerbated because we are in a world of software engineering – the engineers believe they have the ability to *socially* engineer. 'I have worked with Big Tech companies like Google and Facebook for decades,' she says, 'and you have to realise how ideological senior management in transnational companies are. They co-opt globalist causes. On the face of it that can be good, but the causes are corporatised and embedded in platforms.'

Inevitably the political and personal ideologies of the staff, including software engineers, company management and human content moderators, influence the prioritisation and deprioritisation of certain viewpoints. This human fallibility has the potential to magnify in effect as we move into virtual and augmented realities, as environments are programmed even further with moral codes and values.

'Googling' is now synonymous with searching and a vital part of the modern-day professional and personal functioning. In their 2004 founders letter – 'An Owner's Manual' to shareholders – Google's Larry Page and Sergey Brin argued that their search results were 'unbiased and objective'. Nowadays, search is increasingly politicised, as well as influenced by advertising, sponsorship and paid-for optimisation. Research on the 'search engine manipulation effect' has found that Google's ranking of results on political candidates can shift the voting preferences of swing voters by up to 20 per cent.[33]

In the name of public safety, but without public consultation or accountability, Big Tech took assertive steps to control misinformation during the Covid-19 pandemic. This was purportedly for the common good, but mistakes were made.

Google pushed certain approved content to the top of search results via knowledge panels, downlinked Covid misinformation and removed apps relating to the virus from the Google Play app, as well as some videos from YouTube.[34] Facebook censored stories that Covid was a man-made virus leaked from a lab, and then stopped. Likewise, YouTube censored videos that claimed masks didn't work, and then stopped. These policy changes reflect that the facts, or at least the accepted facts, change. If misinformation can become good information, then was it ever really misinformation in the first place?

An article by Professor Carl Heneghan published by *The Spectator* about the landmark Danish mask randomised controlled trial (RCT) was labelled as containing 'false information' on Facebook. The company boasted in 2020 that when people see such warnings, 95 per cent of the time they would not click on the post.[35] Professor Carl Heneghan is a GP, clinical epidemiologist and a Fellow of Kellogg College, the director of the University of Oxford's Centre for Evidence-Based Medicine and Editor-in-Chief of *BMJ Evidence-Based Medicine*. Science should encourage enquiry, debate and differing ideas. If he wasn't qualified to comment on an RCT, who was?

You might have been censored without even knowing it. Not long ago, the idea of 'shadow banning' (whereby the search results are suppressed) was considered a conspiracy or hoax. Yet, in a blog post in September 2021, Facebook admitted to shadow banning accounts that it believed to be guilty of misinformation, although the company called it 'content ranking' and 'reduced distribution'.[36] Anyone's account could be effectively silenced if they shared misinformation, or content that is 'broadly disliked', sensationalist, or provocative, even if it doesn't contravene the community guidelines or law.

Were millions of posts, videos and stories censored in error? Who can be trusted to state with absolute certainty whether information is good or bad? Tedros Adhanom, Director General of the World Health Organization, said, 'We're not just fighting an epidemic; we're fighting an infodemic. Fake news spreads faster and more easily than this virus and is just as dangerous.' But the UK's Royal Society reported that there is little evidence that calls for major platforms to remove 'offending content' will limit harm, and even warned it could drive misinformation to harder-to-address corners of the internet and exacerbate feelings of distrust in authorities.[37]

Using different search engines rather than relying upon the almost monopolistic Google can yield different results – but even that isn't a failsafe. DuckDuckGo – favoured by those who want to avoid Google's privacy-invading trackers – announced it would combat Russian disinformation by using 'down-ranking'. The search engine was keen to justify this decision by differentiating between 'down-ranking' and outright censorship, and by making a value judgement that the content of disinformation sites is lower quality. But what if, for some reason – and you are entitled to your own reasons – that's exactly what you want? Maybe you want to know how Russian state media is reporting the war in Ukraine. Is it the business of search engines to decide to make that difficult for you? Conducting multiple searches using different search engines, and also searching within news sites, might help to counteract the impact of up- and down-ranking.

Some people know how to game the algorithms. Prior to May 2022 if you wanted to read stories about the controversial cheese and wine parties at Number 10 Downing Street held during lockdown, and you searched for 'Boris Johnson cheese', you would have found the sort of stories you were expecting. But, after May 2022, the same search would yield stories about Boris Johnson saying he can't work from home, because cheese and coffee are too distracting. Images of lockdown-breaking wine-swilling parties were pushed down on Google, and stories about quirky loveable BoJo salivating over cheddar and coffee were pushed upwards.

Gareth Morgan, founder of SEO and Digital PR firm Liberty, believes this was an example of search engine optimisation cleverly deployed for reputation management by spin doctors. By pushing out this rather eccentric story about cheese – greedily picked up by the media – the older story was down-ranked in search results.

As Morgan says, there have been

> many bizarre stories about BoJo and the cheese story might not be the only example of reputation management. Crazy personalities can get away with crazy stories. Do you remember the story about Boris Johnson painting wine boxes to look like buses? Maybe they were trying to push down the story about the Brexit bus. You have to wonder if the bizarre answers he gives in interviews are actually cleverly calculated messages his advisors prep him on, to change the online narrative.

Since reputation managers try to 'own' the first page of Google, Morgan suggests you make a 'verbatim' rather than 'all results' search, using the tools selector. Also, look at the second and third pages of Google search results, and even beyond. Finally, be suspicious of eccentric stories. They might be a cyber magician's trick designed to dazzle and distract you from the 'real' story. As Morgan says: 'If Boris Johnson had a weird crazy story out my first thought would be, what story in the past is he trying to cover up?'

The bot squads

Automated accounts, called bots, also game social media. Their sole purpose is to shape the online narrative by disseminating and amplifying information, or disinformation. When clusters of accounts (sometimes known as bot squads) share the same message, or retweet the same post, it creates the effect of amplifying a message, often for political ends. In other words, it is a form of propaganda. It's not always easy to spot, or identify, which actors are behind it, but it is a serious problem. It is estimated that 9 to 15 per cent of Twitter accounts are bots.[38]

A 2017 study 'How the Chinese government fabricates social media posts for strategic distraction, not engaged argument' estimated that from two hundred and fifty thousand to two million Chinese people are hired by their government to post approximately 448 million 'fake' social media posts per year.[39] These undercover pro-government commentators set out to be ordinary citizens as they steer conversations in the 'correct direction' for the Chinese Communist Party. They are referred to as the '50c army' as they are reportedly paid 50c per post.

Propublica analysed fake and hijacked Twitter accounts and found more than ten thousand suspected fake Twitter accounts pushing propaganda about Hong Kong.[40] Accounts then switched their focus from Hong Kong to Covid-19. These tweets were not aimed at the Chinese living in China, as Twitter is blocked by the Great Firewall. Some were in Chinese and aimed at ethnic Chinese living overseas, but many of the tweets were in English. They were aimed at us. And they waged an unofficial PR campaign in support of the Chinese government's handling of Covid.

Bots have been studied by academics for over a decade, and are one of the scourges of social media. Elon Musk's purchase of Twitter was held up by a dispute over the number of bot accounts on the platform. As bot detection methods evolve, so do the bots, but fighting this phenomenon is proving difficult. A 2017 study declared that 'neither Twitter, nor humans, nor cutting-edge applications are currently capable of accurately detecting the new social spambots'.[41]

Bot use is not limited to China. There are 'Kremlin bots' too. There are bots all over the world and of all political persuasions. One analysis of bots in Italy found that they were affiliated to (but this does not mean managed by) all political parties, various newspapers, soccer commentators and even the Catholic Church.[42] It's very hard to detect which actor might be behind particular bot campaigns.

Strangely, in the course of writing this chapter, Laura noticed that there was an orchestrated bot campaign on Twitter using a quote from an article she had written. The quote, from an article about detransitioners, published in *The Sunday Times*, had been tweeted by J. K. Rowling on 12 July 2020: '"I fear that the detransitioned women I interviewed are canaries in the coalmine. Not only for detransitioners, but for womanhood. They all, in some combination, found being a woman too difficult, too dangerous or too disgusting" – Laura Dodsworth.'

At the time, it was retweeted by genuine accounts. But nearly two years later, in May 2022, a cluster of accounts started tweeting the exact same quote, with Laura's name. Why, and to what end?

Laura contacted Twitter about the bot campaign, and asked the following. How can people report a suspected bot campaign? What does Twitter do about these suspected bots and organised campaigns? How many bot accounts does Twitter suspect may be operating on the platform and what volume of content do they generate? How can Twitter determine who was behind this campaign? And does Twitter investigate who is behind organised campaigns?

A Twitter spokesperson said they would not be able to facilitate an interview, did not answer the questions and deleted the bot accounts.

How did we know they were bots? First, Twitter effectively confirmed this by deleting the accounts. Second, although it is not always easy to identify more sophisticated campaigns, these accounts bore classic hallmarks, with cartoon avatars and little to no engagement with other accounts. This 'squad' all tweeted about NFTs (Non Fungible Tokens) or mentioned them in their bios, and commonly tweeted about Elon Musk, Tesla, NASA and President Joe Biden, and they all first tweeted in early summer 2022. Why these accounts were set up, who was the originating actor, and why this quote was chosen, all remain a mystery.

An insight into the characteristics of bot campaigns came from Dennis (not his real name), who used to work at an agency that undertook work for the Research, Information and Communications Unit (RICU) of the UK government. The unit's stated ambition is to use strategic communications to 'effect behavioural and attitudinal change'. It works with third parties so that these ambitions do not appear to be connected to the UK government, covertly engineering the thoughts of people by using chosen 'grassroots organisations and NGOs, providing financial and technical support from the government for the production of their multimedia campaigns, which purport to be "grassroots"'.[43]

When Dennis worked at the agency contracted by RICU they were running social media accounts, not troll farms, but they were analysing social media identities and building profiles of Twitter accounts to appear authentic:

> In the early days, we weren't running troll farms, we were running official social media accounts. The techniques have evolved a lot since I was at [the agency]. It wouldn't surprise me if they now copy the Russian disinformation bot campaigns they used to be so worried about. We had a presentation on Twitter tribes the agency wanted to access. This woman was high up in the agency, she was public school, middle class, she probably lived in Clapham. She was talking about 'Muslim football fans'. Football badges represent identity but she saw them as 'fans'. You'll notice time and time again that football accounts pile on to the controversial news like 'anti-vaxx' stories and it's weird they would comment on that. The people that run these campaigns don't seem to know that football fans don't talk about vaccines all the time, and there is an artificiality to these bot campaigns.

In relation to the bot campaign quoting Laura on detransitioners, does this mean that someone, or some agency, thinks that NFT collectors who support Barcelona FC and admire Elon Musk are likely supporters? It seems improbable. It was artificial enough to get our attention, anyway.

Perhaps these bots were using some of the six techniques that are believed to be used to influence public opinion online.[44] For example, 'forum sliding' is where a tsunami of unrelated posts are used to flush critical opinions out of public sight and mind. 'Consensus cracking' involves immunising people against opposing arguments by using a fake account to post a weak version of their argument and then having many other accounts take it apart, making your side of the debate look strong. 'Anger trolling' is where you find out the sensitive buttons of the most volatile members of your opposition, and troll them into a fit – distracting your opposing team and making them look deranged in the public's eyes.

Escaping *The Truman Show*

Social media and search are awash with propaganda and misinformation (define it as you will), so how do we protect ourselves? First, we need to consider why the susceptibility may at least partly lie within ourselves. As we citizens have obtained the means to broadcast for ourselves, particularly via social media platforms, we too have become propagandists. The blurred lines start with us.

When you post on social media, how strictly do you adhere to the truth? Do you tend to share the successes, holidays and wins, but ignore the failures and depressing days on Facebook? Do you take 20 selfies in order to select the most flattering example for Instagram? Do you apply a filter? Does it look like such an idealised version of yourself that it bears little resemblance to the real 'you'?

A century ago, a commissioned portrait or self-portrait would have taken hours, or days, and required costly materials and some talent. These days you can take a burst of ten photographs per second on a smartphone and slap a filter on. While the portraits of the past and today's selfies could both represent a form of self-flattery and propaganda, today's efforts are accessible and at scale. In our efforts to present the most sparkling version of ourselves for personal, social and professional reasons, we have become consummate propagandists. The self has been replaced by the selfie.

'Snapchat dysmorphia' describes when someone wants to look like their social media selfie. The term was coined by cosmetic surgeon Dr Esho. Before social media, his prospective clients would want to look like the stars they saw in magazines and on TV. Then social media changed everything. It gave people the ability to edit themselves using filters. The angle of the smartphone camera added the first degree of distortion, different to a mirror. Then filters and apps added an additional layer of unreality. It has changed people's expectations of how they want to look and created unrealistic expectations of cosmetic surgery. 'People ask for their pores to be removed,' he said. 'That is not possible in real life. In images it's because of makeup and filters. Sometimes it shocks people I can't remove pores. People don't know what's real anymore. They want bigger eyes, smaller noses, a sharper jaw and cheekbones, arched brows. We can do some of that, but not all of it.'

Esho describes this as a '*Truman Show* effect', referring to lifelong publicly viewable identities. Our babies are born into a world where their first portraits are shared by us, proud parents, online. It starts there. Teenagers now remove photos from their platforms if they don't get enough likes. And at the most extreme end of the scale, how we present ourselves online can render us almost unrecognisable. Dr Esho says that he frequently doesn't recognise clients in consultation from the photos attached to their online profiles.

Thanks to the lockdowns, this phenomenon has spread to the older generation. Esho now has an older set of clients who want to look like their Zoom selves, since it introduced filters and they became accustomed to their bright eyes and smooth, tanned skin.

But this is about more than how we look. Social media puts pressure on how we want to *be*. Esho knows a blogger who is verging on agoraphobic because they don't want to be seen in public and compared to their social media self. Or worse, not recognised. The social media guru also told us that 'a lot of influencers find social media a big strain. It's stressful behind the scenes.' And these influencers are influencing *us*.

There are various steps you can take to minimise the impact. First of all, acknowledge that social media is not real. 'Today's beauty ideals are not real,' says Esho. 'The Kardashians don't look like the Kardashians. So no one else is going to look like them either.' He refuses to treat people with Snapchat dysmorphia and instead refers them for counselling.

Leaked research findings showed that Instagram and Facebook know exactly how harmful their environments are to teenage girls.[45] The *Wall Street Journal* reported on a leaked presentation which revealed that Facebook made body image issues worse for one in three teen girls. And nearly a third of teen girls said that when they felt bad about their bodies, Instagram made them feel worse according to a subsequent presentation reported in March 2020. Worryingly, among users who reported suicidal thoughts, 13 per cent in the UK and 6 per cent in the US traced them back to Instagram.

Social media companies can flag up when an article might be 'misinformation' but they show little interest when an image has been filtered into an unrealistic representation of a human. Consider whether it helps you to apply visual filters to photographs or metaphorical filters to the representation of your life. It's possible it could create lower self-esteem in the long run.

Esho is hyper-aware of his role as a cosmetic surgeon and the impact on his own life. He has taken a decision to 'post wins and losses'. He advises that:

> You don't have to go deep, dark and grim, but you could share day-to-day reality things like not getting a contract, or a result that you wanted. It's not about advertising you are a failure but showing you can move on and grow, and that is a good thing for people to see. We need to know the difference between real and fake. So be present in your real life. Smell the roses. Have the little moments. If your kids say something beautiful to you, or if someone says 'good job', then take time to be present in real life, not social media.

Do not disturb

The various harms of social media are clear. So, why do so many of us use it?

Your phone dings, you pick it up, and then you are on it for an hour. Or more. Welcome to the 'Attention Economy', first theorised by economist Herbert A. Simon. Techno futurists say that the products of the future are our brains. Quite simply, social media is designed to be addictive and the social media companies want our minds.

We wake up, check our email and our social media platforms, then the weather and the news, then we do it all again. Sometimes we complete the circle twice before we even get out of bed. We check our phones while watching TV, or at the table over a romantic dinner. We can't read books like we used to. We post on social media about what we are doing with our friends rather than just enjoying it. Half of the public say they sometimes can't stop themselves from checking their smartphones when they should be focusing on other things, despite their best efforts.[46] We also check our phones about twice as often as we think we do. One study found that people guessed they check their phone 25 times a day, but in reality it was between 49 and 80 times a day.[47]

Social media affects concentration. One study found that it can take about 23 minutes to fully resume focus after an interruption and we are more stressed afterwards – how often do your smartphone notifications interrupt you?[48] It's unsurprising that half of us feel that our attention span is shorter than it used to be.[49]

Various studies have shown that using smartphones and social media can affect your brain. One study showed that the mere presence of a smartphone reduces available cognitive capacity.[50] The researchers found that participants with their phones in another room significantly outperformed those with their phones on the desk, and they also slightly outperformed those participants who had kept their phones in a pocket or bag. Although this study has suffered with replication, many others have proved the same point. For example, the more people use the search engine phone on their smartphone, the less thought they put into answering questions.[51] People who take pictures of museum exhibits score worse on a quiz about the exhibits.[52] We outsource our thinking to 'the brain in the pocket', and this makes us vulnerable to manipulation: if you don't think for yourself, the algorithms will do it for you.

Many of us have seen someone we love taken down by addiction, be it to alcohol or drugs, or gambling, food or sex. But how many of us are prepared to admit we are among the fallen? Sure you could just not look at your phone. Or close your social media account. Or set a time limit. But it's not that easy, is it?

Twitter even acknowledged its addictive power, tweeting, 'one more Tweet and then it's bedtime', 'one more scroll' and 'and an all-nighter later'. Some of us were there for it, eyes held open with matchsticks, helpless in the face of tweets cascading like a mesmerising waterfall. It's not so funny now.

Twitter's mission statement is 'to give everyone the power to create and share ideas and information instantly, without barriers'. Twitter isn't going to give you any barriers, so you will need to erect them yourself. In the UK, 73 per cent of people think that there is non-stop competition from social media platforms for our attention.[53]

Social media taps into our reward-based learning processes: trigger, behaviour, reward, dopamine rush. Clickbait headlines draw you in. Social media videos autoplay. Notification symbols pulse and sound, creating a Pavlovian response. 'Love' symbols lure you. Timelines refresh like a casino slot machine. This all takes time away from other pursuits, affects concentration and of course maximises your susceptibility to the nudges and propaganda on social media.

This book's authors feel your pain. We are not paragons of social media moderation. Patrick's wife has the security code to his smartphone settings to help him limit the time he spends on social media. Laura has tried everything to break her addiction, including staying on a silent device-free retreat in a convent.

'Some people are addicted to Twitter,' Father Colin, a Catholic monk, suggested. 'People are frightened of not having the constant interaction. They are frightened of the silence. They need constant affirmation and contact, this many people liked my post, this many people have contacted me.' Did the monk have a direct line into our souls?

Like Dr Esho, Father Colin observed that social media makes us less present, and points out that the answer is simultaneously simple and difficult:

> People complain they are bombarded with emails and tweets. The answer is you don't have to be. They complain about it but in a funny sort of way they must enjoy it. I can understand the addiction. But what it means is we have become not attentive to the present.
>
> We have the opportunity to know what is going on all over the world all the time, but what is interesting is we are not very good at living in the present. We are worried about what happened in the past or anxious about what will happen in the future. People are distracted and blown about. It is difficult for people to be in the present.
>
> You can complain about it, but the answer lies in oneself. Social media can be moderated. It is difficult, but it is possible. Switch it off. The answer lies in your hands.

Research abounds with studies showing the importance of switching off. Kids put into a screen-free camp scored higher on emotional intelligence.[54] Switching off notifications reduced symptoms of ADHD in a non-clinical sample.[55] Deactivating Facebook for four weeks reduced political polarisation and increased subjective wellbeing.[56]

The irony is that you probably don't even need social media, from a functional point of view. A 2022 meta-analysis of 76 studies found that social media had no, or barely no, effect on political knowledge.[57] The authors concluded that 'the contribution of social media toward a more politically informed citizenry is minimal'.

If the answer doesn't lie in your hands, there are apps to control time limits. Or you might need to put the security settings password into someone else's hands to fast track your control.

Smartphones are not all bad. Who would want to give up real-time weather, navigate a city without maps, share photos and arrange social gatherings in seconds?

But there are dangers. Remember, techno-future fan Yuval Noah Harari doesn't even own a smartphone. Stories proliferate about tech industry bigwigs limiting screen time for their families. James Barrat, author of *Our Final Invention: Artificial Intelligence and the End of the Human Era*, even told the *Washington Post*, 'I don't want to really scare you, but it was alarming how many people I talked to who are highly placed people in AI who have retreats that are sort of "bug out" houses, to which they could flee if it all hits the fan.'[58]

Social media and search engines are now embedded with increasingly personalised and sophisticated behavioural science techniques. Perhaps the smartest thing to do with a smartphone is ditch it. However, we don't want to do that, and we expect you don't want to either. Even Father Colin recommends moderation and not abstinence. But at the very least you must do your best to maintain safe social media distancing.

The rules:

- Social media entails many harms as well as benefits, so give it up, or at least use it mindfully and minimally, and assess whether you need to temporarily unplug, do a digital detox, or get help with 'addiction'.
- To maintain privacy and reduce manipulation you can have multiple accounts and identities on social media platforms if you want to sandbox your interests, and choose to 'like' and engage less.
- Use multiple search engines to ameliorate bias, and set your social media timelines to chronological to reduce algorithmic influence.

7

Death and tears in the absence of Twitter

By Laura

It's not what I expected. The large trees must once have sat within the grounds of a gentrified estate, but the convent in front of me is charmlessly utilitarian. It is not the cloistered classic I had imagined. This is Lewisham, not Lindisfarne. The sun beats on my head as I open and close the rusty green driveway gates manually. A dusty chalkboard 'Welcome' greets me.

A smiling sister ushers me though the front door. I sign in. Neither of us knows the date – ah, we are sisters in our unworldliness. She provides a guided tour through cool corridors. The interior is wood, vinyl, linoleum, floral fabrics and religious paintings, just as you would expect. It smells of church, village hall and washing powder, which is to say it smells of safety, community and motherliness. Smell is an affecting sense. I already want to stay and nestle and be protected for longer than the 24 hours I have booked. My eyes mist. I knew this would happen.

Just before leaving I'd told a friend that I was going for just 24 hours. That's quite specific, he laughed, *just* 24 hours. The thought of even 24 hours in a silent retreat with no phone or computer made me feel itchy inside and out – the mark of a true addict.

I sensed that pressing pause on my frantic life as a single mother, hustling for work, writing a book, renovating a house, seeing friends – oh you know how it is – could potentially cause *something* to surface.

For one thing, I'd have to confront my social media problem. Hello, my name is Laura and I'm a Twitter addict.

Addiction is often about pain and numbing feelings. Just 24 hours is enough time to greet feelings in the silence. Goodbye noise, goodbye Twitter, hello me, hello thoughts and feelings that I normally like to push away. This silent retreat is all about tackling Twitter. I am writing about the need to practise 'social media distancing' and I have to walk the talk. I've tried lots of techniques and, frankly, I am at the cold turkey stage.

Social media both captures and scatters my attention. I find concentrating on books more difficult. I can doomscroll for a good hour after I intended to go to bed and I'm overwhelmed by information. I begrudge the personalised social media environments designed to manipulate me. I only have to look at a smartphone screen and I feel alpha waves emanate from my brain. I know that when my life flashes before me – hopefully not for a few decades – I will not wish I had spent more time on Twitter. And that is what brought me here.

A card with my name marks my bedroom door. A single bed, a view of trees, and quiet. Without busyness, I feel the weight of life. As my bedroom door soft closes the sadness is irrepressible. I kick things off with a cry.

I look at my phone. I know, I'm not supposed to. But there are two watertight reasons; honest, I promise I am not in the bargaining phase of the addict. First, I have to pay the ULEZ road charge I incurred driving through London. Second, I am a mother and need to know whether my children need me. I despatch the ULEZ toll, but maternal duty will provide permission to check my phone a number of times in 24 hours without my halo slipping.

It turns out Son Number One has already messaged me. I respond. See, this minor infraction is worth it, I am a Good Mother, and doing what needs to be done.

He reminds me that I said I would not use my phone. I point out that my children are an exception. Natch.

Then I check my email. Oops, there is no watertight excuse for that. Then I have a little word with myself and I put the phone down. Believe it or not this is an accomplishment. I have not looked at Twitter.

I eat my packed lunch and make a coffee.

I feel tired. So tired. It is morning, I have just arrived and I have done nothing except cry and eat houmous and falafels, but I take a nap for an hour and a half. It seems that by putting Twitter and my life down, even just for a few hours, I have lifted the lid on a well of emotion and tiredness.

When I wake up I visit the convent chapel, which is round and pointed like a Kentish oast house. I recite the Lord's Prayer, the only one I know, but the words feel empty. Perhaps the squat spire is not sufficient to direct my prayers heavenward. I read a Christian feminist prayer book. I've been off Twitter for a matter of hours and I've read a book, which is amazing.

I walk in the garden. The roses and I play a wilting competition in the heatwave. It's so hot I feel like I am in a film experiencing a fictitious British summer.

A newborn baby cries in the neighbouring stuccoed flats. My heart pangs for when my children were babies and I cry. I want to rewind 17 years and do it again. Does the sound of a baby crying do this to all mothers? In the future, will the sound of shouting and a slamming front door make me want to repeat teenage years?

I feel god in the dead grass, the distant barks and the gruff cawing from the trees. I am not missing Twitter. I feel present and weightless, but maudlin. The sadness soars from my throat. I want to cry *again*.

I find a skull. I think it belonged to a fox. The sister warned me there are many foxes in the grounds, and they are bold. They think they own the garden. I should be careful, she said, and she seemed pretty pleased about it.

I cradle the skull in my lap and, finally, I pray. Dear Creator, please help me live a good life. In the time between now and when I die, please help me be a good person, a good mother, to make the people I know feel good, and to do good work. Please help me use social media less and write more. On my deathbed I want to know I did my best. Amen.

I place the skull next to my can of Diet Coke and handbag on a dirty plastic chair next to me – a surprise low-rent tableau vanitas. Now I am on a silent retreat.

The evening music in the chapel is enchanting. The Church underrates female pitch. However, I maintain my silence, because I don't know the words or the tunes and my throat feels tight. There are only six of us, three nuns and three visitors. While five are singing beautifully, I have my eyes shut, embarrassed, at the chair furthest in the corner.

Evening light kisses a vase of flowers in front of the altar. This is a tender chapel. Nuns do it differently.

The gospel reading speaks acutely to a family problem I need to fix. I join the Lord's Prayer out loud because I know the words, and this time I feel it.

I stay after the others have left, the lights extinguished aside from the sanctuary candle and the sunset. I hold the unused hymn sheets in my lap. What I feel is indecipherable.

In my bedroom I check WhatsApp to see if my children have messaged me. The truth is, I miss them, but I am also craving communication. I've handwritten pages of notes. There are various ways to circumvent silence. But they have both messaged me and our exchanges make me happy. I don't check Twitter. And I don't care.

At 9pm I go to bed because there is nothing else to do. Optimistically, I think I will wake for sunrise, but I sleep for 11 hours. Sweet Mary Mother of Jesus, I must have been tired.

In the morning I go to find the fox's skull. It is as white, delicate and pretty as coral. It's hard to believe that it once held desires, fears and love. I sniff it. This part smells meaty, musky and edible. This part here reminds me of the comforting smell of my dog's fur after a long walk. This part smells of urinals. I put it down.

It's funny really that the most significant aspect of the retreat was a fox skull. I could have found one anywhere in the countryside where I walk my dog. But my head might have been too busy to notice it. I wouldn't have held it so long, and so silently. I definitely wouldn't have prayed. The skull was the catalyst, the silence and the retreat were the crucible.

I'm home now. I kept the skull. It's a totem, reminding me of death, as well as what I stand for in life until then.

And I need to confess. Forgive me, Reader, for I have sinned. I opened Twitter. I'd like to say I was testing myself, but actually it was picking at me, picking, picking, picking – pick me. But I didn't like it very much. I have no desire to carry the weight of the algorithms, the noise of dispute and opinion, the irritations of politics. Not yet anyway. Life is quieter and I like it better this way. This isn't what I expected.

8

Turn off your TV

Television is relaxing. But it is also a source of direct and indirect propaganda. It shapes your perception of reality. What's more, you are more likely to be 'programmed' by the programming when you are relaxed. You should turn off your TV, or at least watch it less and watch it mindfully and purposefully.

The power of television

At 13 years old, Tsering became a Buddhist monk so he could watch television.

He had never seen a television – nor cars nor aeroplanes – in his remote village in Nepal. When his Buddhist older cousin visited the family after years in a monastery in Kathmandu, Tsering was captivated by the stories of modern life, enough that he begged his father to allow him to become a monk.

His father consented and Tsering left his village for Kathmandu to embark upon life as a monk. He travelled alone by train for the first time. When he arrived in the city, he had to make a further transfer by bus, which he said felt like being in a house that moved. In just one day, he was catapulted into modernity.

In those days there was no internet, and no telephone calls to the village. He once went two years without speaking to his family. But cars and aeroplanes became a normal sight, and the boys at the monastery were allowed to watch cartoons on television on a Saturday.

The boy who became a monk in order to watch television, and who 'loved to watch funny cartoons', spent the rest of his life learning principles and practising techniques to detach from undue influences – including the temptation of television.

Monks are one of the groups of people who can teach us something about how to resist the lure of television, and this chapter will conclude with their advice. But what is wrong with the allure? Why should we resist? 'The Sun Always Shines On TV' goes the hit tune by Norwegian pop band A-ha. Phil Waaktaar, the writer of the song, explained that even on a rainy day, 'the power of television and the way television presents life' can brighten everything.

Since its invention, the power of television has even entered our dreams, literally. You might take the colourisation in your dreams for granted (though not everyone dreams in colour) but in the 1940s and 50s, many people reported that they dreamed in black and white.[1] Researchers can't be sure whether people *did* dream in black and white, or just believed that they did, but either way television did impact on people's perceptions of the world.

And in 2019, several news outlets reported on how American children were speaking with a British accent – which they had picked up from watching *Peppa Pig*.[2] If programmes can affect language, they can by extension affect perception.

This is how television works to wash your brain. It saturates your mind with imagery that you use to define reality. If you close your eyes and think about New York, the mental imagery probably comes more from *Friends*, *Seinfeld* and *Sex and the City* than it does from visiting the city. The television has constructed a reality of New York for you – and it does the same for relationships, rites of passage and systems of power. What effect, for example, has a show like *Friends* had on how Millennials worldwide think friendships should work?

The Greek philosopher Plato argued that people live stuck in a cave looking at shadows dancing on the cave wall, flickering from the fire. People think these shadows are reality; they have never stepped outside of the cave to see the beautiful truth of daylight. Today, the television literally flicks light against the cave wall, and we take it to be reality, when it is not.

For example, the British population is about 3 per cent black, yet black people make up about 8 per cent of on-screen contributions, according to a report from the Creative Diversity Network.[3] A YouGov poll found that Brits estimate the population to be around 20 per cent black.[4] Of course, there is nothing wrong with black representation; the issue is that the media presents a distortion, which seems to be affecting the public's perception of reality.

We imagine the television screen shows us the world but, in a sense, the opposite is true. The history of the screen is that it was used to cover things up – fires, drafts, sunlight. Screens do not show the world, they obscure it. The television screen erects visual screens in our mind; it constructs a fake reality that obscures the truth.

But surely television is an endangered species, the dinosaur of the entertainment world, you cry. 'Old media is dead. Long live new media!' You are a modern product of a modern world. You might spend as long, or longer, on social media compared with television. Even Tsering the monk now uses his smartphone, not the TV, to keep up with world news. Yet despite new media alternatives, television is still the most popular recreational pastime in the United Kingdom[5] and the United States.[6]

Not only is it popular, but it's also potent. Television viewing can be addictive, including heavy viewing, problem viewing, craving for viewing, and withdrawal symptoms.[7] Heavy viewing can be associated with negative body image,[8] problems with sleeping,[9] a possible contribution to Attention Deficit Hyperactivity Disorder (ADHD),[10] and a sedentary lifestyle.[11]

Watching TV might make you more violent, too A report in 1969 from the US Surgeon General's Scientific Advisory Committee on Television and Social Behavior contained a number of provisos, but concluded that viewing violent entertainment generally increases the likelihood of subsequent aggressive behaviour.[12] Researchers found that children under certain conditions were apt to reproduce aggressive acts after observing adults exhibit aggressive actions on the screen.[13] Namely, kids who watched footage of an adult battering a doll of a clown with a hammer, went on to treat the doll in kind, though it should be noted that the effects of media on aggression are fiercely debated by psychologists.

It's even claimed TV makes you stupid. Well, a study examining the viewing habits of 599 American adults between 1990 and 2011 found that those who watched an above-average amount of television showed reduced volume in their frontal cortex and entorhinal cortex.[14] Perhaps TV viewing really *can* reduce your grey matter.

In an article about giving up TV, *Fast Company* quoted brain health expert Eric Braverman: 'The boob tube turns you into a boob. Television mesmerizes people and turns them into intellectual spectators.'[15] The effect is indeed hypnotic. Neurosurgeon Adam Lipman, in the same article, explained that EEG studies have demonstrated how television induces an alpha wave state in the brain, associated with daydreaming and reduced critical thinking.

Perhaps this partly explains why television viewers have often proven so gullible over the years. On April Fool's Day in 1957, the BBC current affairs programme *Panorama* aired hoax footage presented as fact, about spaghetti growing from trees.[16] Afterwards, some viewers called the BBC for advice on how they could grow their own spaghetti. In 1992, the BBC aired a mockumentary 'live' ghost-hunting programme called *Ghostwatch*, hosted by trusted broadcaster Michael Parkinson.[17] Many viewers believed it was real; one vulnerable young man killed himself out of fear. His mother said he had been 'hypnotised and obsessed' by the programme.

We can all be transfixed by television, but young children are perhaps the most vulnerable. *Teletubbies* epitomised the allure and success of children's television. It was a British children's television show exported around the world for an audience of pre-schoolers, featuring the carefree lives of four colourful childlike creatures.

Teletubbies has provoked much theorising about the symbolism imbued in the programme. Are the antennae on their heads Satanic symbols? Are their primary colours a homage to the Pride rainbow flag? Crazy theories aside, these funny little humanoids do possess an unusual and intriguing feature inlaid within their stomachs.

In each episode, the magic windmill transmitter whirrs and emits stars into the air. The Teletubbies run from their grass-covered bunker into the bright sunshine and up the hyperreal hillside, to get better reception. They coo, smile and squirm in rapture at their television screens as they wait for one lucky Teletubby to receive the signal to play a video. Thus, every episode is at once an entertaining and quirky piece of children's programming, but also a self-referential, meta-programme reinforcing the power of television.

This chapter cares not whether you are a couch potato, nor whether your children are babysat by screens. It intends to convey to you, rather, the serious power of the television to nudge and manipulate you.

Sugar-coating for mind pills

'Entertainment is sugar-coating for mind pills,' Edward Hunter said sagely in his book *Brainwashing: The Story of Men Who Defied It*. (He might have described the Teletubbies as a pure glucose spinal tap of entertainment ...) Hunter interviewed Korean War veterans who survived POW camps and civilians who were in China about their experiences of brainwashing and how they survived. The 'mind pills' relate to the 'saturation treatment' in society, where the routine of each day and night was arranged so that people simply could not escape from the sight and sound of communist propaganda, where writings were prescriptions, not stories. He said that communist literature had to be written by the group, not any one single person, to make sure the right psychological effect was achieved.

Even today and in democratic countries, storytelling and creative authorship are not the sole preserve of the artist, author or scriptwriter. There are other parties involved in influencing you through sugar-coated television programming.

The late nineteenth and early twentieth centuries were periods of expansion and development in propaganda. Mass media enabled access to mass audiences. In *Brave New World Revisited*, Aldous Huxley predicted 'the Age of Television Addiction, the Age of the Soap Opera'.[18] Television has contributed to propaganda and persuasion becoming increasingly sophisticated, widely practised, and accepted as part of modern society. Despite complex media ecosystems and the fragmentation of audiences, people continue to regard television as an authoritative source of information and fount of entertainment. According to Ofcom, TV is still the UK's most popular source of news.[19]

Television can enable regimes to tighten their rule using 'soft autocracy'. Just like drugs, entertainment media undo your sophistication and make you more susceptible to propaganda. In other words, the advent of television and entertainment media has enabled autocratic regimes to maintain resilience and avoid costly heavy-handed approaches. One study of a Chinese audience showed that an increase in people's interest in entertainment media was associated with an increase in both their satisfaction with the current regime and their anti-Western hostility.[20]

Dr Colin Alexander, Senior Lecturer in Political Communications at Nottingham Trent University, specialises in propaganda and communications, and put it simply:

If you just watch programmes that you like then you are relaxed. If you are relaxed you are more programmable. Whatever the communication, always consider what the purpose of the communicator is. To create content requires time, effort, money, skills. You can consider this at the authorship level or the editor level. Media content often has a political, ideological purpose behind it, even kids' TV. Sometimes the purpose is to sell products, or there might be another purpose. Walk back that process to deliver the media product, from a tweet through to a blockbuster film, it all has purpose.

Generally we connect television propaganda with authoritarian and communist countries. *Squirrel and Hedgehog* was a North Korean animated series that ran from 1977 to 2013. The industrious squirrels in Flower Hill represent the North Koreans. Flowers are a symbol of resistance, dating back to opposition to Japanese rule. The squirrels are pitted against the weasels – sneaky creatures – representing the Japanese, who are in league with wolves, the Americans. The lowly mice in the cartoon stand in for South Koreans, and they humbly serve the Japanese weasels. Thus, *Squirrel and Hedgehog* offers a political allegory of 'good versus evil' propaganda. Or, as the Visit North Korea website puts it: 'It's the story of industrious, loyal, innocent and devoted young patriots who seek to deliver servitude to their land against a treacherous series of adversaries.' Patriotism or propaganda? It's all a matter of framing.

During Putin's first two terms as president, Vladislav Surkov was regarded as the Kremlin's 'grey cardinal', due to crafting Russia's system of 'sovereign democracy' and directing its propaganda principally through the control of state-run television. He would allegedly meet once a week with the heads of the television channels in his Kremlin office, instructing them on suitable subjects to allow on TV, who should be banned and how to present the president's image. According to an article in

The Atlantic, Surkov would, 'pluck a theme (oligarchs, America, the Middle East) and speak for 20 minutes, hinting, nudging, winking, insinuating, though rarely ever saying anything directly, repeating words like "them" and "the enemy" endlessly until they are imprinted on the mind'.[21] The peddling of propaganda by communists and authoritarians is no surprise. But even in democratic countries there can be an unofficial relationship between government and entertainment media. According to the book *Propaganda and Persuasion*, there is cooperation between Hollywood and the Pentagon at times in the provision of assistance in the production of war movies and, 'This fact provides much fuel for those who see in this cooperation the potential for covert government propaganda.'[22]

Top Gun featured never-seen-before aerial action, made possible by extensive support from the US Department of Defense, particularly the US Navy. The use of real equipment made the film look like a commercial for the Navy and recruitment surged. Lawrence H. Suid, historian and author of *Guts and Glory: The Making of the American Military Image in Film*, wrote that *Top Gun* completed the rehabilitation of the American military after it had been savaged in Vietnam. Unsurprisingly, Hollywood and the military have long seen one another as partners, ideologically and economically, and it's no secret.

Top Gun: Maverick (the highest-grossing film of 2022) signed a Production Assistant Agreement with the Pentagon. The producers could access the military's planes, ships and locations, but in return the Department of Defense could review the script and 'weave in key talking points'.[23]

The Department of Defense, for their part, denied that they influenced the creative process: 'The film-makers are the creatives. We're not the creative force … our job is to support them, really, not to push an agenda on to their story.'[24]

Nudges in your favourite shows

More covert propaganda does edge its way into movies and television. The UK's Behavioural Insights Team has helpfully published revealing reports. Colloquially known as the Nudge Unit – after a form of behavioural science called Nudge Theory – it was once part of the UK government, although it is now independent. While still one-third owned by the UK government it published a report entitled 'The power of TV: Nudging viewers to decarbonise their lifestyles'.[25] This collaboration with the broadcaster Sky made some startling admissions: 'Behaviour change via broadcasting and traditional media has historically been aimed at improving public health, boosting gender equality, and reducing violence. Imagine the potential for emissions reductions if the same methods were used to encourage sustainable behaviours!'

The key word is 'historical'. If you have ever suspected that social and political issues were being confected somewhat artificially in TV programming, you were right. This is an admission of social engineering.

Watching TV is known to encourage normative behaviour. In defence of North Korea, what we perceive as propaganda targeting children, the regime presumably intends to be positive and prosocial. One study observed that people learn from television and thus it can no longer be regarded as mere entertainment: 'It is a major source of observational learning for millions of people. In that role it may be one of the most important agencies of socialization in our society.'[26] It's an important point to consider. Although this book is written to help you defend yourself against nudge, manipulation and brainwashing, you may find yourself aligned with those very intentions. The case can be made that the nudgers and manipulators have your best interests at heart, and that you share their causes. But this also creates a feedback loop, where the deliberate agenda-setting inherent in the programming, from news, to soap operas, to documentaries, influences your beliefs about priorities and solutions. For instance, one study found a correlation between reports of high-profile crimes on American television news and a significant increase in public belief that crime and violence are the nation's foremost problem.[27] That, in turn, could influence political leaning and, in the case of televised violence, may increase dependence on strong-arm politics.

The Behavioural Insights Team and Sky may genuinely believe that climate change is an urgent problem. You may believe that too. And if you don't yet, perhaps you will after watching enough of Sky's TV output. For the report proposes an audaciously bossy suite of suggestions that would run through the entire gamut of programming.

Advice such as, 'Frequency of exposure to green themes could be enhanced by building ecological beliefs and traits into core characters within a show so that green issues can fluently be raised time and time again,' sounds potentially tedious, although it might be effective. You would see fewer characters 'carelessly drinking from a plastic bottle'. The report cleverly proposes more kids' programming to centre on green issues to promote 'intergenerational spillover'.

Suggestions continue with 'a family could discuss reducing their waste' in a comedy show. Making that funny is quite the gauntlet throw. News segments could 'explore barriers to acting green and share stories for overcoming them', which doesn't sound particularly newsworthy. (And yes, you read that correctly, a quasi-government behavioural science unit colluded with a broadcaster about news programming.) An episode of a drama could include references to buying an electric vehicle and, of course, characters should order vegetarian options in restaurants. They intend to shove that plant-based, planet-saving burger down your throat.

In addition to Sky, another 11 major UK media brands, including the BBC, ITV, Channel 4, RTE, BritBox and

Discovery, have pledged to adopt a hard editorial bias and increase the amount and quality of their climate coverage.

This collaboration between different broadcasters explains how, during COP26 (the United Nations Climate Change Conference), storylines in multiple soap operas converged on the environment. Each soap filmed scenes that covered different aspects of climate change, the shows referenced each other and characters popped up in different soaps. What better to wash your brain with than *soaps*?

Technocratic policy advisors and activist journalists appear to have taken it upon themselves (presumably with the government's blessing, if not an actual directive) to subliminally influence viewers. Although they clearly believe in the urgency of a climate change problem, it is nevertheless a controversial political goal. And rightly so, since the UK government's Net Zero pledges means the British public must don a number of hair shirts, such as eating less meat and dairy, switching to electric vehicles, using public transport and switching to green pensions.

As an aside, Sky's Chief Executive Dana Strong commuted between the US and UK by private jet for some months in 2021.[28] Perhaps watching her own channel's programming would cure her of such devastating climate-destroying behaviour. (In response to the criticism, Sky said, 'Many CEOs leading multinational companies have schedules that mean it is appropriate to use different modes of transport ... It is critical to counterbalance this, that is why we offset carbon emissions caused by the business travel of Sky employees.'[29]) Essentially, wealthy people live differently, and that includes their TV viewing habits. According to the book *Rich Habits: The Daily Success Habits of Wealthy Individuals*, only 23 per cent of millionaires watch more than an hour of TV a day, compared with 77 per cent of everybody else.[30]

To summarise the Nudge Unit and Sky collaboration plainly: a once-government-owned unit of behavioural scientists and a licensed broadcaster collaborated on plans to subliminally affect viewers of all ages. They want to nudge the British population into prioritising climate change behaviour, and soften them up for tough policies. As it is often considered that 'the science is settled' on climate change, there would be little requirement for introducing opposing points of view. This plan to harden the editorial bias is propaganda. And it is taking place in a modern, democratic country. Even if you agree with this action, will you necessarily agree with the next one?

We might have a broad tolerance and expectation of propaganda in wartime. But a war against climate change apparently means the 'ends justify the means'. Similarly with the war on a virus: Covid-19.

A scriptwriter (who wants to remain anonymous) was invited to attend a summit for film and TV writers in the US, 'Educating Audiences on the Covid-19 Vaccines'. The email invitation read:

> Film & TV writers have incredible persuasive power and reach to educate audiences through authentic and resonant storytelling. That's why we hope you'll join the Ad Council and COVID Collaborative in the largest communications initiative in U.S. history: a massive public education campaign to inspire more confidence in the COVID-19 vaccines.
>
> On June 29, hear from market research and messaging experts from the Ad Council, for an in-depth briefing on all the ways you can help – including how your scripts and storylines can integrate the key vaccine facts and framing that resonate with hesitant audiences.

The email entreated scriptwriters to 'make a difference – and help save lives'. But this particular scriptwriter was horrified that he had been asked to 'tell people what to do with their bodies'. He felt that a line had been crossed.

> I couldn't go. It would have made me feel angry,' he said. 'I'd have thrown my laptop out of the window. It's my place to examine the human condition in a way that is universal and timeless. I don't want to write about one issue that is just 'right now'. No one tells me what to write.

Despite that bold statement, the scriptwriter did concede to a request on a TV series. A producer told him that there was a crisis because 'there weren't any transgender people in the show'. After a little debate it was agreed that they would create a minor character who had about three lines so they could 'tick the box and say job done'. It all became a bit confusing:

> We had a male character who we decided to make a trans man, and so we cast a trans man in the role. But the wardrobe people got it the wrong way round and thought it was a man transitioning to a woman so they did up the trans man as a woman. This woke creation blew up in our faces.

The use of entertainment as a vehicle for social agendas is nothing new. Consider the film *Dirty Dancing*. You might think it is just a nice, light rom-com about a friendly girl who wants to dance with Patrick Swayze. In fact, the movie's screenwriter, Eleanor Bergstein, has described the movie to magazine *Vice* as a vessel for a social agenda – making abortion palatable to Middle America at the time.[31] The catalyst for the film is a dancer, Penny, who is unable to dance (and thus is replaced by the protagonist) because she falls pregnant and wants an abortion. The storyline normalised abortion for 1980s audiences – and, more implicitly, the message is that your carefree, romantic life will be taken away by 'Baby'. As Johnny says, at the end of the film, 'Nobody puts Baby in a corner.' Putting the plot secondary to the social engineering, Bergstein told *Vice*:

> There are six social classes in 'Dirty Dancing', there's the Vietnam War, and there's all the stuff about race relations, and those were things that I cared about, but I felt that the only way to get people into theatres to see them was to have them instinctively move into the film's fabric of love and wonderful music and dancing.

Of course, there is little argument with the excellent intentions of some of these campaigns. The intersection of anti-smoking messaging with the Superman franchise resulted in Nick O'Teen, a baddie who tried to recruit children to his army of smokers. The rationale was to target children who were thought to be easily led to unhealthy choices, but also that the children as 'agents' would persuade parents not to smoke. The good intentions were transparently contained within advertisements. This is a world apart from news, editorial and entertainment being covertly influenced outside of the transparent framework of advertising, which is subject to regulation.

Using television for social engineering is not the sole preserve of British behavioural scientists. India and Mexico, for example, have actively used soap operas to deliver prosocial messages on issues such as breast-feeding, birth control and consumer fraud. *Propaganda and Persuasion* explains that these programmes are 'designed to be as involving to viewers as any regular soap opera, [and] have been carefully crafted by script writers working with social scientists to ensure that these "positive" propagandistic messages are smoothly integrated into the plot'.[32]

Mindful watching

The power of television, and other screens, is here to stay – worldwide. It's a powerful mode of entertainment and education. And it's simply too useful for propagandists and advertisers to influence us while we are in the resulting state of passivity and relaxation. In George Orwell's *1984*, the telescreen is an obligatory screen in every home, broadcasting propaganda but also keeping the inhabitants under surveillance.[33] The telescreen 'could be dimmed, but there was no way of shutting it off completely'. Fortunately for us, we can turn off our televisions, and we should.

Many studies have linked television viewing hours to negative outcomes, like obesity and depression, but few have looked at the power of unplugging. However, a researcher at Eastern Washington University split participants into two groups: those who were instructed to reduce the consumption of screen-based media, and those who weren't.[34] The first group reported higher levels of subjective wellbeing thanks to the experiment. The BBC programme *Panorama* worked with a media psychologist to devise an informal experiment in which families had their TVs and other screens taken away for two weeks. The result? Families interacted more, kids got more sleep and woke up feeling refreshed, and they spent more time on their homework.[35]

Tsering became a Buddhist monk because he wanted to see televisions and cars. Even as an adult he says car advertisements can prove a distraction to his faith and a temptation because they cause 'a kind of jealousy, attachment, and anger'. His solution is not to avoid all television, or screens or modern technology, but to consciously moderate his use of them. He advises, 'If you use media purposefully and carefully it can help you and be good for you. Beyond certain limits it is harmful to you. For instance I am using WhatsApp at the moment so I can connect with you and share something with you. But if I used it for idle and unnecessary talk then it would be harmful. You must try to be conscious and aware when you use the media.'

Father Colin, also resists the temptation to watch television because it is 'a waste of time and it over-stimulates you'. In his opinion, heavy viewing presents people with 'an alternative existence which can be entertaining and funny and interesting', which makes them less attentive to the present. As a man of the cloth his concern was that this detracted from faith since 'We can only meet God in the present', but he observed that the 'secular equivalent is we can only meet ourselves in the present too'.

His advice is simple:

> You have to resist. You should resist looking at stuff because you want to be entertained. It is better not to watch too much television so that you are more attentive in life. It is hard to feel discernment about the right course of action in your life if you watch TV all the time, or you are on Twitter all the time, because you are affected by other people's ideas. You have to switch off your TV and your phone to avoid being bombarded. It is that simple.

Father Colin's astute observation that television exposes you to 'other people's ideas' is both a blessing and a curse. Drama, art and documentaries do originate with other people, and storytelling is as old as language itself. Storytellers want to affect you. As this chapter has demonstrated, sometimes it is because they think they know what is best for you, or the country as a whole, or even another country.

Father Giles is a Catholic hospital chaplain and was discomfited by the discrepancy between TV news and his own experiences during the Covid-19 pandemic: 'Everyone in hospital took Covid seriously, but a lot of the panicky and inflammatory stuff on the television didn't seem to add up. We were treating sick people, which is what hospital is for, but it didn't get overwhelmed. You'd see someone on TV who was very drained and talking about their hospital about to fall over, but that never accorded with what I saw where I work. On TV it was the end of the world, here in the hospital it was Tuesday. I think that journalists accentuate the sense of peril to produce a better story.'

Beyond the news, Father Giles is also aware of more subtle messaging, such as 'political messages about going electric' in a motorbike series. It's an indication that the covert messaging might be more obvious than the nudgers think. 'Things are being snuck in to change how you think,' he observed. 'Storylines are politically influenced.'

But is it a good thing, to use prosocial engineering on TV, or a bad thing?

Father Giles mused: 'It's being done deliberately and so that's a bad thing. It creates tension between how things are and how they want things to be. There is an intentional shove in terms of what you are supposed to consider normal.'

Another report from the UK's Nudge Unit, 'Mass media, behaviour change & peacebuilding', proposes using mass media to reduce violence.[36] The authors pronounce idealistically that 'mass media can also promote peace' and achieves this 'through sharing stories':

> The impact of art and media – such as books and movies – is a result of taking the perspectives of the characters depicted within the story. As described by Wayne C. Booth, 'art is a bridge between one mind and another … it's a primary way in which people create and exchange meaning'.
>
> … By putting these stories into the homes and phones of people across the globe, mass media can create a bridge between ourselves and others in a way that other forms of communication are not able to. It is this that gives mass media the potential to reduce conflict at a global scale.

If the UK behavioural scientists don't quite see themselves as the architects of your mind, they do see themselves as political civic engineers, building a bridge from their minds to yours. While global peace is a lofty aim, this report is another illustration of the sheer scale of the desire to influence you through your television.

You don't have to find God to free your mind from TV's nudge and propaganda influences. But you can learn from monks and millionaires – and watch less TV.

The rules:

- Remember that TV content is not just influenced by an editorial team – governments, policy makers and advisors have their fingers in all types of TV programming in order to deliberately and covertly influence you.
- If you don't turn the TV off altogether, watch less TV in order to minimise influence and potential harms, and watch it 'mindfully', i.e., with a purpose.
- If something about the TV programming strikes you as 'different' compared with real life, or out of place (from green product placement to exaggerated news stories), be aware you might have spotted attempted social engineering.

9

Get it in writing

An image tells a thousand words, and seeing is believing. You tend to be more easily persuaded by images than you are by words – and video is more persuasive still. On the other hand, reading leaves more breathing room for critical thinking.

The picture superiority effect

'You don't put stuff on your head if you're president. That's Politics 101.'

So said Barack Obama when invited to try on a Navy football helmet.[1] Perhaps he was thinking of 1988 presidential hopeful Michael Dukakis, who lost the election to George H. W. Bush thanks in part to a cringeworthy photo opportunity featuring a helmet, a tank and a dopey smile. The picture may have sealed Dukakis's fate as forever a presidential hopeful and nothing more.[2]

British politician Ed Miliband joined Dukakis in the goofy runners-up club after his failed campaign for prime minister. The day before the election, Britain's most popular newspaper, the *Sun*, published a front-page photo of Miliband ungraciously stuffing a bacon sandwich into his face.[3] Ask any Brit what comes to mind when they think of Ed Miliband, and it could well be his awkward snack.

Politics can be defined by imagery. Even a powerful metaphor or visual statement can be enough to stick in our minds. Donald Trump's political career was defined, in part, not by a complex and abstract immigration policy, but by something visualisable and literally concrete: a wall. On the other hand, *Dilbert* creator turned political commentator Scott Adams believed this kind of visual metaphor almost sunk Trump's presidential hopes when he was alleged to have 'groped women like an octopus'.[4] Adams said, 'The "octopus" line about Trump is engineered persuasion of the highest order. It makes the story deeply visual and extra-creepy.'

Mental images grab us and viscerally insinuate themselves into our mind's eye. They are powerful persuasive tools, and often drive political movements forward, like the tragic image of a Syrian child refugee lying face down, drowned, on a Turkish beach, his little shoes facing the sky; or the image of a starving African child stalked patiently by a vulture, an image so haunting that the photographer took his own life a few months after winning a Pulitzer Prize. These visuals stay with us, and they drive us to action. A study found that those who stored in their memory shocking images about 9/11 (like the famous 'falling man') were consequently more concerned about terrorism.[5]

Psychologists tend to concur when it comes to the sticking power of images. There is a principle called 'the picture superiority effect', which refers to the very consistent finding that images are more memorable than words. One study exposed people to a mix of 612 images and words for six seconds each; asked later which ones they recognised, 98 per cent of pictures were recognised compared with 90 per cent of words.[6] Elsewhere, a study of news broadcasts found that 16 per cent of stories were remembered when heard over the radio, compared with 34 per cent when seen on the television.[7]

Not only are images more memorable, but seeing is believing. Consider how, in 2022, a physicist hoodwinked thousands of people with his NASA photo of a star – which actually turned out to be no more than a piece of chorizo.[8] This is to say nothing of the ability of AI-generated images to fool us – like the fake photograph of Donald Trump being arrested that went viral in March 2023.[9] We tend to have faith in images, and why wouldn't we? Technically, there is nothing to dispute. A photograph is a snapshot of space-time, disconnected from context and from cause and effect. There is no argument, only a frozen frieze. The only question that can be asked of a photograph is if it is real; if so, there is no debate.

Besides, once we store an image in memory, we tend to believe it even if it is later proven to be inaccurate. During the Persian Gulf war, Americans who watched footage of high-precision bombings concluded that the military strikes were state of the art – but when they were later informed that only 7 per cent of bombs hit their targets, they found it hard to discard their previous impressions.[10] A more recent study found that Covid-related news was significantly more believable when consumed in video format compared with reading the transcripts of the videos.[11]

Daniel, a former military intelligence analyst, explained how terrorists harness this effect.

> The Islamic State noticed that fictional executions on social media created as much terror as the real executions. The same with the fake destroying of antiques in Syria. This still created anxiety and fear and terror. Even if people know some of them are fictional, they still think, 'It could happen to me (even though I've seen the same guy executed three times!).'

Part of the reason for all this has to do with how we process information. Psychologists believe there are two ways we do this: a 'central' route where persuasion happens through thoughtful engagement with descriptions; and a 'peripheral' route where persuasion happens through repetition and emotional factors like attractiveness.[12]

The emotional route tends to come into play when a message is presented visually. Our ancestors have had eyes for over 500 million years, whereas we have only had speech for the last 50 thousand and writing for the last four thousand.[13] Images engage our so-called lizard brains, whereas words have to contend with our rational brains. Is it any wonder that a study found that newspaper stories about Iraq war casualties elicited greater emotional responses and lower support for continued US presence when they were accompanied by photographs?[14]

Images are also great at grabbing our attention. Eye-tracking studies have found that newspaper readers typically enter articles through photographs, especially larger, colour photographs.[15] This is particularly true of the moving image: videos are significantly more memorable than static images, and fast-moving videos with lots of edits are even more memorable still.[16] Pavlov called this the orienting response, or the 'what is it?' reflex.[17] When there are sudden changes in our environment, like the images flashing on a TV screen or a colour photo set against black-and-white text, we will involuntarily pay attention to it before we've even consciously identified what it is.[18]

Plus of course, there is truth to the old saying that a picture is worth a thousand words. The 'dual-coding' theory of psychology suggests that words are only stored in one system of the brain (verbal), whereas images are encoded in both the verbal and non-verbal systems, because when we see an image we automatically think of words to describe it.[19] Images activate a wider array of memories in the brain; whereas text is processed one word at a time, pictures automatically and simultaneously convey a vast depth of meaning. In a matter of milliseconds, we can see, for example, the injuries inflicted by a terrorist attack, the victims' socio-demographic backgrounds, the location, the rubble from buildings and so on. Researchers have discovered that people find it easier to extract meaning from televised news stories than they do from radio or print.[20]

One of the implications of being bombarded with 'a thousand words' in this way is that it overloads the critical-thinking abilities that could protect you from brainwashing. When you're faced with fast-paced television content, more brainpower is allocated to processing that content, which could otherwise be used for paying attention to details and thinking critically. An illuminating study had one group of students watch news stories, while another watched them in a typical CNN format, with infographics flashing on-screen and text scrolling along the bottom.[21] The multimedia format 'exceeded viewers' attentional capacity': the more info we are bombarded with, the less able we are to critically scrutinise what we're seeing.

As communications theorist Marshall McLuhan put it, media is 'the juicy piece of meat carried by the burglar to distract the watchdog of the mind'.[22]

The medium is the message

Amusing Ourselves to Death is an important book about the effects of the media on society.[23] Its author, Neil Postman, decried the fleeting nature of television:

> There is no murder so brutal, no earthquake so devastating, no political blunder so costly ... that it cannot be erased from our minds by a newscaster saying, 'Now ... this' ... we are no longer struck dumb by a newscaster who, having just reported that a nuclear war is inevitable, goes on to say that he will be right back after this word from Burger King.

Postman quoted news anchor Robert MacNeil, who said the idea of television news 'is to keep everything brief ... to provide constant stimulation through variety, novelty, action, and movement ... to pay attention to no concept, no character, and no problem for more than a few seconds at a time'.

The research suggests he's right. An article in *Biologist* noted that, in the quarter-century since *Sesame Street* had been on the air, the number of edits per episode had doubled.[24] Another study, titled 'Image bite news', reported that between 1968 and 1992, the average length of a journalist shot in a news programme decreased from 33 to 14 seconds, while the number of insertions of film or video per shot increased from 5 to 27.[25] The trend is towards more, faster and simpler – and less thoughtful. As Ray Bradbury wrote in *Fahrenheit 451*: 'Whirl man's mind around about so fast under the pumping hands of publishers, exploiters, broadcasters, that the centrifuge flings off all unnecessary, time-wasting thought!'

In the study 'Are U.S. presidents becoming less rhetorically complex?', researchers analysed the text in political leaders' speeches and found a downward historical trend in complexity.[26] Biden's debate performances and Trump's inauguration speech, for example, were so low in complexity they even outpaced this downward trend. 'Together,' said Trump, 'We will make America strong again. We will make America wealthy again. We will make America proud again. We will make America safe again. And yes, together, we will make America great again.'[27]

This is a stark contrast to the politics of yesteryear. *Amusing Ourselves to Death* gives the example of the debates between presidential candidates Abraham Lincoln and Stephen A. Douglas in the 1850s. In one, Douglas delivered a three-hour address; when it was Lincoln's time to respond, he reminded the audience that it was already 5pm, that he would probably require three hours himself, and that Douglas was scheduled to give a rebuttal; he proposed that the audience go home, refresh themselves, and return for four more hours of debate, which they did. The dialogue itself used complex rhetorical techniques like paradox, metaphor and fine detail, and used formal syntax akin to print. Appeals to emotion rather than reason were discouraged. Douglas said, 'My friends: silence will be more acceptable to me in the discussion of these questions than applause. I desire to address myself to your judgement, your understanding, and your consciences, and not to your passions or your enthusiasms.'

Could the attention span of a 2020s citizen, who must be told to 'watch until the end!' even for a TikTok video, endure this kind of prose for seven hours? Audiences in the 1850s must have had extraordinary reasoning abilities compared with audiences of today. In fact, some studies have found that mathematics scores, verbal proficiency and reading comprehension have been dropping in the US.[28] The potential for brainwashing via imagery is greater than ever.

Could it be that fast-paced, visual content is contributing to an inability to think rationally? Could it be that, as Aldous Huxley wrote in *Brave New World Revisited*, 'inured to television and radio, [the] audience is accustomed to being distracted and does not like to be asked to concentrate or make a prolonged intellectual effort'?[29]

Do you, personally, find it increasingly difficult to concentrate on long-form content, or stick with your train of thought?

In 'The immediate impact of different types of television on young children's executive function', researchers studied whether a fast-paced television show affected four-year-old children's abilities to concentrate and inhibit impulses (a process that's called 'executive function').[30] For nine minutes, the children either played with crayons, watched a public broadcasting documentary with an average scene change every 34 seconds, or else watched a 'very popular fantastical cartoon about an animated sponge that lives under the sea' with a scene change every 11 seconds. Compared with the crayons or the documentary, the fast-paced cartoon had a significant negative effect on executive function.

While this study only looked at the short-term impact, others have found a link between early television viewing and trait deficits in executive function, as well as speech delays.[31] In other words, it can potentially reduce attention spans. Rapid presentation of events on screen captures attention emotionally and automatically, rather than nurturing more logical processes in the prefrontal cortex. Even studies with mice have found that overstimulation of new-borns' brains can shape the architecture of their minds for the worse, for life.[32]

Yet the cartoon about the sea-dwelling sponge is almost *War and Peace* by modern standards. Where the aforementioned study noted a scene change about every 11 seconds, the animated nursery rhymes of *CoComelon* change every one to three seconds by one amateur count.[33] A popular post on Instagram pondered whether *CoComelon* is 'essentially baby cocaine – an intense and dangerous stimulant, which will likely result in an entire generation of children with attention, behaviour, and executive functioning disorders'.

In an email to us, *CoComelon*'s production company Moonbug said, 'We strongly disagree with your assertions that *CoComelon* is potentially addicting and damaging to children. Moonbug creates content for children that supports our key values of compassion, empathy, and resilience.'

They argued that none of the studies cited here specifically looked at *CoComelon*, that one of the studies was conducted solely with a small sample of Malay families, that another study with a much larger sample in the US found no link between television viewing in infancy (of any kind, regardless of pacing) and visual motor skills at age three, and that TikTok videos and Instagram posts are not a reliable nor accurate source.

Elsewhere, TikTok use has also been found in academic research to have a direct, negative impact on concentration spans.[34]

Marshall McLuhan famously said that 'the medium is the message'. What matters is not so much the content, but the format through which this content is delivered. Communication technologies can change the way we think, or don't think; they change who we are as individuals and as a society.

An illustration comes via *Amusing Ourselves to Death*: when philosopher Friedrich Nietzsche began using a typewriter, one of his friends noticed his writing style had, like the machine itself, become more efficient and forceful. 'You are right,' replied Nietzsche. 'Our writing equipment takes part in the forming of our thoughts.'

Even before television, the telegraph had, wrote Neil Postman, trained minds to be 'suited only to the flashing of messages, each to be quickly replaced by a more up-to-date message. Facts push other facts into and then out of consciousness at speeds that neither permit nor require evaluation ...'

The impression is of a maelstrom of superficial, fleeting information, with little room for deeper meaning and connection.

Take, for example, the crisis in Ukraine in 2022. Few stories besides Covid-19 have received so much attention in modern history, and most of us have a strong opinion on the matter. Yet, how many of us could name the prime minister of Ukraine at the time? No, not Zelensky (the president). Did you know Ukraine had a prime minister? When did Ukraine declare independence? From whom? Everyone has an opinion on Ukraine but, as Postman noted about Iran, 'it is probably more accurate to call them emotions rather than opinions, which would account for the fact that they change from week to week'.

Similarly, Postman explained (all the way back in 1985) why television news is, by its very nature, 'disinformation':

> What is happening here is that television is altering the meaning of 'being informed' by creating a species of information that might properly be called disinformation. I am using this word almost in the precise sense in which it is used by spies in the CIA or KGB. Disinformation

does not mean false information. It means misleading information – misplaced, irrelevant, fragmented or superficial information – information that creates the illusion of knowing something but which in fact leads one away from knowing.

A return to the word

So, if imagery leads us to instability, emotionality and irrationality, and makes us vulnerable to brainwashing, what is the cure?

Interestingly, an analysis of the 1988 Canadian election measured people's media consumption as well as the stability of their attitudes over time.[35] Those who watched large amounts of television content were more unstable in their views. Their opinions were as fleeting as the images on the screen; they dashed from one 'current thing' to another. However, as exposure to print media went up, so too did stability. Other academics have found that print media allows more opportunity to process information compared with the transient nature of electronic media.[36] As a result, it is more likely to produce thoughtful cognitive responses such as counter-arguing.[37] As Postman wrote: '[Reading] means to uncover lies, confusions, and overgeneralizations, to detect abuses of logic and common sense. It also means to weigh ideas, to compare and contrast assertions, to connect one generalization to another.'

The solution, therefore, is to get it in writing.

Only through writing can we engage rationally with concepts. Some religions, for example, perhaps forbade iconography because images are a crude representation of abstract truths – just as a photograph can only capture a tree, not 'tree', images cannot capture something so abstract as 'God'.

In contrast to the shallow nature of images, reading involves a deeper style of thinking. It engages profoundly with an inward world of ideas and emotions. It demands sustained focus, the inhibition of impulses, and the strength to ignore distractions – all of which strengthen our executive function skills. That is, reading makes us more thoughtful and rational.

And in contrast to imagery, reading is slower; it gives us room to breathe and to digest the information. Psychologists have demonstrated the power of 'the shower effect' – that is, taking breaks gives our unconscious mind the time it needs to solve a problem, resulting in better decision making.[38] When we're faced with something like rapid-fire content, our conscious brains turn into little more than TV sets themselves, picking up fleeting signals moment by moment but not processing them deeply or storing them in long-term memory. Instead, they vanish and are replaced by the next thing. Reading, on the other hand, provides a small but steady drip of information that can be integrated into our long-term memory.

When we're faced with powerful imagery, it affects us emotionally, and we rarely take the time to deeply consider the nuance or context involved. Would we, for example, have been so easily led into the first Gulf War were it not for the shocking mental imagery evoked by tales of Saddam Hussein's soldiers pulling babies out of incubators, later shown to be a fabrication amplified by public relations firm Hill & Knowlton?[39] Or indeed, would we have been so easily led into the second Gulf War were it not for Colin Powell being photographed holding a vial of anthrax before a UN security council as a demonstration of weapons of mass destruction, which were ultimately never found?[40]

Perhaps not.

The rules:

- Free your life of overstimulating content, since it can potentially harm your attention span and reduce rationality.

- Build reading habits, since they can help to strengthen your critical-thinking skills and give you 'breathing room' to digest information.
- Watch out for the manipulative use of images or mental imagery: if a story is very easy to visualise, there might be an agenda behind it.

10

Watch out for the blip

You are most vulnerable to manipulation when you're going through a 'blip', a period of disruption that breaks down your critical defences, whether it's a fleeting sense of confusion, or a long-term life change. Day to day, watch out for downbeats like hunger, anxiety, loneliness and tiredness.

A hurricane in the mind

Manuel Noriega was not exactly what you'd call a virtuous man. He ruled Panama as an authoritarian dictator who trafficked in guns, drugs and murder. So, when the US invaded in December 1989, his decision to seek sanctuary in the Vatican embassy might have seemed odd. In fact, it was incredibly shrewd. The United States was forbidden by treaty to invade the embassy, meaning Noriega was safe within its walls.

Unable to reach him physically, US forces mounted a psychological assault instead. Operatives made as much noise as they could at all hours of the day and night, revving the engines of armoured vehicles against the embassy walls, and landing and despatching helicopters nearby. They also set up loudspeakers at full volume, led by 'someone who identified himself as a member of the PSYOPS team from Fort Bragg', according to a military report.[1]

Noriega, apparently an opera fan, was treated to a round-the-clock playlist of heavy metal turned up to 11, including hits like Van Halen's 'Panama', as well as Rick Astley's 'Never Gonna Give You Up' (though that may have been aimed more at the embassy staff).

Within the embassy walls, the papal ambassador Monsignor Laboa was waging some psychological warfare of his own, to 'weave a sort of spell' around Noriega and convince him he had no choice but to surrender.[2]

On 3 January 1990, after ten days of bombardment, Noriega phoned his family, attended mass and made his decision. He surrendered to US forces. When he reached the front gate, he was confronted by paratroopers, one of whom subsequently described him as a 'broken man'. The psychological assault seemed to have had its effect.

All of us, dictator or otherwise, are particularly vulnerable to suggestion when going through some turbulence in life. It could be something small, like tiredness, or it could be something large, like a never-ending musical assault.

An Oklahoma judge recently ruled that prison officers' use of the children's song 'Baby Shark' ('Baby shark, do-do-do-do-do-do, baby shark, do-do-do-do-do-do, baby shark, do-do-do-do-do-do, baby shark') on repeat for four hours was a form of torture – especially accompanied as it was by a standing stress position.[3] 'The volume of the song was so loud,' read the lawsuit, 'that it was reverberating down the hallways.'

The aim, as Naomi Klein wrote in *The Shock Doctrine*, is to 'provoke a kind of hurricane in the mind: prisoners are so regressed and afraid that they can no longer think rationally'.[4]

Under continued overload, there is a temporary phase – a blip – at which conscious defences are so broken down that the mind becomes a vacuum, open to absorbing new ways of thinking. This is the very essence of brainwashing.

While it is a potent tool for shaping minds in totalitarian regimes, interrogation chambers and cult campgrounds, it also applies to the bamboozlement and discombobulation foisted on us by con-men, advertisers and politicians in our daily lives, as this chapter will explain.

At its most extreme level, however, a CIA interrogation manual explained it like this:

> When [disruption] is achieved, resistance is seriously impaired. There is an interval – which may be extremely brief – of suspended animation, a kind of psychological shock or paralysis ... that explodes the world that is familiar to the subject as well as his image of himself within that world. Experienced interrogators recognize this effect when it appears and know that at this moment the source is far more open to suggestion.[5]

Destroy to rebuild

The underlying principle is death and rebirth – destroying a person psychologically so that they may be rebuilt anew. It is an alchemical process of dissolving and reassembling. As George Orwell put it in his classic *1984*, 'Power is in tearing human minds to pieces and putting them together again in shapes of your own choosing.'[6]

Open any book on brainwashing and you'll find broadly the same process of indoctrination. First, there is a phase of bombardment, which, in its basest form, can involve physical assaults. The book *The Rape of the Mind* described how prisoners at a camp in North Korea were marched barefoot to the frozen Yalu River, where water was poured over their feet, and they were left for hours to reflect on the accusations levelled at them.[7] Hunger can also weaken energy and therefore resolve. The book *Brainwashing: The Story of Men Who Defied It* described how, in Pak's Palace POW Camp in North Korea, the minimum amount of rice a man could eat without starving to death was calculated carefully and then cut by a third; a knife was run over the top of each cup to make sure not one additional grain passed through.[8] The interrogator can also count psychological weapons like humiliation, isolation, confusion and guilt among his arsenal.

'Time, fear, and continual pressure are known to create a menticidal hypnosis', wrote psychoanalyst Joost Meerloo in *The Rape of the Mind*.

Eventually, there is a moment of almost childlike surrender and an attachment to the new authority figure and ideology, as it is the only means of escape from the intense psychological pressure. With this sudden yielding, 'the new phonograph has to be grooved', as Meerloo put it. New thoughts and behaviours are impressed upon the target, who is helped to rationalise and justify them.

Cardinal Mindszenty was the leader of the Catholic Church in Hungary following the Second World War, and staunchly opposed to communism. As a result, he was tortured and imprisoned. Stephen K. Swift wrote an exposé of his treatment, which graphically outlined the three-step process of breakdown, submission and imprinting.[9] First, the political prisoner would be bombarded with questions at all hours of the day, with almost no rest and inadequate and irregular feeding. The cardinal himself was made to stand for 66 hours of questioning. When he asked to be killed, he was told he would not be harmed and could end the ordeal simply by cooperating. Under constant and contradictory questioning, the cardinal was unable to keep his thoughts straight. As a social being like all of us, he also felt an urge for good relationships with his captors. He was burdened not only by insomnia, diarrhoea and backache, but also by loneliness, guilt, uncertainty and a detachment from reality. The torture from within and without urged him towards cooperation in order to seek release – at the very least, to sleep. At this point of submission, he was trained to accept and rehearse his 'confession' in minute detail, repeating the same sentences over and over again.

The key is to give people a sort of shock that discombobulates their critical thinking, making them more vulnerable to suggestion. Meerloo reported how behaviourist Ivan Pavlov showed how *actual* electric shocks – especially when intense, unexpected, or coming when ill or tired – could be used to break down dogs' behavioural patterns as well as build up new ones. The overwhelming stimulation causes a kind of cognitive shut-down.

Every dog, said Pavlov, has its 'breaking point' provided the appropriate stress is applied. Fred Newman, leader of the alleged Social Therapy cult, described his revolutionary psychotherapy as 'the overthrow of the rulers of the mind' – according to Alexandra Stein's *Terror, Love and Brainwashing*.[10] Stein was an ex-cult member herself, and described how cults engineer a 'cognitive collapse' and use the resulting 'cognitive vacuum' to implant new beliefs.

Stein wrote that giving in and ceasing to think are experienced as a relief. It is the end of a struggle, welcomed among those overwhelmed with confusion and exhaustion. In her own journal at the time of being in a cult, she wrote: 'I must take myself in hand. I must struggle and face my fears. This chaos in my head has got to stop or I'll drown. The noise is unbearable ... I will work harder for the struggle. It's the one thing I know I can do ... No more nightmares. I am moving on. I feel as if I've found solid ground. I've decided to join.'

A great example of this kind of sudden conversion comes from Arthur Koestler's *Arrow in the Blue*, which describes his conversion to militant communism.[11] His final decision was a sudden one, following 'a whole series of grotesque events, crowded into one December evening'. He went to a friend's poker party and promptly lost several months' salary, after which he headed to an afterparty to drown his sorrows. He got very drunk and, upon leaving at around three in the morning, broke his newly repaired car. He was spotted by a girl from the party (whom he did not like) and accepted the hospitality of her nearby flat, leading to 'the consequences which were to be expected'. He woke up hungover, anxious, guilty and broke, in bed next to a person he loathed.

'The series of grotesque misadventures on that Saturday night looked as if they had been arranged by a crude jester,' he wrote, 'but the face of a clown, bending close against your own, can be very frightening. By the time I got back to my flat my decision [to finally join the Communist Party] was made, though I hardly felt it to be mine; it had made itself.'

While it can be a single event that triggers the cognitive collapse, more often it is the culmination of undulating waves of bombardment. Like the ocean erodes a cliff by ebbing and flowing, a person or population is worn down by what Meerloo called 'waves of terror'. Each wave is, after a breathing spell, more effective than the last; it reaches its targets off-guard and already softened up by the prior waves.

On a smaller scale, magician and psychologist Professor Gustav Kuhn explained how timing is used in magic tricks:

> Offbeats are very important. They're probably the most important principle in magic. You're dissociating effect from method, because the method happens before the effect. You do the trick when the magic 'hasn't started yet' – for example in a moment of relaxation before the trick begins. Moving backwards causes the audience to relax, whereas moving forward increases the tension. Or you can use rhythm. When you say, 'One, two, three,' people expect things to happen on the third time. It's called time misdirection.

Another technique Professor Kuhn outlined was bamboozlement and misdirection, through tactics like glitzy showgirls, smoke bombs and loud music. 'If you present loads of stuff and bamboozle your audience, it's a lot harder for them to work out how it's done. At a magic show your senses are being bombarded with a vast amount of information.'

First, make them mad

This is why, Meerloo said, an important tactic of totalitarian regimes is to create confusion, so people cannot distinguish true from false. In order to break down people's minds, the totalitarian leader 'first needs widespread mental chaos and verbal confusion'. Many victims of totalitarianism told Meerloo in interviews that one of the most disturbing aspects of the concentration camp was the feeling of the loss of logic. As the famous saying goes: 'He whom the gods wish to destroy, they first make mad.'

Alexandra Stein wrote about how former cult member Juliet was bamboozled by meaningless language. She had not been political, but the group started to talk about political and identity issues more often. They would get together on a Saturday evening, discuss classism, and 'all accuse each other of being this or that and we had no clue what we were talking about – it was just flinging out these words 'cause we were just learning them ... "sexism", "racism", the "isms", you know, and it was hard because I had no understanding of what that meant ...'

So, cults and authoritarian regimes in other countries and time periods deliberately apply pressure and confusion to brainwash people, but it doesn't happen to *us*, in everyday life, does it? First of all, these extreme examples are set out to bring to life vulnerabilities you may experience in a smaller way. But the fact is, our own governments do also use the playbook of bamboozlement.

The aforementioned CIA interrogation manual also outlined what they called the 'Alice in Wonderland' technique of interrogation. People are accustomed to a world that makes sense, 'a world of continuity and logic, a predictable world', and cling to this world to reinforce identity and resistance. The Alice in Wonderland technique is designed 'not only to obliterate the familiar but to replace it with the weird'; it involves asking nonsensical questions, interrupting answers with illogical follow-ups, asking two or more unrelated questions at once, and using voice tone that is entirely inappropriate for the importance of the question. This creates a strange atmosphere in which normal patterns have been replaced by 'an eerie meaninglessness'. As the subject's mind goes into overdrive to make sense of the nonsensical, the situation becomes 'mentally intolerable', and they are more likely to let their guard down.

Another way of disabling people's critical defences is through overwhelming the senses. Aldous Huxley wrote that, 'No man, however highly civilised, can listen for very long to African drumming, or Indian chanting, or Welsh hymn singing, and retain intact his critical and self-conscious personality ... If exposed long enough to the tom-toms and the singing, every one of our philosophers would end by capering and howling with the savages.'[12]

This might be why rhythmic drumming is found in transformative ceremonies and political rallies all over the world. It produces a crescendo of excitement, often accompanied by dancing, which culminates in a point of physical and psychological exhaustion.

Avant-garde artist Maya Deren visited Haiti in 1949 to study Haitian dancing.[13] In her written account, she described how the drums gradually induced uncontrollable movements that climaxed in a feeling of possession. 'My skull is a drum,' she wrote:

> each great beat drives that leg, like the point of a stake, into the ground ... I am caught in this cylinder, this well of sounds. There is nothing anywhere except this. There is no way out ... The bright darkness floods up through my body, reaches my head, engulfs me. I am sucked down and exploded upward at once. That is all ... If the earth is a sphere, then the abyss below the earth is also its heavens; and the difference between them is no more than time, the time of the earth's turning.

Having reached her moment of suspended animation and cognitive collapse, Deren achieved the sort of rebirth experienced by religious and political converts: 'How clear the world looks in this first total light. How purely form it is, without, for the moment, the shadow of meaning ... As the souls of the dead did, so have I, too, come back. I have returned.'

Critical thinking can also be overwhelmed by emotional overload, such as extreme stress, guilt or fear. Cults encourage relentlessly critical 'soul searching' and 'confession', while political movements inculcate intense feelings of guilt around identity politics such as class or race. On re-education camps, Chairman Mao Zedong said, 'The first method in reasoning is to give the patients a powerful stimulus, yell at them "you're sick!", so the patients will have a fright and break out in an over-all sweat; then, they can be carefully treated.'[14]

Recent experimental research has demonstrated that people are more persuadable after they have been emotionally overwhelmed. Of particular note is the 'fear-then-relief' model of compliance; one study showed that people jaywalking were more likely to stop and complete a survey (59 per cent) if they had been startled first by a policeman's whistle from a concealed location, compared with those who were not whistled (46 per cent).[15]

This probably happens because of 'ego depletion'. The brain has limited resources; like a muscle, it can get tired, especially when bombarded with information, sensation or emotion. Students in one experiment who completed a difficult, boring task (crossing out each instance of the letter 'e' except when it was next to a different vowel or one letter removed from a vowel in either direction) were subsequently more likely to agree with the unpopular proposition that new mandatory exams should be introduced.[16] They were less able to resist because they had used up their brainpower on the task.

This is probably why a *Psychology and Marketing* study in 2007 found that some people are more persuadable later in the day because they have depleted their energy.[17] Hitler himself wrote that during the day 'man's will power revolts with highest energy … In the evening, however, they succumb more easily to the dominating force of a stronger will.'[18]

Outside the interrogation room

You may be unlikely to attend a night-time Nazi rally, but these examples all illustrate the power of the 'blip' in its purest form. The basic principles are used across all walks of life, even in your daily routine. Contemporary religions, for example, often involve fasting, chanting and, most extremely, mortification of the flesh, such as self-flagellation, to foster the 'blip' and make the follower more receptive to the message.

Outside of religions, what are we to make of secular initiation rites like freshers' week at university? It bears all the anthropological hallmarks of a 'death and rebirth' ritual. Initiates are wrenched from their home communities and accommodated in new surroundings. At night, when the mind is weakest, students typically break down their critical resistance with a cocktail of alcohol, drugs, loud music and sex. During the day, the softened-up students are introduced to new ways of thinking.

Jennifer (not her real name) explained how her worldview changed radically at university:

> I learned to hate the white man, basically. I never felt like that before uni. My friend would talk to me about systemic this and oppressive that. We would hang out in the bars after classes. I was really lonely at uni, I'd just been broken up with, I had no one to talk to. I remember I had an argument with my sister once because she used the word 'midget' in front of me. I said you're supposed to call them 'little people'. It's so embarrassing to look back on it. A couple years out of uni I went back to normal.

Music festivals are also fertile grounds for indoctrination. Attendees often find themselves filthy and exhausted, having been kept up all night in noisy, uncomfortable tents and eaten too little nutritious food. Their resistance is further broken down by alcohol and drugs, while loud music and fantastical sights overwhelm attendees' senses and emotions. It is under these conditions that what MK-Ultra researchers would call the 'psychic driving' of songs' repetitive messages take root, and esoteric subconscious symbolism can have its effect. Overt political messages, such as Labour leader Jeremy Corbyn's speech in 2017 and climate activist Greta Thunberg's speech in 2022, both from the Pyramid Stage at Glastonbury, are far more likely to receive rapturous applause and take root in receptive minds.

Brands, salespeople and advertisers try to foster a 'blip' of vulnerability too. In a *Journal of Personality and Social Psychology* paper, researchers tested the so-called 'disrupt-then-reframe' technique.[19] They made sales to around 40 per cent of customers when a package of eight cards sold for $3.00. However, when customers were told that 'the price of eight cards is 300 pennies, which is a bargain', sales doubled to around 80 per cent. The unusual presentation of the price in pennies disrupted people's normal thinking, so that the bargain message could be implanted in the vacuum.

Retailers place sweets and trinkets by the checkout, banking on the fact that many shoppers will be too tired to resist their impulses by the time they've made their way around the store. Car rental companies ostensibly use the fact that weary travellers, assaulted by an 11-hour flight and five-hour time difference, can be bamboozled into paying high sums for insurance that only covers scratches measured in millimetres. Outright scams often employ 'the distraction principle': for example, the window-tap technique involves one hustler knocking on the window of a café to ask a patron for the time, while another hustler helps himself to her handbag.[20]

The Shock Doctrine

Disruption can happen on a small scale like this, but it can also be the result of a bigger life event. The National Counter Terrorism Policing's platform Action Counters Terrorism (ACT) explains that 'anyone can be at risk of radicalisation', and it is situational factors such as a traumatic life event that are the biggest risk factors.[21] The book *Cults in Our Midst* described a key vulnerability as being a life 'blip' – a life change like a move to university, a divorce, or a death in the family.[22]

Gerette, a cult recovery educator, said:

> It's not uncommon that people get involved when they're at a transition point in their life. My daughter was born six months before I started. I was a new mum and a bit vulnerable. It was disorienting, a lot of vulnerability. It's not uncommon after a traumatic experience, divorce, death.
>
> I have just heard about a cult that goes through the obituaries and looks for grieving families. People are more easily recruited because a loved one just died. Since Covid, the group has had to strategise because they're not going door-to-door.

An article in *Stuff* reported that Jehovah's Witnesses admit viewing the recently bereaved as 'ripe fruit' for 'grief targeting', according to former members.[23] As well as cold-calling the grieving families found in obituaries, there have been reports about a Jehovah's Witness car being equipped with sound equipment and being driven from cemetery to cemetery on All Souls' Day in Brazil, reaching over 40,000 mourners.

Building on the 'blip' theory, Alexandra Stein continues:

> War, natural disasters or social upheavals – such as the breakup of the former Soviet Union, or the current collapsed states of Syria or Somalia – can contribute to weakening family and community ties leading to increased social fragmentation and isolation. Simply living in the contemporary developed world, with fewer neighborhood ties and more dispersed families, means most of us live in increasingly vulnerable social networks.

When a society is wracked by shocks like a war, pandemic or economic crash – or deregulatory earthquakes like Brexit – it is more malleable. This is what Naomi Klein called 'the shock doctrine' in her book of the same name:

> the original disaster – the coup, the terrorist attack, the market meltdown, the war, the tsunami, the hurricane – puts the entire population into a state of collective shock. The falling bombs, the bursts of terror, the pounding winds serve to soften up whole societies much as the blaring music and blows in the torture cells soften up prisoners. Like the terrorized prisoner who gives up the names of comrades and renounces his faith, shocked societies often give up things they would otherwise fiercely protect.

The war in Iraq offers an example. The US military, said Klein, used a Shock and Awe technique to try to transform and exploit the country. An ex-CIA operative explained that 'the fear and disorder offered real promise': his private security firm won $100 million in contracts.[24] Klein expounded: 'Fear and disorder are the catalysts for each new leap forward.'

The Fourth Turning

Which brings us to today. Modern life is atomised and lonely – and above all confusing. Technology and the media overwhelm us daily with sensation, emotion and information. Fact-checker Will Moy, from Full Fact, explained: 'We know that one of the goals of disinformation campaigns is to spread and create confusion where an actor or a group of actors are trying to use disinformation. The goal isn't to convince people of something which isn't true but to create confusion.'

The past several years have been marked by traumatic events and chaos. Academic studies have found that people were more susceptible to hoaxes, scams and phishing during Covid-19, due in part to the debilitating effects of fear on critical thinking.[25] Yet the hurricane in which we find ourselves is a lot more than just Covid-19 – there is also the conflict in Ukraine and economic recession, to say the least.

The world's troubles can be considered a symbolic flood. Floods wreak devastation, but they also sweep away the old and leave the soil fertilised so that something new can grow. It was the Leningrad flood that gave Pavlov the eureka moment that the brain might be wiped clean of previously conditioned patterns of behaviour.[26]

Over the years, many scholars have argued that society goes through cycles of death and rebirth, with destructive crisis points that dissolve old ways of living so that something new can take their place. Neil Howe and William Strauss added detail to the theory in their book *The Fourth Turning*.[27] Their hypothesis was that societies pass through a four-stage cycle much like the seasons every 80 to 100 years (about the average human lifespan). When a society reaches the 'winter', it is characterised by disorder, by the collapse of existing values and habits, before a new paradigm takes their place. Pressure builds at several points – including the economy, faith in institutions, and community cohesion – before erupting into chaos.

According to this theory, the last 'winter' was about 80 to 100 years ago, when the world experienced two world wars, a financial collapse and a flu pandemic. The conditions of pre-Nazi Weimar Germany – hyperinflation, a cost-of-living crisis, a pandemic, an industrial revolution, licentiousness, inter-group conflict, and collapsing faith in politicians and the media – feel eerily similar. The same sort of conditions were likewise found in eras such pre-revolutionary France and the last days of Rome.

Whether or not the cyclical theory is true, there is no denying that Western civilisation is currently going through a crisis point. Faith in politicians, the media and other institutions is collapsing.[28] While many countries are experiencing a literal energy crisis, they are also experiencing a psychological energy crisis: shock after shock is ostensibly weakening people's resolve. YouGov reports that one in eight Brits now feels tired all the time.[29] Economic conditions have worsened in many countries. Food bank use in the UK and food pantry use in the US have increased.

Hunger, stress and exhaustion are the perfect conditions for old ways of thinking to be dissolved so something new can take their place. These are the conditions that totalitarian regimes have fostered in order to implement new ideologies. China's 'Great Leap Forward' agricultural reforms starved millions to death (whether deliberately or not), as the regime sought to destroy the Four Olds: old ideas, old culture, old customs and old habits. The Khmer Rouge revolutionary agricultural reforms also starved millions of Cambodians in their 'Year Zero' attempt to reset society.

Today, our leaders in the West openly view the state of chaos as an opportunity to implant new behaviours and ideals under the banner of The Great Reset and Net Zero – as a prime candidate for the 'shock doctrine'. Proposed digital IDs, central bank digital currencies, and environmental and social agendas wait in the wings.

Just HALT

Whether it's the government bureaucrats pushing a new policy, the phishing scams in your inbox, or the disinformation bot farms on your social media feeds, the current climate of confusion is ripe for brainwashing, manipulation and nudging. Even in the best of times, salespeople and advertisers can bamboozle you into compliance. You can't single-handedly alter societal cycles, but you can improve your own psychological resilience. First, HALT.

Alcoholics Anonymous are experts at maintaining a level head and resisting temptation. Whereas most of us try to avoid manipulation by advertisers and colleagues, people in recovery must be constantly vigilant, lest the monkey on their back persuades them to have just one drink, just one smoke, just one bet. One of the techniques is to recognise when you are in a psychological state that might make you weak to temptation. Specifically, there are four triggers: hungry, angry (or anxious), lonely and tired – giving the acronym HALT.[30]

The next time you're making an important decision, halt, and ask yourself if you're in the best frame of mind to do so. If you've just stepped off a long-haul flight, have only eaten airline food, or are worried about getting to your next destination, that may not be the best time to deal with a car hire company. Instead, it might be better to first have something to eat or take a power nap. Similarly, try not to make important decisions when life has bamboozled you: if you've had a recent divorce, it might be better to rethink that self-improvement course until a later date.

Likewise, watch out for techniques designed to bamboozle you and put you under pressure. Former FBI hostage negotiator Gary Noesner explained, 'My book's called *Stalling for Time*. Whenever someone's trying to put pressure on you, just slow things down. Ask them to help you understand why it has to be done right now. At least you have the time to work it out in your mind.'

Ultimately, it's important to try and get out of a 'hot' decision-making state, and into a 'cold' one. That is, try to remove pressure and take your time to cool down. This is what social media companies do when they ask if you're sure you want to post something: behavioural science consultancy Irrational Labs reduced shares of flagged content on TikTok by 24 per cent by introducing this kind of prompt ('Are you sure you want to share this video? This video was flagged for unverified content.').[31] The agency's report read, 'TikTok is a fast platform where users often act in hot states. By slowing people down, we hypothesized that we could decrease the sometimes overwhelming power of emotion.'

Whether you're a kid scrolling TikTok, a shopper seduced by snacks at the till, or a Panamanian dictator holed up in an embassy, it seems the key to surviving the 'blip' is to slow things down to a halt.

The rules:

- Remember to HALT when making important decisions: ask yourself if you are hungry, anxious, lonely or tired, and wait until you're more comfortable.
- Make important decisions in a cold state rather than a hot one, and don't give in to pressures such as urgency or conformity.
- When things are confusing and topsy-turvy, try to anchor yourself to something that's real, to provide certainty among the chaos.

11

Be sceptical of Big Brother

It is comforting to believe that governments and authorities are there to protect and serve us – but you should be wary of Big Brother's arm around your shoulder. Sometimes it is benign and comforting, but at times it has been known to prod, steer and strangle. You shouldn't always look up to Big Brother. This doesn't make you a conspiracy theorist, but even if it did, you shouldn't be afraid of the label.

Ghosts in the machine

Have you ever wondered who's pulling the strings?

Has it occurred to you, as it did to Shakespeare, that all the world's a stage?

Fear not, this chapter is not taking a conspiratorial turn. These questions are posed by a very official source: a US army unit, specifically, the 4th Psychological Operations Group (Airborne), in a recruitment video posted on YouTube. The implicit answer is that there *is* someone pulling the strings: this secretive psyop division.

The video entitled *Ghosts in the Machine* is unnerving and impressive. It warrants a detailed description because it is unlike any army recruitment video you have ever seen. You would be forgiven for confusing it with a Hollywood trailer for an eerie new thriller, a scary age-rated video game, or a well-funded and clever denouement by hackers. We contacted the US army numerous times for interview, and our request was passed between majors like a grenade in a game of public relations pass-the-parcel.

The idea that mysterious forces are pulling the strings is not new. Edward Bernays, the influential psychoanalyst and author of *Propaganda*, wrote about the invisible wires of government.[1] Espionage, foreign intelligence and propaganda have a very long history. The video nods to this: the opening screen quotes the fourth-century-BCE Chinese general Sun Tzu: 'If your opponent is of choleric temper, seek to irritate him. Pretend to be weak, that he may grow arrogant.'

In the video, a marionette on TV tap-dances to atmospheric music; a voiceover adds US commentary about the pro-democracy protest in Tiananmen Square and the fall of the Berlin Wall. Chess pieces reference the 'game' of psyops.

There is footage from riots, protests and wars around the world. We are warned that 'a threat rises in the east'. As the imagery moves between the Russian invasion of Ukraine, and from horses, to tanks, to touch screens, the subtitles read:

Warfare is evolving
And all the world's a stage
Anything we touch is a weapon

The accompanying lyrics talk about shadows, footsteps in the night, wolves hiding nearby. And psyops do normally happen in the shadows. We aren't supposed to know about them. But in an intriguing plot twist, the people who pull the strings are now letting us know they are pulling the strings. They are on the stage, holding the marionette in front of our very eyes, telling us it's an act.

The motto of the 4th Psyop Group is *Verbum Vencet*, which means 'the word will conquer'. The conqueror is a deceiver. But do our governments and military deploy psyops upon their own citizens? One of the troubling aspects of this video is the implication that they do.

While some scenes are clearly set overseas, some appear to be domestic to the US. The subtitle, 'We can deceive, persuade, change, influence, inspire', appears slowly, word by word, to scenes from around the world: girls wearing hijabs in a school, boys somewhere in Africa holding a football, even a member of the Maasai Mara tribe, and people who look like they might live in the US. 'We are everywhere,' says the subtitle to images of a metro train and the Statue of Liberty.

The US army is telling us what it is doing: it is using psyops, everywhere. In an interview in the military journal *Task and Purpose*, Colonel Chris Strangle confirmed that US army psyops soldiers are working daily with over forty countries around the globe.[2] More controversially, 'everywhere' might also mean within the US itself.

The objective of the video is purportedly to enlist soldiers. But if 'anything we touch is a weapon', does that include this video? Is that the point? It is purposefully mysterious and unsettling, after all. As Strangle told *Task and Purpose*, part of psychological operations is creating persuasive media.

If agents of psychological operations 'come in many forms', will you recognise those forms – whether they are sent by an enemy state or your own 'Big Brother'? Some comments under the video question whether US citizens should be more frightened of foreign governments, or their own government. The tension is palpable. It is more relaxing to trust Big Brother.

Big Brother is, of course, a reference to the all-powerful and infallible symbolic figurehead of the totalitarian government in George Orwell's *1984*.[3] The case studies contained within this chapter do not signify that we are living under a similar government; Big Brother is also a symbolic repository, albeit for propaganda, manipulation and psychological operations. In the real and complex world it may be that our governments, and their security services and agencies, protect and serve us while *also* prodding and steering us.

Psychological operations are occurring 'literally everywhere, every day, in every component of our lives' throughout the world, says Strangle. So you need to understand Big Brother's surprising methods as much as you do those of the salesman, the cult leader, the advertiser or the magician. As Machiavelli said, 'Princes and governments are far more dangerous than other elements within society.'

At the time of writing, a contemporary psyop war is playing out in real time. As well as conflict in the physical environment, the 2022 Russian invasion of Ukraine has revealed the role media and social media play in modern warfare. According to Strangle, after the Russian annexation of Crimea in 2014, the US psyop community, along with other NATO allies and special operations communities around the world, helped Ukraine build their own abilities. He believes that Ukraine has been far more successful than Russia in the information war.

Disinformation in war is nothing new – it is common to inflate or fabricate information about everything from military might to supposed atrocities to disrupt information, confuse opponents or boost morale. It is said that the first casualty of war is the truth. So, how is this to be married with the very modern disavowal of misinformation and disinformation? Is lying the preserve of the baddies? Steady yourself for another plot twist, this time in the realm of propaganda.

The Ghost of Kyiv

On 30 April 2022, Ukrainian air force officials admitted that the military hero dubbed the 'Ghost of Kyiv' was fictitious by announcing on Facebook: 'Ghost of Kyiv is a superhero-legend whose character was created by Ukrainians!' The authorities explained that the Ghost of Kyiv was 'a collective image of pilots of the Air Force's 40th tactical aviation brigade, who defend the sky over the capital', rather than a single man's combat record.

This origin story was as made up as the ghost himself. He was not written into existence by 'Ukrainians' but by the Ukrainian *authorities*. The Ukraine Security Service originally showed a fighter pilot on Telegram, with a caption calling the Ghost of Kyiv an 'angel' for downing ten Russian planes. The Ukrainian military released a photograph on Facebook of the Ghost of Kyiv in March 2022 with the caption, 'Hello, occupier, I'm coming for your soul!'

His name evoked the dark hero of a fairy tale. His feats were exaggerated, gathering mythic status. Whereas an 'ace' might eliminate five enemy aircraft, the ghost was reputed to have downed about 40 Russian pilots. He didn't seem real, unsurprising given he was a purposeful piece of propaganda, just as the Second World War Stalingrad sniper duel is also most likely to be a myth. Mythic heroes are invented to emblemise wartime courage, just as Father Christmas does the spirit of giving. Human beings will always love legends. And propaganda boosts morale. But it also breeds chaos and mistrust. And we don't normally find out until after the fact.

We are constantly warned about the dangers of misinformation, by fact-checkers, BBC disinformation specialists, the government and various concerned busybodies. The Online Safety Bill is constructed partly around this purpose. There are social and professional penalties for spreading misinformation. So it was interesting that this admission of fiction passed without judgement. In fact, a BBC news report about the Ghost of Kyiv story was remarkably forgiving.[4] It condescendingly explained that legends are 'not surprising', 'there is plenty of room for embellishment', heroes enter 'national mythology', and quoted Justin Crump of the security consultancy Sybilline, who said the Ghost of Kyiv legend is important because in our social media age 'people need myths, heroes and legends, to provide cohesion and meaning'.

This leniency is entirely at odds with the hard and proactive line we have come to expect about misinformation and disinformation. It effectively endorses a government making up the Santa Claus of fighter pilots. And that relegates us to credulous infants. The Ghost of Kyiv may have been coming for the occupier's soul, but propaganda comes for everyone.

The point of this is not to single out and judge Ukraine. Russia delivers a 'Firehose of Falsehood', according to social scientists Christopher Paul and Miriam Matthews, using a large number of channels and messages and 'a shameless willingness to disseminate partial truths or outright fictions'.[5]

The Ghost of Kyiv wasn't a particularly believable hero. Yet he proved that a fiction that conforms to our side's values and mission is a legend, not a lie; it's myth-information, not misinformation. He proved that elaborate bedtime stories will be told.

Both Ukraine and Russia are utilising bot armies to create angst, fear and worry in their cyber warfare, using words like 'president', 'government' and 'leadership', and 'shame', 'terrorist', 'threat' and 'panic'.[6] Tweets have also been used to influence people's decision about whether to flee their homes or not, something that has not been observed before.

While this is a very new field of study, it's obvious that deliberately malicious Twitter campaigns seek to control the narrative and drive polarisation. Stating the obvious, this makes social media – and especially Twitter in this case – a confusing and unreliable source of views, news and sentiment. The old term 'stranger danger' takes on new meaning: is that account you don't know trying to drum up support for a foreign power, petition your president to take action, or exaggerate risks and make you run for your life? Put simply, you can't trust what the world's 'Big Brothers' are doing online.

The UK government funded expert research to expose how the Kremlin was using a troll factory to 'spread lies on social media' during the Ukraine invasion, including targeting politicians, deliberately amplifying 'organic' content supporting the Kremlin's position, and recruiting and coordinating supporters. The operation was detected across eight social media platforms including Telegram, Twitter, Facebook and TikTok.

We know there are Chinese and Russian troll farms and sneaky social media accounts. It would appear that Ukraine is not just responding but possibly winning the online war. But do the bastions of democracy also use ersatz social media accounts? In short, yes.

On home turf

The *Washington Post* reported in September 2022 that the Pentagon had ordered a sweeping audit of how it conducts clandestine information warfare after 'major social media companies identified and took offline fake accounts suspected of being run by the US military in violation of the platforms' rules'.[7] Apparently, Twitter and Facebook have closed the accounts of more than 150 fake personas and media sites created in the United States in the last few years. Anonymous officials pointed the finger at US Central Command. Some accounts involved posts that advanced anti-Russia narratives, some were countering disinformation spread by China about the origins of Covid-19, and one fake account claimed that relatives of deceased Afghan refugees had reported bodies being returned from Iran with missing organs. As one defence official said, if this was organised by the US military, it would 'absolutely be a violation of doctrine and training practices'.

Dennis (not his real name) used to be employed at an agency that undertook work for the UK government's Research, Information and Communications Unit (RICU). According to Dennis, propaganda is outsourced from RICU to external agencies, which then work with NGOs and grassroots organisations. This means that the parties involved and the people they are trying to influence – who might otherwise be suspicious of the government – are more easily hoodwinked. It also enables the government to stay distanced from the propaganda and deny direct involvement. Dennis's account is confirmed by investigations undertaken and reported by openDemocracy,[8] as well as Middle East Eye.

If you came across these grassroots communications you would not be aware you were watching or reading propaganda. The people who created them might not be aware either. Dennis recommends being suspicious 'if the quality is too good to be credible'. He said they produced 'very high end stuff, too good for grassroots'. The agency would have what is known as a 360 degree deal, whereby they would manage the social media channels, build their website and produce videos. 'Most charity videos (not the big ones with offices in Islington and Battersea) are not that good. We were making videos for Somali youth that were really high quality. People should be able to spot that.'

The unit's early propaganda efforts appear to have been largely turned towards attitudinal and behavioural change among Muslims – in other words, changing the way that British Muslims think and act. Dennis was keen to stress that this came out of a well-intentioned government desire – fuelled by pressure from the public and the media – to do something about radicalisation and extremism after the war on terror. However, he said the efforts became 'bloated', and the unit and agency were producing campaigns to 'justify their existence'. Over time, the work felt dishonest: 'Even if the political project is "nice", it's political and it's trying to change the way people think. And it's paid for from government money.' By which he means taxpayers' money, of course.

After the terror attacks on London Bridge in 2017, there were bunches of flowers and graffiti messages of solidarity behind the cordons at the scene of the attack. On social media there were outpourings of support and positively themed hashtags, such as #TurnToLove, #ForLondon and #LoveWillWin. Local officials were told, 'We're sending you a hundred imams.'[9] The media resounded with comments from faith leaders and politicians. Much of the response was not truly spontaneous, but reportedly pre-planned by the UK government. The purpose was to dampen public anger towards Muslims and move swiftly to the 'recovery' stage of the disaster with no riots or retaliation.

Disaster and recovery planner Lucy Easthope, Professor in Practice of Risk and Hazard at the University of Durham, wrote for the *Guardian* that 'the "I heart" messages that appear in cities in the wake of a terrorist attack are not always spontaneous' but 'carefully planned in advance'.[10] She told us that she herself has penned the pre-emptive plans, which include staged displays of positive emotion and resilience. However, after the 2017 Manchester bombing, she had a change of heart about the level of guided response when she realised that people needed a window of raw grief: 'I was wrong to insist in my training that the first message should be "we will overcome" as if the enemy was on the beaches and weakness would be letting someone or something win ... the fight rhetoric has gone too far and instead what we need to do is to admit how much this hurts.'

These operations that contingency planners term 'controlled spontaneity' are designed to prevent unrest and riots, and to ease people through shock and grief, even if the pace is too fast. They are clearly well intentioned although artificial. Is it healthy to disguise, constrain and rush natural emotional responses to a disaster?

How can you be aware if spontaneity – yours or that of those around you – is being controlled? If a response feels fast and unnaturally positive, or if shock, grief and especially anger are minimised, then they may be signs the response is controlled. It might be wisest for your long-term emotional and psychological health to stay in tune with your natural responses.

Although the UK government has labelled Russian bot activity 'insidious', it also undertakes social media campaigns of its own. It certainly uses non-bot accounts to launch campaigns and hashtags, as 'Dennis' who worked on covert campaigns, told us.

The use of fake social media accounts, troll farms and deliberate online misinformation spread by governments, their agencies and military prove better than we ever could that the modern-day battlefield is your mind.

What if your mind isn't just the terrain, but the target?

Nudge

Governments have always drawn on knowledge of human psychology to shape the behaviour of citizens. But, in the early 2000s, the UK and US governments began to more overtly incorporate psychological and behavioural factors into policy making and regulation.

After the publication of the seminal book *Nudge* in 2008, one of the book's authors, Cass Sunstein, was appointed Head of the Office of Information and Regulatory Affairs under President Obama. Sunstein was able to intervene on a range of regulatory issues, particularly through the use of executive orders, such as enabling the Environmental Protection Agency to regulate greenhouse gas emissions and set fuel economy standards without congressional approval. In the UK, the Behavioural Insights Team, colloquially known as the Nudge Unit, was set up under David Cameron's newly elected coalition government in 2010.

Behavioural science had come to the attention of government officials following the publication of the discussion paper, 'Personal responsibility and changing behaviour: The state of knowledge and its implications for public policy', authored by David Halpern, founder of the Nudge Unit, among others.[11] It set out three reasons for governments to use nudging.

First, that achieving major policy outcomes requires greater engagement and participation from citizens – 'governments can't do it alone'. Essentially, personal behaviour must be changed. The authors give the example that improving health requires willingness to exercise and change diet. This rests responsibility for ill health upon the individual, rather than, for example, taking into account socio-economic factors, which require a different form of government intervention. It also assumes that the individual wants to improve their health, and that the government knows best how to achieve that.

Second, the paper claims that there are strong moral and political arguments for protecting and enhancing personal responsibility. This assumes that individual responsibility and choice are preserved in the system of choice architecture. But nudging and choice architecture work because we are nudged *subliminally* to one choice before others. Once you are aware of the nudges and choices, you can truly exercise choice. If you can't see them, you are not 'empowered'.

Third, the paper posits that behavioural science is a cost-effective way to encourage take-up of policies. If it works (and there are studies and theories debating just how successful nudging is), then it is cheaper than the consequences of not nudging. Of course, it is also less costly in terms of debate, which – one suspects – is a huge draw for policy makers.

The use of nudging has inspired inflamed commentary and negative feedback for years, yet governments have persisted. The reasons are clear. Nudges are not mandates, so they are implemented without debate and disagreement. That means they are implemented without you being aware of it. Nudging is also relatively cheap. It is what some academics would label as non-consensual propaganda: people are not informed, and they are not free to opt out.[12]

Government nudges rest upon the assumption that they know what is best for you. As Cass Sunstein, the person who coined the term 'nudge', said, 'By knowing how people think, we can make it easier for them to choose what is best for them, their families and society.'[13] Isn't it great that there are people who know what is best for you?

Yet what Cass Sunstein seemingly fails to realise is that every human being is biased – including the nudgers themselves. The people who think they know what's best for us are just as irrational as everyone else, and the combination of their blind spots and their unchecked power can be disastrous. There are many examples of unintended consequences from government interventions, but perhaps the most famous is the 'Delhi cobra effect'.

The British Raj once wanted to reduce the number of cobras in Delhi, so they introduced a nudge: for every dead snake handed in, they would pay a small incentive.[14] It appeared to be a great success, with so many dead snakes the Raj assumed the problem was fixed and ended the scheme. In fact, the locals had been breeding the snakes to claim the reward. When the scheme was ended, new cobras were released and the problem was made that much worse. Elsewhere, for example, no-smoking signs have been shown to increase smoking (by reminding people of their cravings),[15] and 'beware of pickpockets' signs may actually make the problem worse (because passers-by see the signs and automatically check their valuables, letting would-be thieves know what they have and where they keep it).[16]

It is hard to take exception to campaigns to reduce tobacco use and pickpocketing. But do these worthwhile-sounding initiatives assault people's capacity to make up their own mind? If someone does not give up smoking, it may be because they want to continue despite the risk, not because they are incapable of understanding risk or can't give up.

Governments that nudge have accepted manipulation and deception as a prominent feature of how they do business. Behavioural economics assumes that we are not rational, that we know this, and we welcome the release from anxiety and guilt. A UK House of Lords select committee report noted that when the government guides our decisions for us it 'acts as surrogate willpower and locks our biscuit tins' – acting like the parents of a naughty child who's unable to stop scoffing biscuits by themselves.[17] Essentially, clever people like Sunstein and Halpern make sure that non-clever people do what they want.

In 2010, the authors of 'MINDSPACE: Influencing behaviour through public policy' at the Institute for Government think-tank included a whole chapter on the 'legitimacy of government involvement in behaviour change' because it is 'controversial'.[18] Although they say that 'public acceptability' should not be the determining condition for going forward with behaviour change, they acknowledge that the use of behavioural science 'has implications for consent and freedom of choice' and offers people 'little opportunity to opt out'.

The US and UK governments acknowledge that companies are negatively impacting on customer choice and market competition by deploying nudges and choice architecture. In September 2022 the US's Federal Trade Commission published 'Bringing dark patterns to light' to review how manipulative online design patterns harm consumers.[19] The UK government's Competition and Markets Authority (CMA) published a discussion paper, 'Online choice architecture: How digital design can harm competition and consumers', which focuses on the harm that can arise from the way in which choices are presented, which can lead to distorted consumer behaviour and competition and suboptimal decisions.[20]

Concerns in this area are sometimes referred to as 'dark patterns' and 'dark nudges'. Common examples include the order of products in search results, the number of steps needed to cancel a subscription, or whether an option is selected by default, hiding crucial information, setting default choices that may not align with our preferences, or exploiting the way our attention is drawn to scarce products.

But should the UK government apply the same overdue scrutiny to its own use of choice architecture?

The Scottish Centre for Crime and Justice Research published a briefing paper, 'Influence government', in September 2021, regarding the fusion of behaviour change, sensitive personal data and targeted advertising by the UK government, public bodies and law enforcement to alter behaviour.[21] This marks a fundamental shift in the relationship between people and their government, but the report received little media attention.

National and local governments have turned to targeted advertisements on search engines and social media platforms to try to 'nudge' the behaviour of the country. As with 'controlled spontaneity' programmes and Prevent (a UK government programme to tackle radicalisation), these are sometimes outsourced to third party agencies, thereby evading scrutiny and transparency.

One example in the paper claimed that the Home Office used the purchasing data of people who had recently bought candles to target them through their smart speakers with fire safety adverts. Reducing house fires is well intentioned and has clear benefits. But the rise of influence government can be more harmful in other contexts. It involves using personal data – for instance, using notes from an interview under caution to build a profile of a typical cybercriminal. It can also focus negative attention on vulnerable and disadvantaged groups in ways that could be counterproductive. As an example, one set of anti-knife crime adverts was targeted at fans of drill music on YouTube. This area of pre-crime is disturbingly reminiscent of the futuristic surveillance-state in the film *Minority Report*. But the other problem flagged by the researchers is that being followed around the internet by mentions of knife crime could make young people more likely to think that knife-carrying was common, and ultimately help convince them to carry a weapon.

The research found that targeted adverts based on online behavioural profiles, the use of influencers and 'influence operations', and advanced marketing strategies are now being used as part of frontline public service and law enforcement. This allows public bodies to reach increasingly specific groups and tailor messaging accordingly. This might have benefits, but it makes the nudge hard to observe in an increasingly personalised online world. The online environment and therefore subsequent behaviour have been shaped by the government in ways that people have not consented to, such as when people search for particular topics, use particular language on social media, or view particular content. Do you recall a political party promising to ensure that you would get the search results and content it deems most suitable for you? It doesn't sound like a vote-winner. It also covertly shapes the cultures of groups deemed 'at risk' of engaging in particular kinds of sanctioned or harmful behaviour. Some of this might achieve the desired effect, but it might also create 'blowback' and unexpected negative responses. If the community knows it has been targeted in this way, how will it respond? Will it trust the government more or less?

The government's own online choice architecture practices seem to fall foul of the CMA's areas of concern, including choice pressure, privacy invasion and discrimination against personal characteristics. Most importantly, given a nudge is supposed to be a choice, these are not choices you can ignore as they are covertly embedded in technology.

Crucially, this form of influence government is at odds with democracy. It is 'top-down', providing public bodies with a unidirectional capacity to shape the online environment, behaviours and cultures of their citizens (and 'those groups who fall under their control but are denied citizenship', as the report points out). There has never been a consultation with the public about the validity of these programmes.

As governments scrutinise private companies for abuses of choice architecture and nudges, it seems they may need to get their own houses in order. In a more extreme example, an All-Party Parliamentary Group Report into the loan charge scandal linked HMRC's use of 30 behavioural insights in communications to one of the seven known suicides of people facing the loan charge.[22] The report was clear that a full independent inquiry should include 'looking into HMRC's use of behavioural psychology / behavioural insights'. There has been no inquiry and HMRC continues to nudge to 'apply pressure to taxpayers'.

Nudging has changed our relationship with government. This was foreseen soon after the inception of the Nudge Unit. A Science and Technology Select Committee's investigation into behaviour change noted that there are 'ethical issues because they involve altering behaviour through mechanisms of which people are not obviously aware'.[23] And 'MINDSPACE' warned:

> People have a strong instinct for reciprocity that informs their relationship with government – they pay taxes and the government provides services in return. This transactional model remains intact if government legislates and provides advice to inform behaviour. But if government is seen as using powerful, pre-conscious effects to subtly change behaviour, people may feel the relationship has changed: now the state is affecting 'them' – their very personality.

The calls to conduct a public consultation into the use of nudging have not yet been heeded.

We asked Cass Sunstein whether he believed there is a democratic mandate for nudging by government. He said the current focus is on 'sludge', which is administrative burdens and barriers, or frictions that make government work less well. Which is to say, he dodged the question. Sunstein possibly errs towards caution in interviews, since he got into hot water in the past for his proposals for how to deal with conspiracy theories.

Conspiracy fact or fiction

Conspiracy theories often claim to expose secret machinations of powerful people, sometimes the government, who act to accomplish nefarious plans. While there are different ways to define a conspiracy theory, the key part is generally that the precise mechanisms of the plans cannot be detailed. Conspiracy theories are generally thought of as unverified, implausible, unwarranted, unnecessary, stupid. In fact, groups, especially powerful ones, have always conspired to advance their own interests, and it would be irrational *not* to theorise about that.

But the term 'conspiracy theory' has had a bad reputation since it was popularised by the philosopher Sir Karl Popper in the 1950s.[24] Before that point, the world somehow managed without it. Since then, the conspiracy theorist has been viewed as a problem for society.

In a 2008 academic paper entitled 'Conspiracy theories', Cass Sunstein and Adrian Vermeule put forward a policy idea they termed 'cognitive infiltration' to counter the 'serious risks' of conspiracy theories.[25] It's worth noting that the paper labelled conspiracy theorists as 'extremist groups', which in itself is an extreme label for theorising. The authors suggested that, rather than just ignore theories or rebut them, which might give them credence, government should attack the 'supply side', and change people's minds from the inside. This could involve hiring credible private parties to engage in counter speech, and introduce cognitive diversity in groups suffering from social conformity and informational cascades:

> Government agents (and their allies) might enter chat rooms, online social networks, or even real-space groups and attempt to undermine percolating conspiracy theories by raising doubts about their factual premises, causal logic or implications for political action ... If government is able to have credibility, or to act through credible

> agents, it might well be successful in dislodging beliefs that are held only because no one contradicts them.[26]

Smart, or sneaky? The suggestion drew fire from many commentators. Conspiracy theories resonate because people mistrust the government. The concept of cognitive infiltration does not inspire trust in government.

It may never have been implemented. It was just an idea up for discussion (we hope), in an academic publication. But Sunstein isn't a 'nobody', he is a lauded behavioural scientist and friend of President Obama. He has advised officials at the United Nations, the European Commission and the World Bank. In 2020, the World Health Organization appointed him Chair of its technical advisory group on Behavioural Insights and Sciences.

His proposal rested upon the assumption that conspiracy theories tend to be false, unjustified and harmful. Sunstein claimed that conspiracy theories are usually unjustified and false because they cannot remain secret for very long in open societies with a free press and institutional check and balances. But this is not true. Some conspiracy theories have taken years to be proven correct. Even the paper acknowledges this, offering MK-Ultra (the secretive CIA-funded mind-control research) as an example.

MK-Ultra is not the only time governments have misled citizens or experimented on them. Here are just a few more examples that prove conspiracy theories sometimes turn out to be true.

Porton Down, the UK's infamous scientific establishment, deliberately released anthrax on the Northern Line of the London Underground in 1963, presumably to study the impact of biological weapons, although there was no warning or apparent follow-up on the health of Londoners.

Over two hundred similar covert experiments are believed to have taken place between 1949 and 1979, to help the Ministry of Defence assess Britain's vulnerability if attacked by the Soviet Union. One report reveals that military personnel were briefed to tell any 'inquisitive inquirer' that the trials were part of research projects into weather and air pollution. A chapter of one released report, 'The fluorescent particle trials', reveals that planes dropped zinc cadmium sulphide on the population ranging from north-east England to the tip of Cornwall.[27] Cadmium is considered a probable human carcinogen.

Operation Northwoods was a proposed false flag operation against American citizens. The plan would have been for CIA operatives to stage and commit acts of terrorism against American military and citizens, and blame it on the Cuban government to justify a war against Cuba. The proposals were rejected by President Kennedy.

More recently, disclosures on news stories that were once labelled 'conspiracy theories', such as Hunter Biden's laptop,[28] have led some to joke that the only difference between a conspiracy theory and the news is about six months.[29]

One of the strangest theories is that secretive government agencies ran harmful projects in the past, but no longer do so. It is logical to assume these practices didn't have a cut-off date. However, it would also be dangerous to assume that every unhappy circumstance is a conspiracy theory, or that all victims of disasters are crisis actors. The next danger is that authorities blame these possibly misguided conspiracy theories upon online disinformation, and do not absorb the blame for behaving in an untrustworthy fashion.

Has the pernicious programme of cognitive infiltration been implemented? To speculate would make us conspiracy theorists. The truth is, we have no idea. But governments have form. One example was COINTELPRO, the FBI's Counter Intelligence Program. It took place from 1956 to 1971, so it happened in real life rather than in chat rooms. As Dr David Coady, senior lecturer in philosophy at the University of Tasmania, wrote:

> [it] was authorised by every American president from Eisenhower to Nixon ... aimed at infiltrating, disrupting and discrediting a variety of political organisations on the political left, including the civil rights movement, the anti-war movement, and a wide variety of feminist, and anti-colonial organisations. Most infamously it led to the FBI's murder of Fred Hampton and, not only the illegal surveillance of Martin Luther King, but also a well-documented attempt to drive him to suicide. Sunstein and Vermeule do not mention COINTELPRO, perhaps because it does not fit well with their narrative, because it was eventually exposed, not by the fearless investigative reporters of the free press or any other institution of the open society, but by a group of leftist 'conspiracy theorists' called the 'Citizens Commission to Investigate the FBI', which burgled the offices of the FBI and stole documents relating to the programme.[30]

As Voltaire said, 'It is dangerous to be right when the government is wrong.'[31] We hope you are unlikely to need to defend yourself against the dark arts of government infiltrators in chat rooms or real-life groups. Probably the most important takeaway is not to be deterred from joining organisations or stimulating debate in your field of interest (which is not to say diving headlong into an irrational rabbit hole). The next is to reject the label 'conspiracy theorist'.

Conspiracy theorists are the modern-day heretics. It often means challenging the powers-that-be. Many theories are true, and reasonable opinion about others is divided. A number concern situations in which there is no controversy about whether a conspiracy occurred; the only issue is which theory is true. Yesterday's conspiracy theories do not always become today's facts, but it happens often enough that there should be some humility about the label.

When 'conspiracy theory' is used as a pejorative, it contributes to an attitude that there is something wrong with questioning, with wanting to investigate the possibility that powerful people might be engaged in deception. The net effect of this is to silence people in ways that suit the interests of powerful people who might be engaged in deception. Thus, a vigorous critique of conspiracy could allow conspiracies to flourish.

Panic about fake news and conspiracy theory might be a reflection of powerful authorities trying to cripple opposing views and theories. The term 'fake news' was coined by Donald Trump (according to him, anyway) but has since gained traction among opponents of Trump as a way of referring to pro-Trump news. As Coady says, his critics take exception to his use of the term, not the term itself. It is supposed to apply to him and not be weaponised by him.

Many countries have introduced laws that attempt to ban fake news one way or another. In France, President Macron passed a law to prohibit it on the internet during elections. He said, 'If we want to protect liberal democracies, we must be strong and have clear rules.'[32] To summarise, the tenets of liberal democracy – free speech and a free press – were banned in order to protect liberal democracy.

What's more, some disinformation specialists and fact-checkers appear to be doing their best to bust myths and put shoddy articles straight. Will Moy, Chief Executive of Full Fact, believes that 'a moral panic about fake news is causing over-reaction in government'. He is concerned about governments removing legal but harmful content as well as about the opacity of algorithms. It is his opinion that Big Tech should be under pressure from government, but at the moment 'private government pressure on Big Tech to remove content or change what people can see or share – i.e. to shape what we can all do online – is happening without any open transparent democratic oversight process'. But it's not all bad. 'It is amazing to live in a time when information is as democratised as it is. Although there are lots of fears about how it will play out, we should embrace it too in all its glory. We should think about the risks and how we should behave personally, but we shouldn't only talk about the downsides.'

Moy's concern about government pressure on Big Tech is understandable, but might it also be related to Full Fact's funding? In 2021 its website reported that they were paid £481,106 by Facebook and £235,222 by Google, plus a monthly payment of £7,300 worth of free advertising by the search giant and Google staff volunteers who helped to build AI tools. Other donations came from WhatsApp and the Vaccine Grant Program, among others. Does this funding compromise Full Fact's integrity and create bias towards Big Tech? In its favour, Full Fact offers complete transparency and suggests people judge for themselves.

Alongside the standard debunking of politicians' overblown promises and claims, not all of the organisation's fact-checks later hold up to scrutiny. This is one of the fatal flaws of a fact-checking service: facts change as information evolves.

A fact-check in August 2021 quoted the Royal College of Obstetricians and Gynaecologists, which said that 'There is no plausible mechanism by which any vaccine ingredient could pass to your baby through breast milk.'[33] By September 2022 a study had reported that messenger RNA from the Covid-19 vaccines had been detected in human breast milk.[34] While the quantity present was tiny, it meant that the mechanism was not implausible, it was plausible. The phrasing 'no evidence for any mechanism' would have been more accurate and fair. Full Fact stated that, 'The information included in this article contains the latest evidence and official guidance available at the time it was written.' But the evidence changed. If Big Tech platforms had used this scientific thinking at the time, and the endorsement of a fact-checking organisation they fund to censor or shadow ban accounts, that would have been incorrect.

The Covid-19 lab-leak origin theory offers one of the best recent illustrations of the fallibility of fact-checking. Various outlets and fact-checkers firmly rebutted the idea of a lab leak. In one typical example, *Forbes* ran an article with the headline, 'The Wuhan lab leak hypothesis is a conspiracy theory, not science'.

Why were fact-checkers and the media so keen to deny one of the plausible origins of the virus, one that looks more likely as time goes on? These fact-checks distorted the public debate and acceptability of ideas just when minds should have been open. In fact, leading public health scientists were privately speculating (in leaked emails) that the virus was man-made and accidentally released from a lab, but were concerned that further debate would harm science in China and 'international harmony'. Matt Ridley, co-author of *Viral: The Search for the Origin of Covid*, said: 'These emails show a lamentable lack of openness and transparency among Western scientists who appear to have been more interested in shutting down a hypothesis they thought was very plausible, for political reasons.'[35] In November 2022, the *Telegraph* was reporting that 'UK experts helped shut down Covid lab leak theory – weeks after being told it might be true'.[36]

The stifling of dissent

While fact-checkers suppress debate in ways we can observe, governments do so opaquely. In January 2022, Cabinet Minister Nadine Dorries boasted in the House of Commons that the misinformation and disinformation unit censors citizens' online speech at its own, unaccountable discretion. (She was presumably referring to the Cabinet Office's Rapid Response Unit and/or the Department for Digital, Culture, Media and Sport's Counter Disinformation Unit.) An investigation by Big Brother Watch in 2023 uncovered the scale of secretive government units contacting Big Tech platforms to request that critical, but totally lawful, content be removed.[37] Likewise, in the US, Republican Attorney Generals are suing the Biden administration for censoring free speech and colluding with social media during the Covid-19 pandemic, and also for the suppression of the *New York Post*'s exposé of the Hunter Biden laptop story.

Governments themselves deliberately leak disinformation, although of course when the government does it, it's not called disinformation. After resigning from the CIA, Frank Snepp alleged in his book *Decent Interval: An Insider's Account of Saigon's Indecent End Told by the CIA's Chief Strategy Analyst in Vietnam*, and in subsequent interviews, that the CIA deliberately fed false information to journalists, most dramatically about a possible 'blood bath' in Saigon in the closing days of the Vietnam War. 'Disinformation in the CIA sense is not false information. That is the grossest kind,' he said, 'and that is the kind you can usually be caught out on. When the CIA does it, it's nothing so gross. It's information which keys off of reality, like docudrama. But that's the CIA definition, which is not to take an untruth, but to take a piece of truth.'

Big Brother does seem to be becoming less tolerant these days. A leaked document from the UK Civil Service directs civil servants who arrange for external speakers on 'Diversity and Inclusion' to perform background checks, without the speakers' knowledge, to see whether they have spoken out against the government, its officials or its policies, on social media or elsewhere, within the last five years. The document states that the research has to be done long before the event takes place and suggests viewing approximately ten pages of search results and links, and documenting the results.

A civil servant (who wishes to remain anonymous) said that 'it is gravely concerning that, under the cloak of civil service values, dissent of government policy is covertly stifled, so that only conforming voices may be heard'.

This is an extraordinary act of censorship. Government should be robust enough to listen to its critics, on whatever topic. Taken to the extreme, this would prevent a multitude of skilled experts addressing civil servants if they previously voiced opposition to a single policy of their political masters. But understood in the right way, this shows how deep the rot goes. Dissent is stifled outside government walls, and within.

If the wrong theory doesn't have you written off as a conspiracy theorist, maybe you will be called a lunatic. Dr Rachel Sharman postulated that people who doubt climate change have a mental condition.[38] Coady compares the psychology profession to the Inquisition, because it pathologises conspiracy theory. 'The most extreme examples were in the Soviet Union when they had mental hospitals filled with political dissidents,' he says. 'We are not at that stage in the west yet but we do see people with different political views and scepticism framed as mentally ill or harmful.'

He believes that not only should people refuse to fear the term 'conspiracy theorist'; they should consider it a badge of pride. Just as 'witch' and 'queer' have been used to denigrate people and have been reclaimed, he thinks 'conspiracy theorist' should be reclaimed in the same way.

> The main instrument of manipulation is through language. We always want to be alert to neologisms, new terms which describe the social environment we are in. These terms are almost always tools of propaganda. Conspiracy theory is one such term. Fake news is another. That's a new piece of terminology to manipulate people and censor people. Countries all over the world are introducing laws to ban or prohibit fake news. No one can describe what fake news is. When this madness stops people will see this as utterly bizarre as burning witches and heretics. Conspiracies have always happened

and always will. They have always happened in politics. It's a massive con job.

While you should guard against falling for irrational beliefs, some scepticism is a good idea. To be very clear, this is not a clarion call to nurture and promote convoluted conspiracy theories. Don't get lost down rabbit holes or waste your time. Rather, be aware of the intended denigration of this neologism. It is in the same vein as Scientology calling defectors 'suppressive persons', or the unflattering religious classification of 'infidels' and 'apostates'. To call someone a conspiracy theorist is to label them as a nonbeliever so that everything they say is ignored and discounted. We should be more tolerant of the concept of 'conspiracy theory'. A little bit of heresy does you good.

There is enough evidence to be sure that Big Brother and his agencies use propaganda and psyops not only on foreign populations and governments, but also on *us*. You may be comfortable to trust that your best interests are being served, or you may prefer to be alert and observant. Governments are coming to rely upon nudging populations to fall in line with new policies. They want to affect your behaviour and your personality covertly and subliminally.

And governments do not always act in the individual citizen's best interests – your best interests – because a trade-off may be considered fair game in the pursuit of a strategic goal.

As the famous street art by Plymouth's Nme says, 'The world's not that bad, it's your government that sucks.'

They have told you they are pulling the strings. Believe them.

The rules:

- Be aware that governments, foreign and domestic, are running propaganda campaigns aimed at you, using multiple media.

- Understand that if a grassroots organisation's communications, social media and video production seem too good to be true, they might be.
- Be sceptical, ask questions, and don't be afraid of the term 'conspiracy theorist'.

12

Consider your options

Consent is key for manipulation: you'll only accept your choice if you feel that it really was yours to make. Persuasion backfires when people feel that they don't have control. Often, you have to ask whether you really have a choice, or whether it's only an illusion.

The illusion of control

The devil always gives you a choice.

Whether it's Faust willingly signing away his soul for unlimited pleasure and knowledge, or blues maestro Robert Johnson exchanging his soul for a guitar and an unrivalled mastery of its strings, our folktales are full of examples of people making bargains of their own free will. These stories take place 'down at the crossroads' because the protagonist has their own choice which route to take. As C. S. Lewis wrote: 'All that are in Hell, choose it.'[1]

These stories stretch from as far back as the Bible all the way to modern sci-fi flicks. The Old Testament says we would all be living in paradise were it not for Eve making a choice to try the forbidden fruit; the snake didn't force her to eat the apple but instead exploited her pride. *The Matrix* saw its hero Neo exit virtual reality only when he picked the red pill of his own volition. Later, he meets The Architect of the simulated world, who tells him, 'Nearly 99 per cent of all test subjects accepted the program, as long as they were given a choice, even if they were only aware of the choice at a near unconscious level.'

The important principle here is the 'illusion of control': the idea that people are only happy if they believe they have a degree of agency over the world and their decisions.[2] When this sense of autonomy is missing, the psyche suffers. Imagine a dog that has been trapped inside an inescapable cage and given electric shocks; research has shown that even if the dog is moved into a cage from which it could escape, it will simply lie down and take the shocks, as it has learnt to be helpless.[3] On the other hand, psychological research has consistently linked a sense of control to many positive life outcomes, from increased incomes[4] to longer lifespans.[5]

A large (if contested) body of evidence suggests this illusion of control really is just an illusion. What we believe to be conscious choice may actually be nothing more than a rationalisation after the fact.[6]

This illusion is so important that if people feel deprived of their free will, they become rebellious and show what is known as 'reactance'.[7] This means that when they feel coerced into doing something, they may deliberately disobey. It is what happens when a teenager, told not to smoke, says, 'Get lost, Mum and Dad, I'm smoking the biggest Cuban cigar I can find!'

In fact, anti-smoking messages can have 'ironic processes': trying to scare and shame people into quitting cigarettes may simply cause them to smoke more in order to feel that they have free will.[8] They don't want to be pushed around by some advert, particularly one that is emotionally manipulative.

This is why, as one experiment published in the *Journal of Advertising* found, Uber's 'No Mask, No Ride' campaign may have been counterproductive.[9] It threatened people's sense of freedom and, according to the research, actually made people less likely to comply. It also worsened attitudes towards Uber as a brand.

Manipulators benefit from giving you the sense that you are making your own choice; while they may stack the cards against you, it ultimately has to feel like your decision or you won't accept it. One meta-analysis across 42 studies found using the 'but you are free' compliance technique (ending requests with lines like 'the choice is yours' or 'only if you want to') made twice as many people comply.[10]

Former FBI hostage negotiator Gary Noesner named this as a key principle for getting people to do what you want.

> It's all about being patient, taking your time, not trying to force something on someone. The harder you push, the more likely it is that you get resistance. It turns people off. We joke about the used car salesman stereotype – that high-pressure, hit-you-hard-on-the-lot, gotta-lock-in approach. That's not a good way to sell anything. I look for the guy who's like, 'Look over there, take your time.'
>
> Like mules, people have a stubborn reputation. If you lead them, you may be able to move them where you want. If you get around the back and try to push a mule, its little pea-brain will say they're trying to force me. Frankly, people are no different. If you get the sense people are pushing you too hard, you won't comply.

This is the essence of horse whisperer Monty Roberts' book *Horse Sense for People*.[11] Wild horses aren't tamed through brute force. If you chase them, they will run away, but if you trace your steps back, the horse will stop and then, unthreatened and curious, begin to follow at a distance.

If you feel like your freedom is under threat, you might get spooked. Hence brainwashers use all sorts of techniques to influence your choice while maintaining the illusion that you are still in control.

Choice architecture

Let's try an exercise. Think of a two-digit number. Both of the digits must be odd, and they must be different from one another. The complete number must be between 10 and 50.

Did you pick the number in the footnote below?* Most people do, and they, like you, believe it was completely their decision.[12]

This is because of a principle in magic known as 'forcing', wherein magicians control your choice (of number, for example) without you realising.[13] When asked to pick a number between one and ten, seven is the most popular choice, in what is known as a stereotypical response pattern.[14] Another trick is to make one card stand out more by showing it for slightly longer during a shuffle – this can result in it being chosen by up to 98 per cent of people.[15] More simply, the magician may ask you to choose a card from the deck, without you knowing that all of the cards are the same.

In sales, there is a technique called the 'alternative close', where the salesperson gives you two choices that both benefit them. A classic example is the waiter who asks if you would like still or sparkling water, neglecting to mention tap water or no water, which would both be free. Similarly, 'Hobson's choice' refers to a choice where only one option is really available; it allegedly comes from a stable owner, Thomas Hobson, who offered customers the so-called choice of either the horse nearest the door or no horse at all. They could take it or leave it.

Similarly, the presentation of the options – what is known as 'choice architecture' – impacts on which one you are more

* 37.

likely to select. In Austria, Burger King has ordained that there is a 'new normal' and that meat is 'no longer a matter of course'; their motto is '*normal oder mit Fleisch?*' ('normal or with meat?').[16] Similarly, meat substitute makers Quorn released an advertisement in the UK featuring animals urging humans to eat Quorn and to not even think about 'the alternative'.[17] Both campaigns have cleverly used what's called 'the default effect': when one option is made to seem like the default, people are more likely to choose it.[18] It's socially safer and psychologically easier.

In giving you an illusory choice, manipulators are defining the grounds of engagement and limiting the range of options in a way that benefits them. In reality, there could be infinite other choices outside of their false binary.

An obvious application of this principle is politics. The 'paradox of voting' principle argues that voting is irrational because it involves a lot of time, effort and brainpower to engage in politics, and yet a person's singular vote makes statistically zero impact on the outcome, not to mention the fact that the likelihood of politicians actually keeping their promises, and these promises having any tangible impact on day-to-day life, is small at best.[19] Furthermore, it is highly unlikely that one of two parties could satisfactorily meet all of a voter's complex individual needs. The choice between left-wing and right-wing (two wings of the same bird), or blue team and red team (both playing the same game) may in fact be an illusory one, a false binary. In the UK, an allegedly progressive Labour government introduced an unprecedented system of mass surveillance; following that, a so-called Conservative government legislated gay marriage. Regardless of one's views on either of those issues, these laws run in the opposite of the expected direction of the parties. Would things really have been much different if the other party were in power? Around the world, governments of all types implemented lockdowns in lock-step, whether liberal, conservative or something else. The purpose of voting may not be about having a say but about *feeling* like you have a say. Signing the ballot slip is like signing a consent form to be governed, and it stops you looking at the infinite possibilities that exist beyond the false binary.

Politicians perhaps serve an almost anthropological function, echoing past tribes who used their kings as scapegoats and put them to death when they had served their purpose.[20] The approval rating of any political leader shows more or less the same pattern: approval starts out high and then deteriorates across their tenure as the public vents all of their frustrations on him or her, until the time comes for a symbolic sacrifice and a new king to be crowned. In America, people blame the president for economic woes, in the UK, they blame the prime minister. In both cases, attention is focused on the politicians, and not the financiers and oligarchs who profit. Voting for one politician or another keeps people distracted and feeling like they have a choice.

Besides the false binary, there are many forcing techniques in magic, but they all have two things in common.[21] First, they have to significantly affect the decision or the outcome, and second, the target has to feel free in their choice and in control of the result. This lack of awareness is crucial: the target must not realise that the magician was aiming for a certain outcome.

As a psychology professor and a member of the Magic Circle, Gustav Kuhn has unique insight. He explained, ‘With forcing, you appear to have a choice, but you actually don’t. It’s an illusion of choice. You need to feel you’ve had a free choice or else the magic doesn’t work. Once you know or even suspect that you’re being manipulated, the magic disappears.’ This is why the masters of thought-remoulding, the People’s Republic of China, would not rest until their subjects did not just parrot the party line but truly believed the brainwashing.[22] They wanted subjects to be like Winston Smith at the end of George Orwell’s *1984*: ‘But it was all right, everything was all right, the struggle was finished. He had won the victory over himself. He loved Big Brother.'[23]

In his book *Brainwashing: The Story of Men Who Defied It*, Edward Hunter warned that the 'voluntary submission' of people created a 'robotlike enslavement'.[24]

Illustrating the illusion of choice, Hunter tells the story of a sergeant who was interned in a Korean prisoner-of-war camp in the 1950s. During a series of night marches, a foot and a hand turned black due to frostbite. In his desperation to get medical care, the young sergeant tried to please his interrogator and studied the 're-education' literature devoutly as asked. All the while he was panicked by the periodic losses of gangrenous fingers, but hopeful of saving his limbs.

He was given a test. 'You seem to have learned your lesson well. But are you sincere? That is what the people want to know?' said the interrogator.

The sergeant, desperate for urgent medical care, and mentally destabilised after prolonged interrogation, hunger and study, asked what he must do to prove his sincerity. The interrogator assured him he didn't want him to do anything except voluntarily. What he had to do – of his own free will – was admit to dropping burning napalm and bacteria on the people (when, in fact, he had simply been a gunner).

Ultimately, he relented, 'voluntarily', of course. Unspeakable though his situation was, he still had a choice: comply, or lose an arm and a leg to gangrene. He chose to comply.

Still, he lost his arm and leg regardless.

Does nudging respect 'no'?

In day-to-day marketing meanwhile, nudges may be less effective when people feel that they don't have voluntary control. For example, one study found that when a nudge was communicated as being implemented by a politician or expert, the effectiveness of the nudge decreased.[25] Another study found that nudges are less effective when participants are told the alternative to the nudge is legislation.[26] In other words, when someone feels that a powerful agent (like the government) intends to coerce them whether the nudge works or not, they exhibit reactance and are less easily influenced. This may be why governments only want to gently nudge you – a shove is less persuasive.

We asked the co-author of *Nudge*, Cass Sunstein, how people can avoid being nudged.

> Just by going their own way. Nudges are defined as interventions that fully preserve freedom of choice. If you are nudged to show up for a medical appointment (by a reminder, for example), you can still reschedule it, or cancel it. If you are nudged not to choose chocolate brownies (by a calorie label, for example), you can still choose chocolate brownies.

Sunstein only agreed to an email interview and asked that we print his answers in full, which of course we have done. We don't agree that people can avoid nudges by going their own way, because nudges are not visible or obvious in all cases. They work below the level of consciousness, they are subtle, otherwise they wouldn't work. It is a contradiction that something can both influence choice and preserve freedom of choice.

Do nudgers respect that no means no? Unequivocally, according to Sunstein:

> Absolutely. A central point of nudging is to respect freedom of choice. A GPS gives you a route, but you can choose another route if you like. Automatic enrollment in a savings plan is a nudge, but you can always opt out. Of course it is true that nudges do not exhaust the policy repertoire, and while you might nudge people not to smoke (by disclosing the risks, for example), you might

> also favor cigarette taxes. And while you might favor fuel economy labels, you might also favor regulations designed to require motor vehicles to be more fuel-efficient. But nudges, as such, always allow people to go their own way.

In the case of governments, nudges sometimes appear to be merely the first tool deployed in pursuit of a policy goal, which may continue upon an exorable path of nudges, shoves and pushes, finally culminating in cattle prods. The Covid-19 vaccine is an excellent case in point, because it was promoted with a unique panoply of nudges, before eventually being foisted upon the remaining unwilling unvaccinated population with mandates.[27] Around the world, some of the nudges to entice people to be vaccinated were bizarre. To boost vaccination rates, Washington State offered marijuana joints for jabs. The Funpalast brothel in Vienna got in on the act, offering customers 30 minutes with the lady of their choice in exchange for a jab. In the UK, incentives included stickers, posters, a petting zoo and a skate park to entice children, as well as a Euro football ticket raffle, clothing vouchers, free taxi 'jab cabs', the 'jab kebab' giveaway, and a huge advertising, marketing and social media campaign.

The soft and cuddly nudgers like to assure you that there is always a choice – even the word 'nudge' sounds gentle – but their attitudes can self-evidently be firmer. Richard Thaler, co-author of *Nudge*, Nobel laureate and former advisor to the Nudge Unit, wrote in the *New York Times* that it was 'time to go well beyond nudging' and governments should use more forceful interventions.[28] In essence, polite nudges are great, until they don't convince everyone, and then it's time to put the jackboots on.

Sometimes, persuasive messages explicitly try to ramp up the perception of free will. The salesperson might, for instance, say, 'It's completely up to you.' Alternatively, someone might make you choose the option you think they don't want you to choose. This is known colloquially as reverse psychology and technically as 'strategic self-anticonformity'.[29] For example, pick-up artists might play hard-to-get in order to amplify attraction. In magic, given the choice of four particular cards, most will choose the obvious ace of diamonds. However, given a reactance nudge like, 'This has to be a free choice, do not let me influence you,' most people opt for the less obvious four of hearts – which of course could have been the magician's intention all along.[30]

Persuasion can even be amplified by the persuader being open about their attempts: 'If they admit they are trying to persuade me, I must be able to trust them.' The magician makes no secret of the fact that he or she is tricking you and, in fact, this may only add to an illusion's power. As Gustav Kuhn says, magicians are 'honest deceivers', they inform you that you're being deceived. Even though you know it, your perceptions and beliefs are still malleable. Likewise, research has found that nudges are sometimes even more effective when the source is transparent about what they are doing; and brands like the soft drink Oasis have benefited from being refreshingly honest, with one poster reading, 'It's summer. You're thirsty. We've got sales targets.'

Conspiracy theorists have a term for all of this: 'the revelation of the method'.[31] The idea is that the powers-that-be must subtly reveal their secret agendas through symbolism in things like pop videos, award ceremonies and even world events. So the theory goes, they communicate their intentions to the masses, who become subconsciously aware and therefore, at some level, make a choice to accept it all.

Manipulators also benefit psychologically from giving you the illusion of choice. Victim blaming, for example, is well known as a defence mechanism to reduce feelings of guilt among manipulators: 'if you suffer, well, it was your choice after all.'[32]

Ultimately, this illusion of choice underpins the essence of all persuasion. What are we to make, for example, of Europe's GDPR notices on websites?

Consider the scenario where you go onto a website, and a huge box covers a good portion of the content you're trying to read. You expect information on the internet to be instant and you feel frustrated when little things like this get in the way.

Normally you would just click the biggest, most obvious button to make it go away. You have no idea what you're agreeing to in doing so, but you are agreeing. You are giving your consent.

Maybe one day you feel a bit suspicious of the website, so you decide you don't want to consent. There isn't an obvious button to do this, nothing that says 'Reject Cookies'. So you click on 'Manage My Preferences'. You're taken to a long, confusing list of options, which you have to unclick one by one. You finally reach the bottom and press the big button that reads, 'Accept All', thinking it will accept all your changes. You misunderstood. You should have clicked the less visible 'Save and Exit' button. Oh well, too late now. You consented.

So what is the point of even asking for consent? Why put users through the charade of pretending they have a choice? Because, as we have seen, the illusion of control makes people more passive and pliable, and absolves the data-harvesters of moral responsibility. It reflects a broader social trend called 'responsibilisation': a casino is absolved of responsibility if they have told you, 'When the fun stops, stop'; and the bank is absolved if they have pop-ups warning you of common signs of fraud.[33]

So, the next time someone appears to present you with a choice, ask yourself if you really do have one, or whether it's just an illusion.

The rules:

- Don't be fooled by claims that something is completely up to you – it rarely is and the claim could well be a nudge.
- Look beyond the binary and ask yourself if these are really your only options or if there is something else you could do instead.
- When faced with an unpleasant binary, don't choose the easy option you didn't really want, as it rarely works out for the best.

13

Learn the language of symbols

Symbols unlock hardwired responses from deep within your subconscious. Those who can speak the language of symbols can subconsciously manipulate the uninitiated, while those who are aware have some measure of immunity.

Releasing the innate

Nestled among the rolling meadows and by the sweeping Danube just outside of Vienna sits the picturesque town of Altenberg, and within it the ivory Georgian walls of Nobel laureate Konrad Lorenz's family mansion. Here, the birds Lorenz kept for study sometimes punctuated the quiet with a mad flurry of activity.

Lorenz pioneered ethology, the study of animal behaviour, using experiments on ducks, geese and turkeys. His experiments would see them cheep, scramble for cover and rush their eggs to safety – for they believed they were under threat from a predator hovering above.

The predator was actually no more than a cardboard cut-out in the shape of a hawk, glided through the air by Lorenz. Even though the birds had never seen such a predator in the flesh, perhaps for generations, they nonetheless displayed a hard-wired response to the shape of a hawk. This stimulus, called a 'releaser', unlocked an evolutionary pattern of behaviour known as an 'innate releasing mechanism'. A series of studies found that only the shape of a predator could release the fear response: a simple circle couldn't do it and nor could the shape of a goose. It took a very particular symbol to release a response in the chicks' minds, like a key in a lock.[1]

While the specifics of Lorenz and his peers' studies have been the subject of much debate, the underlying principle is uncontested: symbols can influence behaviour.

Really, the essence of all communication, whether it's speech, text or imagery, is symbols being fashioned to manipulate what is on a person's mind and therefore how they behave. Change people's behaviour, and you can ultimately change reality. For instance, if you wanted to eat some biscuits, but there were none nearby, you might call out to your partner ('Bring me biscuits!'); the symbols of your words would shape what is on your partner's mind and manipulate their behaviour such that biscuits would now appear by your side, where once there were none. In sum, you would have shaped reality through your manipulation of symbols. This is what it means to cast a 'spell': spelling is simply the arrangement of symbols (letters) into words to shape what is at the front of people's minds, influence their behaviour and thus manifest reality.

At the heart of this proposition, there are two realms: a physical outer realm and an imagined inner realm. Symbols are the bridge between the two. Hearing the word 'apple', for example, will generate the thought of an apple in your inner realm. In fact, it is man's unique ability to use symbols and to tap into an abstract universe separate from the physical plane that defines his position on the planet. It is also, however, what makes him uniquely susceptible to brainwashing, and to killing and dying for ideologies and fantasies. (Interestingly, research has indeed found that imaginative people are more suggestible.[2])

The temporary autonomous zone

Although the principle is timeless, it has never been more important to be able to consciously speak the language of symbols. As Dr Rachel Lawes, the author of *Using Semiotics in Marketing*, put it: 'In one sense it's something everyone does all the time. To think and be alive and communicate is to use semiotics. But it is much more prolific now than it was 20 years ago.'

Humanity is a world away from the quiet hills of Altenberg where Lorenz's studies took place. Most of us live in a screen-based universe consisting entirely of symbols, increasingly detached from real life and all of its physical laws. Even outside of screens, symbols, once largely exclusive to religious iconography, now jump on top of us from every billboard, bus stop and brand. As Professor Judith Williamson wrote in her seminal book *Decoding Advertisements* all the way back in 1978: 'Advertisements enclose us more and more in a world that has to be interpreted: a world of significance ... [The] semantic universe provided by nature is now supplanted by a symbolic system.'[3]

With the rise of screen-based symbolism, humanity has fallen down the rabbit hole into Wonderland, where, as Alice put it, we can believe as many as six impossible things before breakfast and ask, 'Who in the world am I?'

Dr Lawes explained that 'There's something called a temporary autonomous zone, which lots of people have discovered as they spend more of their time online. It's a creative space where, for a brief period, there are no rules and no facts which might limit imagination.' This concept, proposed by anarchist Hakim Bey, refers to a space in which all forms of structure and control have been dissolved, resulting in a state of fluidity and hypersensitive paranoia where the symbolic dominates.

> A temporary autonomous zone may be entered into when someone is creating an online persona for themselves and acting it out, making it reality. People who practise magic make great use of this – magical rituals with set places and time limits allow the rules of reality to be suspended. Some writers on magic see that to enter a temporary autonomous zone to perform some magic is to allow oneself to temporarily go insane. The magician steps that far outside the normal rules of reality. It allows for complete creativity, complete rule-breaking; it allows impossible events.
>
> The pandemic accelerated a lot of problems with social isolation and living behind a screen. There are quite a few people, the bulk of their human contact is through things like TikTok. You could imagine yourself to be whatever you want to be.[4]

Perhaps an extreme example is Oli London, a 'transracial' internet personality who, although white, self-identified as South Korean. He reportedly spent over £230,000 on more than twenty plastic surgeries, and had plans for a penis reduction.[5] Only in the symbolic screen-based world could he become so obsessed with South Korean pop culture in the first place and then, buoyed by photo filters and online echo chambers, imagine himself to be South Korean, with the effect so powerful that he began surgically transforming his outer reality to try and match his inner reality.

After coming out as transracial, London then identified as non-binary, using 'they/them' pronouns. This is a striking example of the temporary autonomous zone, where structure has been dissolved to the point that there is no distinction between male and female, nor even between individual people. There is no more 'he' and 'she' – no 'you' or 'I' – just one amorphous 'they'.[6]

Goat-headed deity Baphomet is also non-binary, being shown with both breasts and a penis, as well as being both animal and human; typically, illustrations put the words '*solve et coagula*' on Baphomet's arms.[7] The phrase means to break down and rebuild. This is the essence of the temporary autonomous zone: it is the fluid, formless vacuum of decay that precedes a nascent perception of the world.

While gender identity is a potent example, it's important to recognise that the temporary autonomous zone applies across the political spectrum. In the 2016 US election, Trump supporters engaged in what they called 'meme magic', spreading symbols on the internet to manifest their desired reality – to meme Donald Trump into the White House.[8] Their favourite meme, Pepe the frog, came to be seen by them as a reinvention of the ancient Egyptian frog-headed chaos god Kek (who, it should be noted, had both male and female qualities).[9] Pepe was often depicted as a clown, a symbol of the topsy-turvy subversion of carnival (or 'clown world'), where normal rules are suspended.[10]

Meanwhile, members of QAnon exhibited hypersensitive paranoia when they interpreted secret messages in the dates, post numbers and cryptic texts posted on anonymous image boards. So clued into symbolic meaning were they that they often said of the elites that 'symbolism would be their downfall'.[11] Interestingly, a 2014 report in the *Journal of Nervous and Mental Disease* provided an account of a previously healthy 31-year-old woman who came to believe that a famous actor was sending her coded messages through his tweets, which she increasingly felt were 'meant in a symbolic way'; the authors coined the condition 'Twitter psychosis'.[12]

On the other side of the aisle, mainstream media outlets such as *Marie Claire* reported on how 'real life resistance witches say they're taking down the patriarchy', casting spells on figures like Donald Trump and Brett Kavanaugh.[13] 'Trump's presidency has spawned a new generation of witches,' exclaimed *Wired*.[14]

Manipulating reality

While magic might seem a far-out concept, it is simply, as Dr Lawes put it, 'all signs and symbols. It is an attempt to bring about material change from sheer force of will through the manipulation of symbols.'

Indeed, there is a power differential between those who can understand and manipulate symbols, and those who can't. Aldous Huxley once wrote that 'irrational propaganda depends for its effectiveness on a general failure to understand the nature of symbols'.[15] Freemason Manly P. Hall concurred, saying,

> Every law and power active in universal procedure is manifested to the limited sense perceptions of man through the medium of symbols. By symbols, men have ever sought to communicate those thoughts which transcend the limitations of language. In a single figure, a symbol may both reveal and conceal; for to the wise the subject of the symbol is obvious, while to the ignorant the symbol remains inscrutable.[16]

Take advertising, for example. Adverts often have two layers: an explicit, informational message, and an implicit, symbolic meaning. In *Decoding Advertisements*, Judith Williamson explained:

> What an advertisement 'says' is merely what it claims to say; it is part of the deceptive mythology of advertising to believe that an advertisement is simply a transparent vehicle for a 'message' behind it. Certainly a large part of any advertisement is this 'message': we are told something about a product, and asked to buy it ... [Criticism of this] is based on the assumption that ads are merely the invisible conveyors of certain undesirable messages, and only sees meaning in the overt 'content' of

the ad rather than its 'form' ... 'Form' is invisible: a set of relations, a scaffolding to be filled out by 'content' ...

One of the many examples in the book is an advert for Goodyear tyres. In the ad, a car is stopped at the end of a jetty, surrounded by the sea. The copy reads, 'After a 36,000 mile run-up, I hit the brakes at fifty.' The rational message is clear: the tyres are so safe and durable, you'll be able to brake suddenly without careening off the end of a pier.

Yet there is a symbolic layer to the ad, too. The jetty itself is curved with equally spaced boards giving the impression of a tyre track. It even has tyres hanging off the side to drive the message home. The car is cocooned within the symbolic tyre of the pier and protected from the sea's erosive power. 'Thus what seemed to be merely a part of the apparatus for conveying a message about braking speed,' wrote Williamson, 'turns out to be a message in itself, one that works not on the overt but almost on the unconscious level.'

An illuminating example of subconscious symbolism in advertising comes from marketing pioneer Edward Bernays, who was consulted to help the brand Betty Crocker with sales of their cake mix.[17] Bernays discovered that the brand's target market of housewives felt that using the mix was cheating their family. His solution was to change the recipe so that it required the addition of two eggs. Loaded with symbolism, the eggs made housewives feel they were putting maternal love into the food.

Bernays once said that 'a thing may be desired not for its intrinsic worth or usefulness, but because [the consumer) has unconsciously come to see in it a symbol of something else, the desire for which he is ashamed to admit to himself'.[18] Diamond jewellery, for example, has no intrinsic value except to boost the ego of its wearer; or consider face masks, which, some health officials have admitted, served as little more than a tangible reminder of the pandemic's presence and a symbol of unity and right-thinking.[19]

McDonald's, meanwhile, considered abandoning their golden arches logo in the 1960s, until psychologist Louis Cheskin advised against it due to 'Freudian implications in the subconscious mind'.[20] Based on their shape, Cheskin referred to the arches as 'mother McDonald's breasts, a useful association if you're replacing homemade food'.

The fascinating premise is that these implicit symbols can affect us without our knowing – that is, they operate on a subconscious level.

Psychoanalyst Carl Jung posited that we are all psychologically connected to what he called 'the collective unconscious'.[21] This is an invisible, symbolic universe to which all human beings are attuned. There are, for example, archetypes of human beings, like the jester or the rebel, which we all implicitly recognise and respond to. Symbols of these archetypes release ancient responses much like Lorenz's birds seeing a hawk. As an illustration, dating gurus have recommended that men resonate with these archetypes deep within a woman's subconscious to automatically produce attraction: the dominant ruler in a designer suit, the rebellious bad boy in a leather jacket, the romantic lothario with a foreign accent.[22]

Scholars like Joseph Campbell (*The Hero with a Thousand Faces*), Christopher Booker (*The Seven Basic Plots*) and Sir James George Frazer (*The Golden Bough*) have likewise posited that the same symbols, archetypes and narratives express themselves again and again throughout worldwide human history, stories and religions. Researchers have, for instance, traced a story archetype called 'The Smith and the Devil' (about a man who makes a bargain with the devil for special talents) through several ages all the way back to Proto-Indo-European.[23] Anakin Skywalker, so say some internet nerds, is simply Space Jesus.

Jung wrote that 'myths [have] a direct effect on the unconscious, no matter whether it is understood or not'. In more scientific terms, subconscious symbolism taps into a psychological technique known as 'subliminal priming', where symbols not consciously registered can nonetheless influence behaviour.[24] To illustrate, one study had participants rate pictures of furniture, with erotic images flashed beforehand for 30 milliseconds.[25] Compared with a control group, they were significantly more likely to self-disclose to a potential romantic partner afterwards. A review of brain-imaging studies in 2012 reported that these kinds of subliminal stimuli activate specific regions of the brain despite a lack of conscious awareness.[26]

Although priming is a contentious topic among psychologists, the core tenet of symbols influencing behaviour is fundamental to psychology, and indeed to all human communication.

Ultimately, those who would seek to manipulate us can seemingly do it through symbols. Much like Konrad Lorenz gliding cardboard cut-outs above his chicks, the manipulator – be they a propagandist, advertiser or pick-up artist – will use their secret knowledge of symbols from above to stir the flock below into a frenzy and direct the crowd's behaviour this way or that. They can control people's behaviour through symbols of heaven and hell, and heroes and bogeymen, which reside within the subconscious psyche of us all, like a minotaur interned deep within a labyrinth.

Lorenz himself seemed to understand this. He titled his magnum opus *King Solomon's Ring*, referencing the occult Seal of Solomon that reportedly gave its bearer the power to speak to animals. This is the same symbol seen in the compass and set square on a freemason's signet ring.

Symbolism through the ages

While readers could be forgiven for thinking that subconscious symbolism is a bunch of kooky old mumbo-jumbo (and perhaps that's true), the powers-that-be do not seem to agree.

Political movements have, of course, used symbolism to great effect. The eagle – a symbol of empire – can be found on flags around the world, from Mexico to Albania, tracing its history back to the Roman Empire and beyond. In Mexico, the eagle has in its talons a snake, symbolising dominion over chaos, and mirroring ancient legends like St Michael vanquishing Satan at his feet, or St George slaying the dragon.

The Nazis used the eagle too, of course. Symbolism was integral to the regime. The thesis 'Symbolism and ritual as used by National Socialists' describes the billowing flags, marching columns, imposing monuments, and huge eagle and swastika banners.[27] Hitler himself was often presented as Frederick the Great, symbolising him as a king, representative of the nation itself and the hope of restoring its vitality. 'All symbols,' the thesis concluded, 'were specifically chosen for the impact they would have on the German people.'

These symbols acted as lightning rods around which the German people's deepest unexpressed fears and desires could be galvanised. They served as 'integrating forces that tie the individual to a group or society at large. They tie together ideology and action ... they strike at the emotional and primeval in human nature.' Symbols, noted anthropologist David Kertzer, have no arguments against them since they represent something that is hard to articulate rationally.[28]

Elsewhere, seats of power have a long tradition of esoteric symbolism. The paths and parks around the Capitol Building in Washington, DC, for example, resemble an owl from above (a symbol of wisdom and illumination: being able to see when others are in the dark). The United States Capitol, with its dome and Washington Monument, appears be modelled upon St Peter's Basilica in Rome, built nearly two hundred years earlier. Why, for that matter, would the seat of Catholicism have an ancient Egyptian obelisk at its centre anyway?

In New York, the Rockefeller Plaza, from which NBC broadcasts information onto television screens around the world, sports a golden idol of Prometheus, who mythically fell to earth with the stolen fire of the gods, bringing both illumination and pain to mankind. In New York, the symbolism is not so much in the statue itself, but in its position over the plaza's famous ice rink, where the slippery nature of the ice causes people to fall to earth like Prometheus.

Meanwhile, the world's most powerful people are known to attend esoteric events, such as the Rothschilds' Surrealist Ball at the Chateau de Ferrières in 1972. According to *Vanity Fair*, the exclusive party saw elites like Salvador Dalí, Audrey Hepburn and members of European royalty don symbolic attire.[29] Marie-Hélène de Rothschild wore the mask of a dead stag with diamond teardrops. They all dined on a life-sized naked woman made of sugar for dessert.

Some five years earlier, future US presidents Richard Nixon and Ronald Reagan were photographed at the exclusive Bohemian Grove, where the *Washington Post* noted 'the rich and powerful go to misbehave'.[30] Members of Bohemian Grove take part in a ceremony known as the Cremation of Care, in which hooded figures watch a coffin effigy floated across a lake, placed on an altar and cremated in front of a 12-metre owl.

And just days before the US election in 2016, WikiLeaks released a batch of emails from the Clinton campaign's servers. Buried among them was a single line that took the internet by storm and potentially changed the outcome of the election.

'I am so looking forward to the Spirit Cooking dinner at my place,' wrote performance artist Marina Abramovic to Hillary Clinton's campaign manager Tony Podesta.

Spirit Cooking, for the uninitiated, is a piece of performance art debuted by Abramovic in 1996. A MIT Press article debunked 'the paranoid conspiracy theory posited by the alt-right' by explaining that spirit cooking is 'nothing but a little-known ... performance Abramovic did ... in which she painted apparent instructions on the white wall with pigs blood' (including 666 and an inverted pentagram).[31] The performance was accompanied by a cookbook containing nuggets like, 'Mix Fresh Milk from the Breast, with Fresh Milk of the Sperm, Drink on Earthquake Nights'.

While someone's perception of spirit cooking as a 'Satanic ritual or fun dinner' (as *New York* magazine put it) depended largely on their politics, there can be no denying that it is deeply symbolic, and that some of America's most powerful political players were invited to take part.[32] In fact, Abramovic's influence on American culture is no secret: she has publicly collaborated on content for Microsoft[33] as well as chart-topping artists like Jay-Z and Lady Gaga. The latter attended a three-day retreat on the Abramovic Method and once tweeted to her fanbase (whom she calls her Little Monsters), 'I am very honored to have Marina Abramovic as a mentor. Her believing in me has completely changed my life …'[34]

At the twentieth Watermill Center Annual Summer Benefit, Gaga was pictured alongside Abramovic, tasting a spoon of fake blood scooped from a bath containing a naked model acting as a corpse.[35] When Abramovic organised the annual gala at the Museum of Contemporary Art in Los Angeles, star guests like Will Ferrell, Kirsten Dunst and Gwen Stefani ate at tables with live models' heads poking through the top as if decapitated, and dined on life-size cakes resembling naked women.[36] Readers may note this is reminiscent of the dessert provided at the Rothschild Surrealist Ball some 50 years earlier.

The land of make-believe

Around the time that Abramovic was hobnobbing with America's cultural elite, something odd was happening in the world of music videos: the use of esoteric symbolism became prolific. Katy Perry's 'Dark Horse', as one illustration, saw the pop star dress as the goddess Isis, cover one eye with the Eye of Horus, and make herself the capstone of a pyramid. The video for Ke$ha's catchy, nihilistic hit 'Die Young' is replete with pentagrams and inverted crosses. Perhaps the most common trope is singers covering one of their eyes to reference the all-seeing eye. While mainstream media outlets like *Forbes* and *Slate* have berated conspiracy theories about the symbolism ('your eyes will roll so far back into your skull you'll look like you've been possessed by Baphomet'), none denies it exists.[37]

This was not a flash in the pan. In summer 2022, pop sensation Billie Eilish became the youngest person ever to headline Glastonbury Festival. She sang on the so-called Pyramid Stage, complete with its glowing capstone, wearing a jacket emblazoned with imagery of Aleister Crowley and mottos like 'Lucifer' and '666'. Even The Beatles famously included Crowley on their cover art for *Sgt. Pepper's Lonely Hearts Club Band*.

The video for a gold-selling 21st-century pop song by household-name musicians features sinister insects combined with unsettling sexual imagery, and the artist being pleasured by an invisible being at an altar of a snake. Most disturbingly of all, there are several flashes of scenes less than one second in length, which likely bypass conscious awareness, including bloody body parts and other negative sexual depictions. We can only guess as to the reasons why this video has subconsciously linked sex with fearful and disgusting imagery.

The method of displaying imagery too quickly for conscious recognition is, in marketing, known as subliminal advertising, which goes against regulations imposed by the UK's Advertising Standards Authority (ASA).[38] It is a grey area in other parts of the world, and this is a music video anyway, not an advert – while the flash-frames are disturbing and odd, they are not illegal.

In 2021, American rapper Lil Nas X – previously famed for his family-friendly hit 'Old Town Road', after which he wrote a children's book called *C is for Country* – released a music video for his song 'Montero', chock full of mythological symbolism. The rapper has an erotic encounter with himself, as a snake, in the Garden of Eden, before pole-dancing down St

Michael's spear into hell, where he kills himself, as Satan, and takes his crown. The track was released alongside a limited-edition sneaker containing real human blood and adorned with a pentagram, promoted using imagery in which Lil Nas X covered one eye with the shoe. Only 666 pairs were made.[39]

Remember, a communication has two layers: a surface message, and a symbolic meaning. Content like music videos – or movies – are rarely messages alone. Rather, the stories tend to serve as vessels for symbolic meaning. Take, for example, the highest-grossing movie of 2021 (at the height of government vaccination campaigns), *Spider-Man: No Way Home*. In the movie, the world is doomed to be stuck in an endless time loop, unable to go back to normal, unless the hero can round up a small group of villains and forcibly inject them with a serum for their own good. The movie was filmed in the winter of 2020–21, when the script was constantly being rewritten, according to star Tom Holland in an interview with *GQ*.[40]

In 2022, one of the highest-grossing movies was *The Batman*. Released amid a tide of growing anti-government resentment, the movie has Batman growl, 'I am vengeance' at the start of the movie, a line that is reflected back to him by one of the incel-esque domestic terrorist villains at the end (having Batman meet his shadow, in Jungian terms). Batman is then shot, falling into a pool of water (signalling his psychological death and rebirth), before pontificating on the importance of choosing hope over revenge. The movie's villain, The Riddler, believes that the political system is broken and that only radical activism can make a difference. The movie's hero, The Batman, is a billionaire with insider access who operates outside of the law. The symbolic message, ultimately, is that the public should not take matters into their own hands but should leave the elite to sort things out among themselves.

At this point, readers may be forgiven for scoffing and rolling their eyes. It is difficult to empirically prove the use of symbolism, which takes its power from representing the unrepresentable, or the occult, which is by nature hidden. The rational counterargument is that we tend to jump at shadows and see patterns in symbols where they don't exist. The scientific name for this is 'pareidolia'; an example might be so-called ghost-hunters alleging they can hear voices in static.[41]

Paradoxically, a heightened sense of paranoia – a temporary autonomous zone – increases awareness of symbols as well as susceptibility to them.

While it might be paranoid to suggest that there is a Satanic cabal of celebrities manipulating the public for nefarious ends, there can be no denying that symbols like inverted pentagrams and the all-seeing eye do have some kind of psychological impact on viewers, and that cultural elites are indeed using them.

Grant Morrison is a prolific comic-book writer who has crafted stories for both DC and Marvel. He is also a practising 'chaos magician'. Chaos magic is a New Age religious movement that believes that reality can be shaped by beliefs, and beliefs can be changed by breaking down conscious barriers – creating the chaos of the temporary autonomous zone discussed previously – and seeding symbols within the psyche. Morrison described some of his work as a 'hypersigil': 'a dynamic miniature model of the magician's universe, a hologram, microcosm or "voodoo doll" which can be manipulated in real time to produce changes in the macrocosmic environment of "real" life'.[42]

Alan Moore, creator of works including *V for Vendetta*, *Watchmen* and *From Hell*, likewise considers himself a magician. 'Art,' he said, 'is like magic, the science of manipulating symbols, words or images to achieve changes in consciousness.'[43]

Elsewhere, Moore explained, 'The only reality we can ever truly know is that of our perceptions, our own consciousness, while that consciousness, and thus our entire reality, is made of nothing but signs and symbols. Nothing but language. Even

God requires language before conceiving the universe. See Genesis: "In the beginning was the Word."'[44]

In Hollywood – the land of make-believe – actors are honoured with an Oscar statuette, which some suggest is modelled after the ancient Egyptian god Ptah.[45] Ptah conceived of the world and brought it into being through his word and by waving his staff (his *holy-wood*). Might Hollywood serve this function in the modern era, crafting the world's perception of reality through the use of symbols?

Yet the power of motion pictures pales in comparison with virtual reality. Mankind is heading via technology to a symbolic crisis point. In November 2021, Facebook announced the release of their new brand, Meta. An advert accompanied the launch. 'Step into a world of imagination with Meta and explore endless possibilities as two dimensions become three,' read the YouTube description.[46] The video itself was titled 'The Tiger & The Buffalo' – a hip, urban retelling of Isaiah 11:6 ('The wolf will live with the lamb …'), an impossible fantasy of peace and equality much like the Disney film *Zootopia*. Meta seems to consider the Metaverse a kind of paradise on earth. More interesting is the artwork on display in the advert, namely, an eye-like sun atop a pyramid, painted by Swedish mystic Hilma Klint. Klint claimed to have created the pictures via a stream-of-consciousness technique often using séances. She claimed to be a vessel for the meaning coming from another dimension: 'I had no idea what they were supposed to depict … I worked swiftly and surely, without changing a brush stroke.'[47]

The Metaverse is sure to be a land of unfettered symbolism. It will connect all our streams of consciousness into one symbolic soup. It will be a *permanent* autonomous zone, a land of 24/7 deep fakes, a true post-truth reality. In this realm, those who control the symbols will truly control reality – not just the perception of reality, but reality itself, since reality will cease to be anything but perception. Mark Zuckerberg could turn night into day and day into night, and users would be too out of touch with physicality to know any different. So far, despite billions of dollars of investment, the take-off to the Metaverse has been very bumpy. We may never get there but, if we do, the political split of the future might not be left–right or libertarian–authoritarian, but reality–fantasy.

Reality check

This all begs the question, how to escape from the symbolic world?

The first step, of course, is to take a real reality check – that is, to close the laptop, switch off the phone and look out of the window. While the news might be screaming 'red alert' and 'one person killed' in a storm, simply looking outside would confirm that it is, in fact, just a bit windy.

As Dr Rachel Lawes explained: 'The way I see the temporary autonomous zone is as a delicate and fragile bubble. It will burst all too easily if you have any connection to "the real world" that you normally experience. A bit like meditating. The hard part is concentrating. The easy part is opening your eyes and allowing everyday thoughts about emails and publishers' deadlines to flood back in.'

The second step is to become semiotically literate. Dr Lawes continued: 'You can't really break out of culture. But what you can do is become a user of symbols and become aware you are that. If you are consciously aware, that's where the fun really starts – you see it everywhere. It's every single thing all the time. A switch in the head. Once you've seen an alternate reality you can't unsee it.'

We human beings are unique in our understanding and manipulation of the symbolic realm. Unlike Lorenz's chicks, we have the power to repurpose and refuse the symbols lorded down from above. We hold the very spirit of creation in our tongues.

The rules:

- Look beneath the surface for the symbolic meaning of any communication; pay attention to the form as much as the content.
- Become familiar with the esoteric symbols that are commonly used by reading up on ancient mythology and classic fairy tales.
- Disconnect from the symbolic world and come 'back to reality'; otherwise you might get swept away by someone else's fantasy.

14

Brainworms and love bombs on transgender subreddits

By Patrick

I was harassed, love bombed and blackmailed on a transgender forum – or at least, my alter ego PatrishiaXO was.

I was there because I wanted some answers as to why, according to UCLA, the trans youth population has doubled in the last five years.[1] And why, indeed, the transgender category on Pornhub grew by 75 per cent in 2022 to become the seventh-most popular category worldwide.[2]

While many people have suggested that this is simply because there is less stigma (which is a fair point), others have argued that elements of popular culture may actually be *making* people trans. Scholars have variously pointed the finger at anime, pornography and social media; some have said it may be a form of social contagion spread through sites like TikTok and YouTube. A (heavily criticised) study published in 2018 surveyed 250 families whose children have come out as trans around puberty, and found that around 80 per cent of them had not observed signs of gender dysphoria in childhood.[3] Almost two-thirds of them reported that their child exhibited a marked increase in internet usage just before announcing they were trans.

Being trans is undoubtedly tough. Trans people often have to contend with isolation, stigma and mental health issues. In fact, life for *anyone* is tough, and if a person finds purpose and satisfaction living as the other gender, then I say, fill your boots. It is a given that everyone deserves dignity and compassion, no matter their path in life.

However – a man is not a woman, and a woman is not a man.

These are basic facts. Male and female is a fundamental building block of reality, like day and night, or north and south. To deny this is odd. And yet the fact-checkers and the Oxbridge academics never debunk this most obvious piece of misinformation that a woman can have a penis.

In this way, could some instances of transgenderism (not all, of course) involve a sort of brainwashing? For a biological man to think he is a woman (or vice versa) is to be objectively separated from physical reality. So, I decided to investigate whether principles of influence are at play in parts of the transgender community.

After I had chosen my Reddit username, PatrishiaXO, I scrolled past the posts about Marvel movies and soy-based meat and headed to a subreddit called /r/AskTransgender.

'I think I might be trans,' I posted, 'but I don't know where to start. Can anyone help?'

Reading the other posts, I was struck by just how broken and traumatised some of the users were. The forums were full of lonely wanderers scrabbling for meaning and bearing the desperate weight of their struggles.

I had already started to receive replies on my post. One user in particular was keen to help. He told me he was a twenty-year-old college junior who wanted to be a girl. He wasn't in classes at the minute because he was being bullied. Specifically, he volunteered, he was being harassed in the locker-room showers by a big, black quarterback with a big, black penis. (He used a different word.) I was beginning to have my doubts.

My mentor asked me to send pictures of myself. When I explained that I was new to this and didn't have any, he told me I could download apps to feminise my face and transplant it onto a woman's body. One of the subreddits was full of these photoshops – glassy, almost-female faces morphed with bikini models and pornographic GIFs.

Duly, I downloaded FaceApp, fed it one of my photos, and changed my gender to Female 1.

I posted the image to a subreddit called MtFSelfieTrain and was flooded with hundreds of upvotes and dozens of positive comments. I was told repeatedly that I was beautiful. A drip of direct messages turned into a flood – mostly from men who, after a bit of small talk, wanted to know if I had any more pictures.

'Huh,' I thought. 'Maybe I would have made an attractive woman.'

The brainwashing had begun on two fronts here. First, and most importantly, I was being drawn into a symbolic world, detached from reality. Of course, in real life, I would never look like the Patrishia of FaceApp. These photoshops allow people to live in a fantasy world that was impossible before the age of screens – what Jung called 'chimerical wish-fantasies', unreal images of heaven and hell that push political movements to and fro here on earth.

Second, I was receiving a lot of positive attention – what is known among cult scholars as 'love bombing'. I got the kind of validation for my picture that I would never get as a man. It's nice to be told you're attractive, even if the context is utterly deranged. In my conversations with other users, I also received affirmations and reassurance. We know that people with low self-esteem are particularly vulnerable to brainwashing. There is always the promise of a better life, whether it's through religious conversion, exterminating a political scapegoat, or, in this case, surgically removing your penis and testicles.

Fortunately, my self-esteem is fine, and I was very much on guard when receiving these comments. Users told me I looked beautiful, but they also said the same for every other poster – even the many ageing men in fishnets with concealer shoddily pasted over their five o'clock shadows.

From reading other posts, I could see that these communities might possibly create an insecure attachment style among their members and sever their old social ties. Adherents were told to cut from their lives 'toxic' people who did not agree with the gender ideology; the forums were their 'new family', where they could find an 'adoptive mother' in the form of an older transgender person. Indoctrination is most effective when people are loosened from their old attachments (family, tradition, community). It is about emptying people so they can be filled with something else.

The forums sometimes employed various linguistic tricks common to brainwashing. The process of conditioning was evident in the concepts of gender 'euphoria' versus 'dysphoria'; any thoughts and behaviours in line with the ideology were praised and rewarded, while any that ran counter to it were *verboten*. Dissent was discouraged, even within the adherent's own minds. Doubts or misgivings were labelled 'brainworms' (defined by one user as 'Trans-related thoughts/belief systems that are negative, hurtful, and untrue. For example, a cis-passing trans man who's convinced he's clocky [easily identifiable as trans]'), as if they were pathological voices to be ignored and repressed.[4] When I told one of my interlocutors that I wasn't sure if I was trans, they told me that doubt and denial are common signs that I was, in fact, trans.

As in totalitarianism, all roads lead to being trans. If you think you aren't trans, that means you're trans. Every doubt posted by users was rationalised as a reason for why that really means they're trans after all.

Many of the posts were confessional in nature. This is common in brainwashing: highly charged emotional episodes are used to break down critical defences in an iterative process of death and rebirth.

After an interesting day role-playing as Patrishia, I closed my laptop and went to bed, breaking wind (loudly) to reaffirm my masculinity.

The next day, I awoke to an email in my work inbox. It had been sent through my personal website. The subject line was blank, and the message read, 'hi is that Patrishia can I talk to you'.

It was probably an attempt at blackmail, given the unique spelling of my pen name. I was astounded. Of course, I hadn't given any of my personal details to the perverts on Reddit. The only part of me I had shared was my photoshopped picture. After a quick Google, I discovered a search engine called PimEyes, where you can upload a face photo and it will use facial recognition to find any other instance of that person on the internet. I tried Patrishia's photo, and it returned dozens of other pictures of me (the real me), including the one on my personal website.

I quickly purged my Reddit account. I was too ashamed of being outed, even though it was book research. I mean, that's what Pete Townshend said, but would you let him babysit your kids? Mud sticks, and the thought was humiliating.

For many, this would be the ultimate brainwashing denouement – the severing of their old ties, leaving them reactive to bind to their new identity. It also speaks to the importance of living without lies – your secrets can be used against you by manipulators.

Patrishia is dead now, but *xer* legacy lives on.

I learnt there is an element of manipulation to transgenderism, at least in certain corners of the internet. It thrives on symbolic fantasy, and it uses tools like isolation, inversion and confession to destroy adherents' old identities and build something new.

I also reaffirmed that transgender people are, of course, deserving of compassion. Many of the people I saw were going through difficult times in their lives even before they wrestled with the mind-bending complexity of questioning their gender.

Naturally, my experiences were not representative of the whole. Many people sincerely feel they were born into the wrong gender. Yet others, in their vulnerable states, may well be victims of a sort of brainwashing.

With more and more people, including children, coming out as transgender, this begs the question: should more be done to investigate?

15

Be the first to speak up

Conformity and crowds can be dangerous. Leaders can be fallible. Faced with this, it is vital to have the courage of your convictions and speak up. Practise being like the boy in 'The Emperor's New Clothes' and speaking first. It will change the dynamics of the group around you and, most importantly, it will change you, making you more psychologically independent.

The Emperor's New Clothes

An emperor hires two weavers to make him some new clothes. The weavers claim to make the most beautiful clothes in the whole world. In actuality, the weavers are tricksters who convince the emperor they are using a magic fabric that appears invisible to anyone who is too stupid to see it.

Of course, all the courtiers who are invited in to view the weavers' work pretend that they can see it, for fear of appearing unfit for their role. Likewise, they are keen to see if any of their neighbours are 'faking' their cleverness.

No one feels able to challenge the weavers' integrity. One influential person after another crumbles when put on the spot, each in turn reinforcing the 'validity' of the cloth. After some time, the weavers report that the suit is finished and they mime dressing the emperor, who then marches naked before his subjects.

The townsfolk uncomfortably go along with the pretence, not wanting to appear stupid. Finally, a child in the crowd blurts out that the emperor is wearing nothing at all and the cry is then taken up by others.

'The Emperor's New Clothes' is a tale that raises questions about self-deception, conformity and obedience to authority. Like all good fairy tales, it attempts to convey a charter for human behaviour – learning to speak first, like the boy, is good practice and will help you develop psychological resilience to mindless conformity.

As we know, the weavers were not weaving material fabric, but they were playing with the fabric of social relationships and truth, exposing how 'the system works'. They exploited human psychology, specifically by playing upon people's shame of being seen as not good enough, and their fear of loss and expulsion.

How different would the story be if the crowd had not been silent? Obviously, it would be shorter, but it would also be unfaithful to human psychology.

Most people like to think they would not simply go along with the crowd. But it is the norm. In *Battle for the Mind*, William Sargant pointed out that,

> A person is considered 'ordinary' or 'normal' by the community simply because he accepts most of its social standards and behavior patterns; which means, in fact, that he is susceptible to suggestion and has been persuaded to go with the majority on most ordinary or extraordinary occasions. People who hold minority opinions, even though these may be posthumously proved correct, are often called 'mad' or at least 'eccentric' during their lifetime.[1]

Psychologist Philip Zimbardo, who ran the infamous Stanford Prison Experiment, concurred: 'To be a hero you have to learn to be a deviant – because you're always going against the conformity of the group.'[2]

Herd-poisoning

The theory of nudge is predicated upon conformity. Cass Sunstein, lawyer and behavioural economist, put forward two explanations for this human tendency in his book of the same name, *Conformity: The Power of Social Influences*.[3] First, informational influence happens when people adapt their behaviour in order to be 'correct' – we often look to others whom we perceive are better informed. Second, normative influence stems from the need to stay on the right side of people and not be punished by them. In combination, these two principles explain the silence of the courtiers and the crowds.

Sunstein also calls these signals to conform 'cascades'. In an informational cascade, people cease relying on their private information or opinions, and instead rely on the signals conveyed by others. Not meeting the 'norm' can result in being shamed and potentially outcast. In essence, people like to be right and they like to be liked.

In the famous conformity experiments conducted by Solomon Asch in the 1950s, he demonstrated the influence of group pressure on opinions.[4] These experiments revealed the degree to which a person's own opinions are influenced by those of the group. Participants were shown a line and then asked to choose the matching line from a set of three lines of different lengths. Asch found that people were willing to ignore reality and give an incorrect answer in order to conform to the rest of the group (in this case, actors instructed to deliberately give the wrong answers).

The need to follow the group is so hardwired that it is observed in animals: they assume that if other members of the flock are doing something, it must be safe and appropriate. A Larsen trap, for example, uses a cage from which a bird cannot escape once they have entered. Normally, birds would be rightly suspicious. Yet this trap has a special compartment in which a sort of 'turncoat' bird is kept fed and watered. Wild birds see there is a peer already safe in there, and head on into their doom.

Aviculturist Zoe Owen, of East Sussex Smallholders, explained to us how, 'Birds like chickens, ducks and turkeys will want to lay their eggs where other birds lay theirs. They think the other bird who got there before them must think it's a safe and good place – and so they all follow suit. In the same way we all want the desirable postcode of the catchment of a highly rated Ofsted school.'

Asch found that conformity increases when more people are present, when the task becomes more difficult and when other members of the group are perceived as being higher status.[5] Conversely, conformity decreases when people are able to respond privately. This is why the courtiers are embarrassed to look stupid in front of the king, and the townsfolk in front of their 'betters'. It takes the innocence of a small boy to pierce through the crushing conformity of a huge crowd.

Crowds are not all bad. Feeling identified with a crowd can create a feeling of safety, thanks to our tendency to conform. It can produce reliable decisions. It can even be literally safer in a physical sense – we don't eat the berries from the bush that everyone else avoids. Physical crowds *can* also be safe, contrary to what you might think: one study asserted that 'self-organization in the crowd prevented disaster'.[6]

The fact is that we are social animals that rely upon cooperation and groups. Dr Libby Nugent, clinical psychologist and group work practitioner, explains that, 'If you think of evolutionary development, the group existed before the individual. We need groups. When we talk about a hierarchy of needs, actually our foundational need is to belong, before everything else. We will sacrifice everything to belong.'

Conformity happens for good evolutionary reasons. But great thinkers, studies and entire books have described the dangers of crowds and conformity. In *Brave New World Revisited*, Aldous Huxley said that man is not made to be an automaton, lost in the crowd, and he risks his mental health and freedom if he becomes one:

> To make them more masslike, more homogeneously subhuman, [Hitler] assembled them, by the thousands and the tens of thousands, in vast halls and arenas, where individuals could lose their personal identity, even their elementary humanity, and be merged with the crowd ... They become very excitable, they lose all sense of individual or collective responsibility, they are subject to sudden accesses of rage, enthusiasm and panic. In a word, a man in a crowd behaves as though he had swallowed a large dose of some powerful intoxicant. He is a victim of what I have called 'herd-poisoning'.[7]

Another great thinker of the period, Carl Jung, drew similar conclusions. He lived through the destructive collective movements of the world wars and the Cold War: mass movements, mass hysteria, mental contagions and 'psychic epidemics', as Jung termed them. In his book *The Undiscovered Self*, he offered advice about how to minimise the risks to the individual and to society.[8] The most important thing we can do to resist the lure of the crowd and mass movements is to self-individuate. 'Resistance to the organised mass can be effected only by the man who is as well organised in his individuality as the mass itself.' Jung believed you can self-individuate through meaningful values, work, community, faith and religion. And, of course, the individual will also be more likely to speak up first.

Crowds can grow angry, surge and rampage, but other dangers exist within groups of people, such as professional communities, neighbourhoods, religious groups and more. In the age of social media, this is even more relevant. Groups are collected by interests, coordinated by pages, followerships and hashtags, emojis displayed on bios like the standards of old, yet in reality the people are likely to be physically separate. 'I think we are in a world which has very little understanding of group and large group psychology and that we are increasingly dependent on it,' says Nugent. 'We have the World Wide Web and social media, and we just don't know what to do with it. We have invented the "group psychology atomic bomb" and we're playing with it like it's a toy.'

People have a hardwired bias towards their in-group. They tend to feel more empathetic pain (via 'mirror neurons') when they see a member of their own race experiencing pain, for example.[9] One study found that black Americans were more likely to agree with the statement 'African Americans must stop making excuses and rely much more on themselves to get ahead in society' when it came from a black politician rather than a white one.[10] Countries tend to vote for their geographical or political neighbours in Eurovision.

'Us versus them' is a powerful mechanism that's often exploited by manipulators. So too is 'black and white thinking' more broadly. When people become too attached to identities or ideas, this can be leveraged against them. Research has shown that people with a high 'need for cognitive closure' are more persuadable in some respects.[11] Those who are more comfortable with ambiguity, with saying 'I don't know,' may be less likely to fall for the silver bullets and snake oil of manipulators.

Cult recovery educator Gerette said,

> Cults use black and white thinking – like 'right and wrong'. It's a powerful controlling mechanism. It's done subtly. Pitting one's birth family against the cultic group is classic polarisation. For me it happened very slowly. I

> got to the point that I really believed that my group was the much more important family – to the point I didn't even go to my brother's funeral. His funeral was scheduled the same weekend as a retreat I was already committed to. I created a whole other reality so I could justify not going to the funeral and staying with my cult family.

Groupthink can stifle independent thinking. Gustave Le Bon put forward one of the earliest and most influential theories of group mind theory in *The Crowd: A Study of the Popular Mind*; he believed individuals can lose their sense of self in a group, and become both anonymous and more powerful as a group at the same time. Once an individual is submerged in a group, ideas and sentiment are contagious. Think of individual fishes moving as a shoal. Although more recent theorists have criticised Le Bon's conceptualisation of the crowd as 'mindless', it is self-evident that bad ideas can take hold of groups. Our powerful tendency to conform is supported by reams of scientific experiments – and it is mercilessly exploited by manipulators.

We like to think we come up with our own ideas, and that we wouldn't conform. In fact, we are often swept up. As Carl Jung's famous saying goes, 'People don't have ideas. Ideas have people.'[12] This is relatable in the everyday way; we recognise that ideas take hold of us, like 'She's beside herself today' or 'I don't know what got into me.' Jung's observation can also refer to the psychic epidemics and mass hysteria that can grip people, from small social groups to nations.

There are many examples of history proving the group was wrong, while the lone voice, the 'boy who spoke up', was right. The famous sixteenth- and seventeenth-century physicist and thought leader Galileo championed Copernicus's theory of heliocentrism, which correctly identified that the earth was observed to move around the sun, rather than vice versa. The Pope and priests of the Catholic Church – 'higher-status' officials in the 'crowd' – did not approve of his controversial theory. He was judged to be a heretic, and a fool to boot, and put under house arrest for the rest of his life. In this classic example, Galileo was correct, and the consensus was wrong.

Conformity can be good or bad, says Sunstein, depending on what results. In which case, conformity due to social pressure or false information is fine, if the political goal reached is desirable. But do the ends really justify the means? Do you trust others to know which political views are desirable to *you*?

We see movements today with cascades of conformity so sequential, influential and coordinated that they appear to be choreographed, even if they are actually examples of ideas taking hold of people. Let's take one modern-day example to show how conformity evolves: man-made climate change.

Climate conformity

This is a hot potato. Any smidgen of doubt about climate change risks incurring the label of 'denier'. Regardless of your views on climate change, it's important to understand how such denigratory labels emerge and acquire the power to silence. To be a 'climate change denier' is to be positioned as an outlier, apart from those who prioritise informational and social conformity. The term is designed to constrain serious opposition, just like the term 'conspiracy theorist'. Various countries have pledged to Net Zero targets, some have made legally binding commitments, including the UK by 2050. As such, governments, as well as activist groups, are also committed to persuading you to change your behaviour. The Behavioural Insights Team have noted that 'Delivery of Net Zero depends on substantial social and behavioural change'.[13]

Education, academia, the media, entertainment and the internet have been enrolled to create 'cascades', and this is very powerful. For the purpose of this illustration, it does not matter whether or not you believe in the severity of man-made climate change, the necessity of measures to tackle it, the need for cost-benefit analysis of those measures, or whether you think the whole thing is an exaggerated storm in a modeller's tea cup. Regardless of what you think of the 'ends', these are the 'means'.

On 'Earth Day' in 2022, a new Natural History GCSE was announced in the UK, or 'saving the world' as some described it.[14] It is part of a wider move towards 'greening the curriculum' according to examination awarding body Oxford, Cambridge and RSA. And at COP26 (the 2021 United Nations Climate Change Conference), the Education Secretary Nadhim Zahawi set out his vision for all children to be taught about the importance of conserving and protecting our planet, and declared education to be one of the 'key *weapons* [our emphasis] in the fight against climate change'.[15]

The Behavioural Insight Team published a report entitled 'Net Zero: Principles for successful behaviour change initiatives – key principles from past government-led behaviour change and public engagement initiatives', which said: 'Education also plays a key role in establishing new norms. Indeed, schools have often been a vector for building national identity. Children can then in turn have profound impacts on their parents, or through other means by making new behaviours observable.'

It's hard to put a piece of paper between this observation and Chairman Mao's comment that 'all work in school is for changing the thinking of the student'. These educational developments are designed to influence young minds and conscript little climate footsoldiers. School is the first and perhaps most powerful 'cascade' for building social norms. Regardless of your beliefs about the war, it is hard to deny that children are being deliberately enrolled, especially when the Minister for Education comes out and says so.

In the same vein, the Nudge Unit and broadcaster Sky recommended in a joint report – 'The power of TV: Nudging viewers to decarbonise their lifestyles' – that broadcasters should use children's TV content to encourage 'positive environmental behaviours' among children and their parents due to the multi-generational spillover effect. Of course, there were suggestions for how to infiltrate the full gamut of TV programming with climate nudges to reach people of all ages. The media uncritically reported that during COP26, the storylines of various British soap operas converged on environmental themes ostensibly to establish new social norms.

In *Coronation Street* – which has the UK's biggest soap opera audience with an average of six million viewers per episode – Maria Connor was upset when the field her son played football on was threatened with development. Also, her son's asthma diagnosis was linked to air pollution.

And in *Emmerdale*, grieving doctor and dad Liam created a TikTok video as he worked on his new allotment, to help him deal with his daughter Leanna's death. In an astonishing piece of cross-fertilisation between different soap operas, the video was then seen in *Coronation Street*, when Maria's husband shows it to her, while they discuss the plans for a new bypass.

The storyline seeped into another soap opera as characters in Hollyoaks discuss a news article about Maria's protest calling for action to tackle air pollution, before they talked about doing business more sustainably.

In *EastEnders*, the focus was on cutting meat consumption, with schoolgirl Bailey Baker raising a petition for meat-free Mondays. She tells the other characters that, 'Global livestock production makes a huge amount of greenhouse gases. They need to be reduced to save the planet. It causes deforestation and pollution. Don't you care that there are floods and droughts?' and 'We need to cut down the amount of meat we eat to help save the planet before it's too late. The damage that has been done already is criminal. If we all stop eating meat for one day a week we can all help slow down climate change.'

This was observably artificial in tone and pointed at the audience as much as the characters, causing some viewers to complain on Twitter, with comments about 'the heavy-handed way the soaps are dealing with climate change' and 'another soap lecture'.

Climate storylines were not short-lived but continued throughout the year. The fiftieth anniversary of *Emmerdale* was commemorated with a 'killer' daytime storm. In October 2021 the iconic *EastEnders* closing credits were adapted to show London if sea levels rose by two metres, to promote the final episode of *Frozen Planet II*. The BBC's press information for the show offered this note to editors:

> Some IPCC climate projection scenarios indicate a possibility that by 2100 sea levels could have risen by two metres. If this happens, and no further flood defences for London are built, it's plausible that water levels around the Thames would resemble this digitally-created aerial image.

In essence, the BBC used visual effects to create an impression of a crisis. In fact, a rise of two metres is outside of any plausible projections.[16] Again, Twitter responded with sharp retorts such as, 'We need a bigger Thames Barrier' and calling it 'brainwashing'.

The science is unsettled

Some scientists declared that the climate change science was settled and could not be debated. One study, using the massive psychological pressure of the crowd, claimed that there was a 99 per cent consensus among academics about human-caused climate change in the peer-reviewed scientific literature.[17] It concluded that 'This issue has been comprehensively settled, and the reality of ACC [anthropogenic climate change] is no more in contention among scientists than is plate tectonics or evolution.' Other scientists and journalists *have* disputed this claim and the robustness of the study, but the whopping percentage packs a convincing punch and has the effect of silencing many academics, scientists, journalists and other public figures who do not want to go against the grain. It's also designed to increase credulity among the public. In fact, Mark Lynas, a visiting fellow at the Alliance for Science and the paper's first author, boldly claimed that 'it's pretty much case closed for any meaningful public conversation about the reality of human-caused climate change'.[18] In other words, 'Pipe down, we've settled the science, and you must now believe what you are told.'

That study was then used to promote the idea that social media platforms should censor climate change denial 'misinformation', which would further stifle debate and shape the public narrative and individual opinions.

While one social norm on climate change is presented through the media, the reality of what most people believe may be quite different. The Institute for Strategic Dialogue (ISD) tracked posts by Facebook's own official Climate Science Centre versus accounts it identified as spreading climate scepticism.[19] It found that sceptical content garnered 12 times the level of engagement of 'authoritative sources' on the platform. The sceptical messaging expressed key themes that COP26 was useless, a failure, hypocritical, harmful to the economy, and the product of an eco-fascist agenda orchestrated by climate activists and elites.

The ISD also observed that the official video of David Attenborough's speech shared by the UN Environment Programme generated just over 8,600 views. In contrast, a video featuring Spiked Online's Brendan O'Neill, in which he describes the summit as a gathering of 'hypocrites, narcissists and virtue signallers', received over 34,100 views and was shared five times more than the UN's post. Neither of these videos received much attention, but the ISD was rattled by the difference between them

Rather than engage with why people are sceptical about climate change claims and policies, the ISD considers this sort of content as misinformation and disinformation. If you like this sort of sceptical content, the ISD would probably consider you to be foolish, tricked by hucksters and plain wrong. As such, findings from this report were submitted by Carnegie UK to the UK government committee for the draft Online Safety Bill as evidence that climate change scepticism should be defined as 'harm to public safety, public health and national security' and form part of the tech platforms' harm prevention mitigations, to then be monitored by Ofcom.[20] There are groups of people determined that you must not like the content you like, or share the content you want to share. You see, you simply do not know what is harmful to you, or in your best interests.

The Journalists Resource, run by Harvard Kennedy School's Shorenstein Center on Media, Politics and Public Policy, explains how 'journalists can use scientific consensus to bolster their coverage and battle misinformation'.[21] Assuming matters are settled and reporting consensus opinion is not the pinnacle of fine journalism. The BBC has likewise taken the position that man-made climate change exists and 'deniers' do not need to be platformed in the interests of 'false balance'.[22] The point is to create the illusion of a unanimous collective, to deter dissent.

For example, a global survey conducted among young people reported that they are very frightened about climate change, and concluded that, 'There is an urgent need for further research into the emotional impact of climate change on children and young people and for governments to validate their distress by taking urgent action on climate change.'[23] A closer inspection of the methodology reveals that the research only sought agreement with very negative statements such as 'the future is frightening' and 'humanity is doomed'. Respondents were not asked to agree with any neutral or positive statements. If they weren't frightened about a perilous future at the start of the survey, they probably were by the end.

Going even further, another Australian study claimed that doubting climate change has various causes, not least a form of mental condition – analytical processing is negatively associated with unfounded beliefs.[24] One of the authors did say it was contrary to their expectations that among those who suffer from this alleged disorder, people with analytical abilities were even more likely to be sceptical. She didn't go on to question why their analytical abilities might make them more sceptical. According to the study, 'Since climate change mitigation policies run contrary to the values of political conservatives, it could be that conflicting evidence is intentionally misinterpreted to match one's existing values and beliefs.' This reveals the bias of the authors, since it could just as easily read, 'Since climate change scepticism runs contrary to the values of political liberals, it could be that conflicting evidence is intentionally misinterpreted to match one's existing values and beliefs.' Bias is just one problem with the idea that the ends justify the means.

After all of these examples of cascades of information it is easy to see how conformity is attained. The term 'climate change denier' is likely to strike fear into the heart of someone who wants to retain the approval of the group. It is reminiscent of the most ghastly opprobrium: the Holocaust denier.

Nevertheless, some scientists and politicians are concerned enough about energy shortages and prices to more loudly challenge some climate change claims and goals. Michael Shellenberger, a *Time* magazine 'Hero of the Environment',[25] testified at the US Congress that climate alarmism is not based on science.[26] Four leading Italian scientists undertook a major review of historical climate trends and concluded that declaring a 'climate emergency' is not supported by the data.[27] In June 2022, a further 1,200 scientists and professionals led by the Norwegian physics Nobel Prize laureate Professor Ivar Giaever published a 'World Climate Declaration' to proclaim that there is no climate emergency.[28]

Perhaps the climate tide will turn. A scientific study found that a minority of just 25 per cent is typically enough to tip the majority.[29] Climate protestors similarly quote the 3.5 per cent rule, which says that no government can resist that share of the population mobilising against it.[30] However, a small group of sceptics could mobilise on the other end of the spectrum. What is a government, with their Net Zero diktats, to do? At the moment it appears authorities are deplatforming and censoring to stifle dissent and maintain an illusion of conformity. Yet the ISD research shows the popularity of sceptical content on social media. Can dissent be stifled or merely appear to be stifled? The problem with the mere appearance of conformity is that authorities then perceive agreement where there is none. This then blinds their strategic vision and they may find that they ignore determined pockets of resistance growing in supposedly conquered territory.

The lone voice

From Galileo to volunteer cops, the outliers, pioneers and whistle-blowers change the world. Steve Jobs put it best when he said:

> Here's to the crazy ones. The misfits. The rebels. The troublemakers. The round pegs in the square holes. The ones who see things differently. They're not fond of rules. And they have no respect for the status quo. You can quote them, disagree with them, glorify or vilify them. About the only thing you can't do is ignore them. Because they change things. They push the human race forward. And while some may see them as the crazy ones, we see genius. Because the people who are crazy enough to think they can change the world, are the ones who do.[31]

Sunstein is well aware that when individuals suppress their own instincts about what is true and what is right, it can lead to significant social harm. He argues for a 'voice of sanity' to disrupt and derail the forces of conformity. He writes that 'if a group is embarking on an unfortunate course of action, a single dissenter might be able to turn it around by energizing ambivalent group members who would otherwise follow the crowd'. It takes the innocence of the boy in 'The Emperor's New Clothes' to turn the crowd around.

Being the voice of sanity, the scientific pioneer or the boy who spoke up can be dangerous. That lone voice needs to find internal reserves of strength. To consider how, Dr Naomi Murphy, a senior clinical psychologist, reframed the problem: what makes people suggestible to manipulation and groupthink in the first place?

> Some people are more susceptible to manipulation and group think. There are links with suggestibility. There are four things that are significant. The evolutionary need to belong and cooperate means we are hardwired to want to belong to the group. People who are most able to resist are more comfortable not belonging to the group and being an outsider. Identity is important and some people prioritise being easy to get on with as part of their 'identity', some are more comfortable being contrarian. If you value integrity as a part of your identity, you are more likely to defend your moral position even when it is hard and there is a cost to you. Finally, in terms of suggestibility, some people are more suggestible than others. There are a number of characteristics that make up being suggestible, to do with emotionality, age, self-esteem, assertiveness.

To combat this she recommends people consciously try to develop their self-esteem and confidence to feel comfortable with being separate from the group. It's also important to observe your uncomfortable emotions in relation to speaking up or deviating from the group. She advises you 'notice the discomfort, strong reactions and fear'. You can merely observe or also push through the discomfort. Although you initially face social disapproval, she says, 'the benefit is authenticity and growth, being true to yourself and having principles'.

Another useful tip is to be prepared to acknowledge when you are wrong. Describing a form of psychological sunk cost fallacy, she says, 'Once your colours are nailed to the mast, once you have gone so far down a path, you might not be able to admit to yourself and other people, you were wrong. Try and admit it and become comfortable with it.'

'The human mind is a lot like the human egg, and the human egg has a shut-off device,' said businessman Charlie Munger. 'When one sperm gets in, it shuts down so the next one can't get in.'[32] There is a danger that once an idea 'fertilises' your brain, you will not be receptive to other ideas. Being actively open-minded is an important skill to practise.

Murphy says you can practise being an outlier. You might find yourself automatically outside the group. In which case, you should make the most of it. Murphy says she hated her teenage years. Her family regularly moved home because her father was in the Royal Air Force. She would change schools, adapt to different environments, have to navigate fitting in to new peer groups and also had the 'wrong' accent. But it brought advantages: she developed a 'thicker skin' and discovered 'there is something about being an outsider that makes you able to accept being different to the majority'. She recommends that people embrace out-group experience.

Alternatively, you can make a conscious decision to be an outlier. Another psychologist who has worked at a very senior level within the NHS told us about choosing to stand up to instances of institutional racism and being a 'whistle-blower', because 'it was important. People have to have the courage to call it out, at an individual or a system level.' But it wasn't easy.

> Ultimately it brought the wrath of the system down on me, and it led to malicious allegations against me. People just looked away when I was badly treated. It was an exhausting process to go through. I am about as senior as you can get as a clinical psychologist in the NHS, and I am 50. What would it be like to do this as someone who is younger or junior?
>
> In the end I was exonerated. I am proud of myself for speaking up. Other people knew about the issues and did nothing. I would encourage people to do the same as I did. It's a hard process but you learn a lot about yourself and grow. You end up with new friendships. Effectively you end up with a new 'in-group' of 'out-groupers'. You know they can be relied upon. They have integrity. You know where you are with them. There is solidity about them. The people who wish to be in the in-group cannot be relied upon and there is a selfishness about them. They look less selfish because they are with the group but actually their position in the group is about maintaining their status and their place.

Choosing to be a whistle-blower – despite the knowledge that it could hurt – was a worthwhile experience, increasing this psychologist's resilience. They felt proud. As Joost Meerloo said in *The Rape of the Mind*: 'Whether or not we are aware of it, there is nothing of which we are more ashamed than of not being ourselves, and there is nothing that gives us greater pride and happiness than to think, to feel, and to say what is ours.'[33]

Lee was a volunteer cop, what's known as a 'special constable'. He reported fraudulent behaviour to senior officers within his own police force. His own force didn't take this report seriously, so he then subsequently reported this to the Home Office who did take it seriously. The investigation is still ongoing. He was subsequently suspended and investigated for allegations of gross misconduct. Ultimately, after a long investigation, none of these allegations against him was proven to be true. However, the investigation team later went on to make a further accusation of racism and gross misconduct.

He joined the police to help people and protect them from criminals and was shocked to discover corruption at a senior level. As with the psychologist, it was a difficult experience: 'When I was suspended I was gutted. When I was found guilty [of the subsequent allegation] it was published in the media. You have no idea what that feels like. It feels like the world is coming to an end.' Nevertheless, he stands by his experience of whistle-blowing and is proud of his actions.

Interestingly, like the psychologist, it seems that previous out-group experience may have prepared him psychologically to take a stand:

> I think that because I was born overseas and am openly gay, I don't seem to fit. That's part of who I am. I think it is part of the reason they closed ranks on me. I joined the police force as a gay man in the 90s. If I had come out as gay they would have found ways to get rid of me then. I saw that first hand with colleagues who came out. I was also surprised how racist the force was at the time then. I have to say that fortunately this has changed a lot now.
>
> But being an outsider and doing things differently has given me the psychological resilience to be a whistleblower.

When Socrates was on trial, in his defence he pointed out that dissent, like a gadfly biting and annoying the horse of public opinion, was easy to swat, but the cost to society of silencing individuals could be very high: 'If you kill a man like me, you will injure yourselves more than you will injure me.'

Indeed, it is these gadflies, the people lower on agreeableness – the non-cooperative, the distrusting, the confrontational – who are less compliant, according to research.[34]

Now, what of the emperor? The fairy tale doesn't continue to tell us what happened in the town afterwards. Was his authority punctured? The emperor fell for the lie, and then through his authority he implicitly compelled the people around him to take part in the lie. He could have set an entirely different example. How often are our leaders weak, lacking in courage, conviction and intelligence? Enough, it would seem, that they justify timeless fairy tales and daily political cartoons lampooning their absurdities.

Dr Libby Nugent says, 'We think of the emperor as someone who "knows" things':

> But the definition of an emperor who looks after thousands of people is that they don't know, they can't know, everything. We give them the power of being someone who knows, but in fact they are 'known' rather than knowing. Everyone knows who the emperor is, but he doesn't know who everyone else is. So we ascribe power to the emperor, but because he doesn't know everyone, he will make mistakes left, right and centre. There is a way in which we don't want the responsibility of speaking up. We want the one-sidedness of thinking they know. We need to take responsibility and authority.

This is a revolutionary point. Often manipulators draw power from the illusion of power: they can control us paradoxically just because we think they can. Once we realise their power is a deception, it evaporates. The mighty Wizard of Oz is just a small man behind a curtain.

Manipulators often try to portray themselves as all-knowing and all-powerful. You tend to comply if you think 'Big Brother is watching you'. In psychology it's known as 'the watching eyes effect' – display a poster of a pair of eyes and people are more likely to wash their hands, and less likely to steal a bike.[35] The principle first emerged as a tool of social control from the concept of the panopticon (meaning 'see everything'): prisoners behaved themselves if a guard tower was placed in the middle of the prison, such that they felt like they were always being watched, even if they weren't.

A declassified CIA document outlined an interrogation technique called 'The All-Seeing Eye'.[36] The interrogator pretends to know the whole story, and reinforces the impression by asking a few questions to which he already knows the answer. 'By skilled manipulation of the known, the questioner can convince a naive subject that all his secrets are out and that further resistance would not only be pointless but dangerous.'

During the Covid lockdowns, every new authoritarian diktat was accompanied by stories of people being caught and punished for infringements. The news reported that a pair were fined for having coffee together in a park;[37] that dog walkers in the Peak District were being filmed by police drones;[38] that helicopters ordered sunbathers off the beach in Australia.[39] The impression was that there was no escape from the all-seeing eye of the state; resistance was futile. In reality, the likelihood of penalty was very slim. Only 5 per cent of burglaries and robberies get solved in the UK, for instance.[40]

In both world wars, inflatable tanks were used as decoys to create an illusion of strength.[41] The key to disempowering manipulators is to deflate their illusory power as if popping these inflatable tanks. Like Charlie Chaplin's parody of Hitler, the Wizard of Oz must be revealed as nothing more than a small man. We must point and laugh at his inadequacy.

'In order to see that our emperors have no clothes on, do we really have to wait for a child to say so? Or even worse, wait for somebody's Inner Brat to pipe up?' asked writer Ursula K. Le Guin.[42] 'If so, we're in for a lot of nude politicians.'

One of the greatest acts of ordinary courage is to speak up first.

The rules:

- Speak up first, blow the whistle and be a voice of sanity. You will help the group as well as yourself.
- Observe and challenge the emotions and discomfort that pull you back to the in-group.
- Seek out-group experience and get comfortable with it if it happens to you. It will be easier next time.

16

Don't be a slave to sex

Sex – and in particular, pornography – can be a psychological weapon. It can break down critical resistance and use its powerful reward mechanism to condition new desires and behaviours. Although sex is a natural and enjoyable part of life, it should be treated with the respect it deserves.

A psychological weapon

High up on the Judean mountains, six miles north of Jerusalem, rests the ancient city of Ramallah. In Arabic it means 'God's height'. The city is so ancient, some buildings contain masonry from the period of Herod the Great. It has seen more than its fair share of conflict over the millennia, including in March 2002, when tanks rolled into Ramallah, as the Israeli Defence Forces (IDF) launched Operation Defensive Shield, the largest military operation in the West Bank for decades.[1]

Between the thudding helicopter rotors and the sharp pops of automatic gunfire, the family homes of Ramallah were besieged by noises of an altogether different kind. Among the ancient stone walls, modern television sets panted and groaned, discharging one of the oldest weapons of war: sex.

The *Sydney Morning Herald* reported how, according to irate residents, Israeli troops had commandeered three

Palestinian TV stations in Ramallah and begun broadcasting pornography.[2] An American consulate employee confirmed to the *New York Times* that the programmes were being aired.[3]

During the conflict, people – religious and conservative people no less – would be switching on the TV for news and information only to experience the psychological shock of viewing pornography. One Palestinian mother, Reema, told the *Sydney Morning Herald*, 'I have six children at home; they have nowhere to go with what is going on here and can't even watch TV. It's not healthy really. I think the Israelis want to mess with our young men's heads.' Another mother, Anita, complained about 'the deliberate psychological damage caused by these broadcasts'.

The Israeli military confirmed they had taken over the TV stations and interrupted the programming, but blamed Palestinian leaders for the pornography. Whoever was responsible, what's certain is that pornography was used as a psychological weapon of war – and not for the first time.

All key combatants in the Second World War used pornography as part of their psychological operations, mostly dropping sexual leaflets on the front lines in an attempt to divide and demoralise enemy soldiers.[4] One leaflet dropped by the Germans, for example, showed an American sergeant lying in bed with a British girl, swooning, 'You Americans are so different.' The back of the leaflet reads, 'The Yanks are putting up their tents in merry old England. They've got lots of money and loads of time to chase after your women.'

Sometimes the weaponisation of pornography was a bit more blunt. The US's Military Assistance Command, Vietnam – Studies and Observations Group (MACV-SOG) conducted covert unconventional warfare operations during the Vietnam War. Staff Sergeant Floyd 'Pigpen' Ambrose had a special poster printed featuring a nude, large-breasted Asian woman, and the question in Vietnamese: 'Who's sleeping with your wife, and has she got jugs like these?' As the message got more provocative, the print size got smaller. The Vietnamese soldier would have to step closer and closer to read it properly – thus stepping on the landmine Floyd had planted by the tree the poster was pinned to. Salacious curiosity would be satisfied at the expense of a foot, or perhaps a life. It was described by the author of *SOG: The Secret Wars of America's Commandos in Vietnam* as 'the most mind-blowing dirty trick I ever saw'.[5]

Sex has been a weapon of war as well as a tool of interrogation and torture for aeons. Mass rape has been documented in the Bible; the Vikings pillaged, abducted and raped; and there were an estimated one million rapes that occurred as the Red Army swept into Berlin at the end of Second World War. According to the academic paper 'Explaining wartime rape', the most influential explanation for why this happens is strategic rape theory: 'It is credited with spreading debilitating terror, diminishing the resistance of civilians, and demoralizing, humiliating, and emasculating enemy soldiers who are thereby shown to have failed in their most elemental protective duties.'[6]

Submission

While the use of sex in wartime propaganda in war and strategic rape has no obvious relation to your bedroom, the point is that they convey the powerful relationship of sex to mind and spirit. Ultimately, a big part of sex as psychological warfare seems to be about submission. Sex and its myriad permutations of power and submission have propagated a world of books for the purposes of pleasurable fantasy as well as theoretical exploration. For instance, in *50 Shades of Grey*, the UK's fastest-selling book of all time, a young woman is physically, emotionally and sexually dominated by a billionaire. Then there is the famous saying that everything in the world is about sex except sex – sex is about power.[7]

Hidden away from the rhythm of humdrum public life, and offering insights into principles for brainwashing, there is a thriving subculture of bondage, dominance, sadism and masochism (BDSM). In London, for example, there is a nightclub called the Torture Garden, where up to two and a half thousand people attend every month dressed in fetish gear (if you don't dress the part, you won't get in) and indulge in orgiastic festivals of pleasure and pain set to thumping music.[8] Many more niche underground fetish clubs operate every night of the week in London, and other towns and cities around the world.

A paper in the *Journal of Positive Sexuality* found that BDSM is associated with what's called 'subspace', a submissive psychological state that produces physiological changes, a deep feeling of relaxation similar to floating, and temporary feelings of depersonalisation and derealisation.[9] It is a state in which the submissive can release their analytical ego and transition from a state of constant, anxious thought to total liberation from self. And for the people in that dynamic, the submissive and the dominant, they will achieve satisfaction. In other words, offering total submission is experienced in a positive way. It is a release from the stress and chaos of the world.

Taken to the extreme, submission can result in a complete annihilation of the self. This is characterised to the utmost in *The Story of* O, a classic erotic novel from 1954 about BDSM, which earned both literary prizes and obscenity charges.[10] In it, O's identity is increasingly diminished as her tortures become more severe. In the final scene, at a party, she notes that the guests see her as made 'of stone or wax, or rather some creature from another world'. She blankly, wordlessly, accepts anything that is done to her. Her mysterious name could stand for object, orifice or oblivion. Ultimately, it is oblivion that she craves. In an alternative ending to the book, she asks for death, revealing an existential longing for release. In an interview in *The New Yorker* in 1975, the book's author, Anne Desclos, described O's ultimate dream to be her own 'destruction and death'.

Fantasies about submission can reveal a desire to regress to the responsibility-free state of childhood, when the all-powerful adults were in total control. The impulse that fuels a sado-masochistic personal relationship corresponds to a submissive relationship with the state. Writing in *Fear of Freedom* amid the ruins of the Second World War, Erich Fromm makes the point with regards to totalitarianism.[11] These mass movements do not simply occur because of the urges of the sadists in power, he suggests, but also because of the unconscious masochistic yearning of the masses. In other words, it takes two to tango. Masochistic strivings, according to Fromm, 'help the individual to escape his unbearable feeling of aloneness and powerlessness … The frightened individual seeks for somebody or something to tie his self to; he cannot bear to be his own individual self any longer, and he tries frantically to get rid of it and to feel security again by the elimination of his burden: the self.' The refusal to face the problem of freedom results in alienating strategies of avoidance such as sadism and masochism. Fromm sees them not merely as sexual phenomena but as ways of surrendering the self to another. Within society, en masse, this creates an unbalanced relationship of power between the government and the governed.

In *The Story of* O, O agrees to be branded with Sir Stephen's insignia. Such things do not happen only in dark, erotic stories. In NXIVM (a personality cult whose survivors have recounted stories of group sex and naked meetings, and whose leaders have been indicted for crimes including sex trafficking), the female recruits were brutally branded to be marked as the property of cult leader Keith Raniere.[12] This is an ultimate physical manifestation of sex employed for power, and psychological ownership. It is claimed he had more than a hundred 'slaves', but NXIVM was also a profitable personal and professional development company that operated like a pyramid selling scheme, its tentacles reaching into the worlds of billionaires, politicians and celebrities. Cults ostensibly use sex because they work by creating a disorganised psychological attachment to the group, and particularly the leader. In

NXIVM's case, videos of sexual confessions were also used as *kompromat*, for extra 'bonding', of an immoral, unwilling and illegal kind.

Gerette Buglion, cult recovery educator and co-founder of the cult support website IGotOut.org, concurred:

> Sex is used in cults. Abso-friggin-lutely. I'm not sure I've met a cult that doesn't use control of sex in some way or another. In the group I was a part of there was no overt sexual abuse. It starts out so subtly that you just don't notice it – doing a couple's session every month where all of our intimacies were kind of flayed. We'd open up with something simple – like I wanted a couch – and yet in the processing of that, the group leader weaves in the withholding of sex, or my husband's sex drive. These intimate topics get brought in in a way that confuses and confounds some practical life things.
>
> Wherever sex is brought in I think there is a vulnerability because of its intimacy. The relational part is also very important here. It's not just sex itself, it's also the relationship. Wherever we have a relationship where there is intimacy, there's more charge. In groups there was switching and reforming of couples. I know without a doubt that was orchestrated by the leader. The way he was pulling the strings of intimate relationships is also messing with their sense of sexuality and their identities.

Psychological research has shown that sexual intercourse produces feelings of attachment; it releases the 'love and bonding' hormone oxytocin.[13] It can temporarily disable the parts of the brain that deal with social judgements and self-awareness, resulting in a feeling of dissociation.[14]

Buglion's story exemplifies, in extreme terms, that what we call sexual liberation can be quite the opposite – a vice is something that traps you, not sets you free. In the classic sci-fi novel *Brave New World*, Aldous Huxley painted a dystopia in which sex flows freely between everyone, and monogamy is a stuffy old thing of the past.[15] Even children are encouraged to engage in 'erotic play'. The theory is that sex, like drugs, keeps people in an emotional, pliable state. In a foreword to the book, Huxley wrote:

> As political and economic freedom diminishes, sexual freedom tends compensating to increase. And the dictator ... will do well to encourage that freedom. In conjunction with the freedom to daydream under the influence of dope and movies and the radio, it will help to reconcile his subjects to the servitude which is their fate.

The counterweight to Huxley's view of sexuality and control is George Orwell's. In *1984*, sex is viewed by Big Brother as a disgusting instinct to be suppressed or distorted into other activities.[16] The psychological perspective, put forward in particular by Wilhelm Reich in *The Mass Psychology of Fascism*, argues that frequent sex is necessary to discharge anxieties and frustrations; without it, there is a kind of build-up of energy that drives behaviour and can ultimately be directed into large-scale mass movements.[17]

Reich wrote: 'The suppression of natural sexual gratification leads to various kinds of substitute gratifications. Natural aggression, for example, becomes brutal sadism which then is an essential mass-psychological factor in imperialistic wars.'

Brainwashing in the bedroom

Whether you agree more with Orwell's view or with Huxley's, sex appears to be a powerful psychological tool for control – and there are two reasons for this.

The first is sex's psychologically disintegrating effect; it can be used to break down the mind's defences. The CIA's MK-Ultra spawned a sub-project called Operation Midnight Climax.[18] Senate investigators were told the goal was to study the link between sex and mind control. The CIA paid prostitutes to lure targets back to safe houses where they were plied with drugs and questioned after sex. According to those who oversaw the experiments, people spoke a lot more freely under this cocktail of sex and drugs, their critical defences weakened.

Perhaps this is why the French call an orgasm *la petite mort*, meaning 'a little death', referring to the brief weakening of consciousness after sex. It breaks down the mind's conscious thoughts, creating an imprintable space in the brain – the subspace identified by bondage lovers, the temporary autonomous zone of symbolism, the cognitive vacuum of brainwashing.

Second, sex is a potent brainwashing tool because it is also a means of conditioning: outside of drugs, the orgasm provides perhaps the strongest rush of pleasure one can experience.[19] Pavlov's dog food pales in comparison to the ability of sex to make people salivate. Flooding the brain with serotonin, dopamine and oxytocin, sex is the ultimate reward. Pairing this reward with the right stimulus can radically change people's minds. Any idea can become palatable if it is made sexually desirable first. As radical feminist Professor Catharine Alice MacKinnon wrote: 'Try arguing with an orgasm sometime.'[20]

Indeed, there is experimental research showing that tastes can be moulded sexually. Psychologists have known since at least the 1960s that paraphilias can be conditioned.[21] One such study hooked men's penises up to a device to measure engorgement.[22] When the men viewed pornographic pictures of women, they became sexually aroused. Shown erotic pictures of women in boots, the men became aroused as expected due to the naked women. After a certain number of exposures to the women in boots, however, the men became conditioned to associate the boots alone with arousal. Eventually, just an image of boots was enough to turn them on. They had become conditioned to find boots sexy. An obvious illustration is the use of bikini-clad models to make brands appealing – but could pornography also be warping what people find desirable, and thus their habits and beliefs, on a more fundamental level?

When somebody watches porn on their smartphone, for example, they are forming an attachment not only to whatever is in the video, but also to the smartphone itself. Their brains flood with endorphins while they stare into its obsidian face. Is it any wonder then that psychologists have identified that smartphone owners feel intense feelings of distress when they are separated from their device, as if it were a romantic partner?[23] The Fourth Industrial Revolution, and its merging of man with machine, can only benefit from this.

The case for NoFap

Of course, the effects of pornography are hotly contested. It's impossible to separate science from socially constructed ideology as well as, frankly, whether one likes using it or not. A suspect amount of bias creeps into these perspectives and studies. But the upshot is that the porn people watch can potentially have a massive impact on what they find desirable and ultimately how they view themselves and the world around them.

Pornography usage has been linked to negative outcomes, such as impersonal sexual attitudes, negative body image, more acceptance of sexual aggression, and delayed ejaculation. It is also claimed to have positive effects, such as providing sexual education. Some literature reviews suggest that pornographic images and films can be addictive, particularly when combined with masturbation, while others maintain that data remains inconclusive.

The World Health Organization added compulsive sexual behaviour as a mental health disorder in 2018. While it doesn't single out pornography, it does refer to repetitive sexual activities becoming a central focus of a person's life to the point that they neglect their 'health and personal care or other interests, activities, and responsibilities'.

Yet many people do claim to be addicted to pornography and some are making radical decisions to abstain. The 'NoFap' website promotes the idea of quitting porn as a sex-positive choice. Its Reddit forum has over one million members. No Nut November, which recommends participants abstain from all forms of ejaculation for 30 days, had 137,000 members in 2022. These movements are nothing new. After all, John Harvey Kellogg allegedly invented cornflakes to be so boring as to dull the desire for masturbation. These contemporary movements prohibiting masturbation echo the myriad criticisms of 'self-abuse' to be found in historical religious and medical books.

Billy (not his real name) quit porn at the age of 20 because he had problems achieving orgasm with his girlfriend. 'Porn is an addiction in the end,' he confessed. 'In the same way that gambling isn't a physical addiction, it's not actually in your blood, but it gets into your mind. I used to use porn every day. Quitting porn and quitting masturbation was like a reset. After several weeks I could orgasm during sex again.'[24] He drew an important distinction between men who started watching porn later in life, who know what sex is like and might be better equipped to balance the effects, with younger men who experience more consequences.

Pornography may also be one contributing factor to the staggering increase in elective labia reduction, known as labiaplasty. It is the fastest-growing cosmetic procedure in the world. As with porn addiction and erectile dysfunction, studies are inconclusive about the involvement of pornography in this phenomenon, although the timing correlates suspiciously with the growth in internet porn. Maria (not her real name) underwent labiaplasty and was explicit about the role of porn:

> I thought the area of the vagina should look like the ones that I'd seen in porn on the internet, and they looked the exact polar opposite to mine. Porn made me feel like shit in all sorts of ways – it would be my weight, my boobs, my vagina.
>
> I watched a documentary that talked about porn stars who were having operations to make their labia smaller. I realised it was something you could have done and I went to my GP and I had a bit of a breakdown. I think it was a really low day, I'd watched porn and my body dysmorphia was bad.[25]

The problems for young women don't end there. Pornography can contain very extreme content. As MacKinnon writes: 'With pornography, men masturbate to women being exposed, humiliated, violated, degraded, mutilated, dismembered, bound, gagged, tortured, and killed.'[26] Women's early exposure to pornography is linked with vaginismus, a condition in which the vagina contracts painfully to physical contact or pressure, particularly penetration. It's reasonable to deduce that content that arouses fear and disgust might contribute to this condition.

Disgust is known to be a foundation of moral behaviour.[27] We all understand what it means if someone did something 'sick' or acted in a 'disgusting' way. It prevents the mixing of things that we (rightly or wrongly) intuit shouldn't be mixed; it maintains psychological boundaries. Sex, on the other hand, is incompatible with disgust: both sexual arousal and disgust run through the same pathways in the brain, such that it is less possible to be disgusted when aroused, and less possible to be aroused when disgusted.[28] The consequence is that when people are sexually aroused, it may be easier to rearrange psychological boundaries and cross lines that might not otherwise be crossed. It is, in this way, a powerful tool for brainwashing.

The world's most popular porn website, Pornhub, had 2.6 billion visits in October 2022, each visit averaging eight pages on the website.[29] (By comparison, the BBC had under a quarter that number of visits.) If you happen to find yourself on Pornhub's homepage you will be met with a cornucopia of thumbnails inviting you to click. There's something for everyone. On a single selected day, among the expected interests on the home page were bondage, sex with a machine, and an extremely niche video combining a part of the body painted to resemble a seasonal vegetable – the pumpkin – with a sex act. Videos featuring step-sisters, step-daughters and step-mums convey (and encourage) incestuous desires while circumventing illegality. Teens, babysitters and schoolgirls (all assuredly 18+ but not necessarily looking like it) reflect a taste (and encourage desire) for girls. Which is to say, that one of the most popular pornography websites in the world is rearranging psychological boundaries.

Based on some public statistics and common-sense assumptions, let's say the average boy starts watching porn at 13. He watches it about three times a week, for 15 minutes per session. Each session rarely involves just one video, so let's conservatively estimate that he watches three and that each one is simply sex between a man and a woman. By this rough estimate, he will have seen over two thousand erect penises before his eighteenth birthday. Prior to the advent of porn, this would probably have just been one – his own.

What effect could this unprecedented change be having on the youth of today? The website Your Brain on Porn has archived men's experiences with porn use, abuse and abstinence. A cohort agree that pornography conditioned them into having autogynephilia, an attraction to being a woman.[30] One person, for example, described how in the throes of his heavy porn usage he became so obsessed with watching women have sex, it led to him wishing he were a woman so that he could, as he put it, feel like a slut and be used by men. He even bought some women's clothing and make-up for himself.

Transgender writer Andrea Long Chu presented an academic paper at the Queer Disruptions conference entitled 'Did sissy porn make me trans?'[31] In short, the answer seems to be yes. The paper argues that watching pornography is itself a submissive act – it is a submission to your desires, and the pornographer's desires, and absent of any kind of active participation you might find in sex with a partner – and in this way porn feminises men. Chu writes that 'the pornographic spectator is basically a bottom'. Sissy porn, says Chu, leaves viewers 'simplified, emptied, dumb. The technical term for this is bimboification.'

The link between pornography and transgenderism is not clear cut, and it is important to be mindful about the devastating consequences. Steve (not his real name) echoed Billy's concerns about the addictive nature of pornography, telling us that 'Porn has been a way to drastically kill sexuality. You get so much of it that you flood the mind till it's not healthy.' When he first saw pornography as a teenager he was 'terrified' because it was 'aggressive and violent and monstrous'. It made him feel unsafe around men. He now believes it was part of the reason he started identifying as a woman, when he was in fact a young gay man. Would he have been trans if porn did not exist? 'Probably not,' he said.

He said this is very common among the detransitioned males he knows. They all saw porn at an early age. Tragically, Steve describes himself now as 'a sexless being'. He surgically transitioned when he was 30. 'The second I started coming to [after the operation] I regretted it,' he said.

Billy and Steve's powerful observations about pornography being addictive and killing sexuality reveal the counterproductive nature of the medium. Pornography is supposed to stimulate sexual excitement but is causing some young men to have problems with erectile dysfunction and some young women to have vaginismus and to seek labiaplasty.[32] In the process, it is shaping sexual desire and exaggerating or even creating paraphilias. Considering its powerful effects, it's worrying that porn is so ubiquitous. One survey found that 98 per cent of men and 73 per cent of women had watched porn within the last six months.[33]

This chapter's criticisms of pornography are not based on prudishness. What people do in the privacy of their homes and on their own time is up to them. But avid porn users should be aware that their sexual tastes change, just like the men who came to prefer boots, or the gay men who started identifying as women, or the 3.6 million people who (at the time of writing) had watched the Halloween pumpkin-themed video.

The last days of Rome

If sex changes us as individuals, it follows that sexual mores can change society. Social anthropologist J. D. Unwin examined the data from 86 societies and civilisations over five thousand years of history to see if there is a relationship between sexual freedom and the flourishing of cultures.[34] In the resulting book *Sex and Culture*, he set out that after a nation becomes prosperous, it becomes increasingly liberal concerning sexual morality, which then causes it to lose cohesion, impetus and purpose (consider, the word 'decadence' comes from the root word 'decay'). This, he says, is irrevocable.

Sexual constraints (especially pre-nuptial chastity and monogamy) lead to a flourishing of culture, while increased sexual freedoms lead to the collapse of culture, according to Unwin. The idea of rowing back on sexual freedom is an anathema to our culture today. However, what makes his theories interesting is that we in the West underwent a sexual revolution from the late 1960s and we will soon be able to assess his conclusions for ourselves.

Historical examples are not hard to come by. The French Revolution was preceded by the kind of libertine culture personified by the Marquis de Sade, from whom we get the word 'sadism'. When we say something is like 'The Last Days of Rome', it brings to mind images of orgiastic debauchery. Weimar Germany was famously decadent, before the Nazis.

Today, we dangle precariously at the precipice. There seems to be no recourse to stop events like 'Drag Queen Story Time for Under-Fives' at public libraries, nor surgeons giving double mastectomies or irreversible hormones to teenagers, nor the explosive rise of OnlyFans among young girls. The fashion brand Balenciaga's autumn 2022 campaign included a photoshoot of prepubescent girls playing with teddy bears decked in bondage gear.[35] A handbag was pictured atop printouts from the 2008 Supreme Court case 'United States v. Williams', about child pornography.

This surely is not sustainable. Indeed, societies are exhibiting a sort of immune system response. In September 2022, Italy elected right-wing Giorgia Meloni as its new prime minister. Meloni has assertively defended 'God, fatherland and family' and denounced 'gender ideology'.[36] Russia has introduced hefty fines for those accused of spreading LGBT propaganda, particularly to children.[37]

The issue here is not to police what people get up to in the privacy of their own bedrooms – who cares, really? – but rather to each take responsibility for our own passions. It is up to every one of us to stop watching porn and avoid being a slave to sexual programming. To do otherwise is ultimately an irresistible route to brainwashing and political control.

The rules:

- Stop using pornography, but if you must continue, try to tone down your usage as it can leave you psychologically malleable.
- Treat sex with the respect it deserves: it is a powerful tool for bonding with a partner but can otherwise be a tool for your own conditioning.

- Learn to control your passions and exercise restraint, else society could be heading for collapse, not to mention you.

17

Choose your illusion

The universe is infinitely big, and our brains are minuscule by comparison, so we can each only see a tiny slice of reality. Much of what we sense as reality is actually an illusion and there's no way around that. However, we can use that fact to our advantage, and each choose the perceived world we want to live in.

No one is safe

'I've studied magic for many years and I still fall for magic tricks,' admitted magician and professor of psychology, Gustav Kuhn.

'Just because you know how magic works, doesn't mean you can't be deceived any more. Especially if you change the context. Magicians aren't resilient to fraudsters. I was taken in by a scam once and I know many magicians who've been taken in by them as well. We are all susceptible to these biases and limitations.'

Jason Deverell, Secretary of the Magic Circle, recounted his exam to get in:

> I was two years into my journey in magic and presenting to 70 people. For my first effect, I did something everyone knew but followed up with something they weren't

> expecting, and they all gasped. These are people who know magic, but on the offbeat I caught a lot of people out. So how can you not be fooled? Even if you know the techniques, you follow a train of thought that leaves you exposed to something that's outside of that stage.

The fact is the world is too complex for any of us to analyse rationally and in its entirety, so we all have to rely on time-saving mental shortcuts, even people who are aware that these shortcuts exist. While some measure of immunity is possible, researchers have shown that teaching people about a bias, or even telling them it's about to be used on them, does not always stop it from working.

For example, you might think that behavioural scientists are immune to the techniques of behavioural science. An experiment had over seven hundred psychologists rate the quality of a scientific study, in which the researchers used individual differences to predict behaviours such as drinking alcohol.[1] Half of the psychologists read about a study where these behaviours were predicted by personality traits; for the other half, the behaviours were predicted by astrological star signs. Even though the methodology and analyses were exactly the same for both, the psychologists rated the personality paper as significantly better. Psychologists are more likely than anyone to know about 'confirmation bias' (where you look for evidence to support your prior beliefs), and yet they still fell for it. Similarly, a paper published in *Nature Reviews Psychology* in 2022 suggested that behavioural scientists are prone to 'functional fixedness' (where someone can only fixate on a single solution to a problem – or, in other words, 'to a hammer, everything looks like a nail'), focusing on solving problems with nudges even when it's not appropriate.[2]

A stark illustration comes in the form of UCL psychology professor Susan Michie. Professor Michie advised the British government on Covid-19 pandemic policy as a member of the

Scientific Advisory Group for Emergencies (SAGE) and is now the chair of the World Health Organization's behavioural science advisory group. Given the massive increase in state control and destruction of private industry that happened under lockdown, you might think it relevant that Professor Michie is a communist – not in the metaphorical sense ('John wants lower taxes, *what a communist*'), but a literal member of the Communist Party of Britain. When challenged on daytime television that her politics might influence her recommendations, Michie refused to answer the question, and hid behind some variation of the word 'science' six times in her brief response, including the scoff that she 'agreed to come on this programme as a scientist'. The implication is that Michie's science is pure and untainted by her political perspective – a bizarre claim to be made by someone who has dedicated their career to understanding how bias influences behaviour. The behavioural science community largely leapt to Michie's defence in the following days, arguing that her communism was completely unrelated to her work, and that it was sexist to ask.[3] This might have something to do with liberals outnumbering conservatives in psychology departments by fourteen to one, by one count.[4]

The point is, when even the nudgers themselves are biased and nudge-able, you simply cannot *not* be influenced. As Aldous Huxley said, 'There seems to be a touching belief among certain Ph.D.'s in sociology that Ph.D.'s in sociology will never be corrupted by power.'[5]

Look at the Müller-Lyer illusion below, for example. Which line is longer?

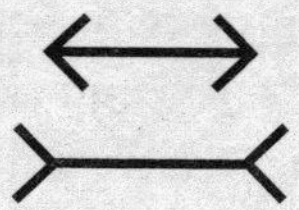

You probably know the answer: both lines are the same length. You know it, rationally, and yet you can't unsee the illusion.

The same is true of persuasion: even if you know about persuasive tactics, you can still be influenced by them. The consumer realities that are crafted for us by the ad men of Madison Avenue are simply inescapable: it is not possible to extricate oneself from culture. A famous ethnographical study of the Burning Man festival (where attendees are encouraged to barter and to express themselves through handcrafting rather than through, say, branded clothing) concluded that 'perhaps it is not possible to completely evade the market': attendees still use Visa cards to pay for their $400 ticket, after all.[6]

You cannot escape the matrix. Even the movie, *The Matrix*, is a great example of the fact. In the film, the characters can never truly leave the fake reality created by a system of corporate interests, which keeps people asleep so that said system can extract their energy. Ironically, the movie itself is nothing more than a consumerist distraction on the silver screen, using the latest computer-generated imagery to bamboozle and amaze its popcorn-grazing audiences.

'*The Matrix* is surely the kind of film about the matrix that the matrix would have been able to produce,' said philosopher Jean Baudrillard (whose book *Simulacra and Simulation* appeared as a prop in the movie).[7]

Short of living in a flotation tank in Siberia, there is no way to avoid social contact and persuasive information – and thus there is no way to avoid brainwashing, one way or another. You are most likely brainwashed yourself. Whatever your opinions and habits may be, they probably originated from an outside source, or at least were influenced by it. You may have learnt them from your parents or schoolteachers, or perhaps they were triggered by a television show or advertisement, or even inspired by watching squirrels frolicking in the park.

This is what makes Professor Michie's suggestion about being an arbiter of pure science so absurd. It is simply impossible to be unbiased – every belief we have has in some way been shaped by the world around us.

Everyone believes their beliefs

People tend to believe they are responsible for their beliefs, and that these beliefs are an unbiased reflection of the real world. This is called 'naïve realism'.[8] We tend to think that our perception is the perception of an objective truth, and that if other people can't see it, it must be because they are bad, stupid, or both.

In short, everyone believes their beliefs, and everyone believes 'the other side' is foolish for not believing them too.

Some people supported Hillary Clinton in 2016 and believed that Trump supporters were hicks brainwashed by Russian trolls; some people supported Donald Trump and believed that Clinton supporters were liberal arts students brainwashed by CNN. Some people believe there is no God and that the faithful are brainwashed by organised religion, while some of the faithful believe the unbelievers are brainwashed by secular society. Echoing CNN's coverage of Black Lives Matter's 'fiery but mostly peaceful protests', psychologists have shown that some people can look at a picture and see a peaceful protest, while others see an unruly mob, depending on their socio-political beliefs.[9]

The point is, every one of these groups has an imperfect view of the truth, and every one of them is right that their opposition is brainwashed in some way. We are all brainwashed. Our view of reality is influenced by the information we are exposed to, and we all believe our view is the right one.

It's like the allegory of the blind men and the elephant. Each of the blind men touches a different part of the elephant, and so each of them is exposed to different pieces of information that informs their perception of reality. The blind man holding the tail believes it's a rope; at the trunk, a snake; at the leg, the man exclaims, 'It's a tree!'

It is unlikely that one side of a debate will ever have a monopoly on the truth. One side could argue, for example, that the vast majority of rapists are men; another side could argue that the vast majority of men are not rapists. These facts are both true, but they are used to support different perceptions of the same reality. The much-derided idea of alternative facts may have some merit after all.

People live in what could be considered different planes of reality. This is especially true today. On both sides of the political spectrum, people are 'awakening' into a new dimension. One side is becoming woke, the other red-pilled.

In a November 2021 YouGov poll taken before the jury delivered their verdict on Kyle Rittenhouse, 45 per cent of Americans said he should be found guilty of murder while 32 per cent said he should not.[10] This polarisation was particularly clear along political lines: 76 per cent of Democrats said yes compared with just 15 per cent of Republicans. It seems that two people could watch exactly the same footage but draw entirely different conclusions. Some saw Rittenhouse as a domestic terrorist, some as a defender of the peace.

Similarly, another YouGov poll found that 9 per cent of Brits believed the BBC has a *pro-Brexit* bias.[11] Former Labour minister Andrew Adonis tweeted that 'the Brexit bias is now so deep the BBC doesn't even realise it'. Accusations of pro-Brexit bias might be surprising to some – a not insignificant number of people could watch the same coverage and have an entirely different perception of it.

These alternate realities may be forming because people like to curate the information they consume. 'Confirmation bias' tells us that people seek out information that supports their pre-existing beliefs,[12] while the 'ostrich effect' tells us that people avoid information that makes them uncomfortable.[13] Having our beliefs challenged produces an unpleasant feeling of cognitive dissonance – it's hard work. As a result, people tend to silo themselves into comfortable echo chambers ('epistemic bubbles', to give them their proper name)[14] by ditching social media contacts they don't like.[15] Media platforms probably compound the problem by disabling comments (in the case of news sites) or dislikes (in the case of YouTube), preventing these bubbles from being popped by external feedback.

People may even create these bubbles in person. A 2020 YouGov poll found that 19 per cent of American adults have zero friends with very different political views, which was up from 7 per cent in 2016.[16] A 2021 Axios poll found that 71 per cent of Democrats would not go on a date with someone who voted for the opposing political candidate.[17] The internet is scattered with stories about people who broke contact with friends or even family members thanks to political disagreements.

In short, people see what they want to see, and they do so to gratify psychological needs.

One academic paper – 'Thirty shades of truth: Conspiracy theories as stories of individuation, not of pathological delusion' – gave 30 people flash cards with statements about 9/11 from which they could construct a narrative.[18] The statements were a range of official (like, '9/11 masterminds were Islamist terrorists, led by Osama bin Laden, to attack the detested Western culture') and conspiratorial (like, 'The US administration had planned and conducted the 9/11 attack to justify the wars in Afghanistan and Iraq'). Only one participant's story contained absolutely no conspiratorial allegations – and she was the only participant to say she had no interest in the topic. The rest of the stories were a mix of official and conspiratorial statements. Everyone constructed their own story, and every story was different. The implication is that people build their own narratives to fit their view of the world and suit their psychological needs. Indeed, researchers have argued that so-called conspiracy theories have psychological benefits, giving people purpose and structure, protecting self-esteem and acting as a warning system for marginalised groups.[19]

Others could argue that the academics, presuming the so-called conspiracy theories are false in the first place, are themselves crafting a narrative that serves them psychologically – a defence mechanism of denial that protects their psyche from the horrifying truth.

The arrogant academic and the kooky conspiracy theorist are both metaphorical blind men grasping at an elephant.

Misdirection and redirection

There is a Gnostic allegory that likens the night sky to a black veil covering reality; the stars are pinpricks in the veil through which the light of truth shines through. Each of us, with our limited brains and imperfect sense perception, is only able to view reality through our own pinhole. A very clever experimental psychology method called the 'moving-window technique' illustrates the point: as people read text on a screen, for instance, an eye-tracking device follows their gaze, while a computer turns all of the text outside of their focus into gibberish.[20] Beyond this very narrow window of perception, participants did not notice the changing text. In life, as in this experiment, we are only able to focus on a tiny slice of the world. We do not have an all-seeing eye capable of processing every piece of information.[21] Brainwashers operate by directing and misdirecting our limited attention.

This is how magicians bamboozle us. As magician Jason Deverell explained,

> If I look at magic, you've got a stage or a close-up mat you're trying to present to a small group of people, and that's what you want the audience to focus on. But it's what's going on outside that space, what the audience *doesn't* see, that creates the magic. You line people up in one direction and the magic is when the direction doesn't conclude in the way they expect.

Our sense-making is not as fixed and objective as we tend to believe – a lot of what we believe to be tangible reality is constructed by our minds. The map is not the territory, so the saying goes.

Take, for example, the eye's blind spot. Where the optic nerve meets the retina, there are no light-detecting cells, resulting in a gap in our vision. Yet our minds fill in this gap with its best guess. For example, close one eye and pick the letter below for the eye that's open (pick R if your right eye is open, L if the left). Focus on the letter and move your head towards it. Eventually the other letter will disappear, and be 'filled in' by your brain with the colour and texture of the page.

R L

Our brain continually constructs reality based on piecemeal fragments like this. Our idea of reality is not fixed, and it is not objective. Many psychological experiments have demonstrated this. Most famously, University of Washington psychologists Elizabeth Loftus and John Palmer had participants watch a film about a car accident, and a week later they were quizzed on what they remembered.[22] Participants were asked if they saw any broken glass (which there wasn't); some were asked how fast the cars were going when they 'hit' each other, while others were asked how fast the cars were going when they 'smashed into' each other. In the 'hit' condition, 7 per cent of participants claimed to remember broken glass, compared with 16 per cent in the 'smashed' condition. Memories were reconstructed in real time according to the information that was fed in. Today, psychologists call this the 'misinformation effect'.

The implication is that you turn into what you tune into; or, as the philosopher Epictetus said, 'You become what you give your attention to.'[23]

Thus, you can brainwash yourself, for the better. You can choose your illusion. By focusing on the good, the true and the beautiful, you can change your perception of reality itself. Many of us consume bilious Twitter feeds, depressing news stories and materialistic advertisements, and these probably colour our perception of what the world is like. In fact, research has linked all of social media consumption,[24] news exposure[25] and prevalence of advertising[26] to negative mental health outcomes.

A consistent theme among the people we talked to for this book was the need to get away from the news. Many of them had stopped watching it. Fact-checker Will Moy wondered whether 'part of the answer is to read less news. I don't think news every second is good for us. We feel bruised by constant exposure to traumatic things.'

Many people believe that the world is literally ending due to climate change,[27] even though the number of people killed by weather disasters has declined from half a million in the 1920s to below eighteen thousand today, and the gloom and doom of the news will rarely tell you that, for example, in 2022 two-thirds of the Great Barrier Reef showed the greatest coral cover since records began, and that worldwide polar bear numbers are at a record high.[28]

Jodie Jackson founded the News Literacy Labs and wrote the book *You Are What You Read: Why Changing Your Media Diet Can Change the World*. She cited a statistic from the 2019 Reuter's Digital News Report that says 46 per cent of people are actively avoiding the news every day because it is too depressing. The news reports on the worst things happening in the world at any given moment, giving us endless coverage of conflict, violence and corruption. The term for this preference for negative content within newsrooms is, 'If it bleeds, it leads.' This focus is because of our own innate negativity bias:

> Both the journalists and consumers have a negativity bias. There is deep value in reporting on and learning about problems. Because unless we are made aware of a

> problem, we are not in a position to be able to confront and correct it. But the excess of negativity means that what was once helpful is now becoming harmful, creating a sense of urgent importance without resolution. We can understand this better by looking at how our relationship with food has changed. Fatty foods and sweet foods used to be adaptive. Evolutionarily it made sense because of lean periods of starvation and the notion that sour foods were more likely to be poisonous. Now that we have sweet and fatty foods in abundance, this adaptive function has become maladaptive. It's the same with our negativity bias. It's not good for the health of our minds to be in this constant state of negativity and sensationalism. Having excessive negative reporting over time can make us generally anxious, depressed, and helpless. It can make us desensitised. If the news were any other product, it would be recalled, or if not, at least relabelled.

Jodie advocates for problems' solutions to be better included into our media diet so that we can seek to understand progress as much as failure. This would increase optimism and hope. 'Just by changing your information space you can change your whole environment,' she says. 'That's so powerful.'

So, what if we consumed something different? What if we could brainwash ourselves? If we made a point of reading poetry rather than the news, would we not live in a more poetic world?

Scientific studies do in fact show that reading poetry can improve wellbeing.[29] Others support the power of positive self-affirmation: if you repeat to yourself that you are a certain way, it becomes a self-fulfilling prophecy.[30] You can indeed 'fake it until you make it'.

Alan Gray, a psychologist specialising in online influencers at influencer marketing agency Tailify, made a profound point:

It's hard not to be influenced by influencers! But influence is not all bad. You can select to be influenced for the better. You can choose who you're going to follow and who will have an impact on your life. You can choose, for example, to only follow people with the same passions and values as you. You can add and follow people on a whim, but maybe that's something that shouldn't be taken so lightly. We don't just pick up any book. Just like you might read poetry to help you reach an ideal self, maybe that can be true of the people you follow too.

Whatever our vision of reality, we can change it. Remember, Plato's allegory of the cave suggests that most people watch flickers of firelight on the cave wall, believing the dancing shadows to be reality. Our minds are too small to step out of the cave and into the vastness of truth. All we can do is move from one cave to another.

If you don't like your cave – if it's dark and dirty and depressing – why not leave it? If you are going to live under some form of illusion, why not choose it yourself?

The rules:

- Recognise that your view of the world is imperfect and that those you disagree with believe their beliefs as surely as you believe yours.
- Take control of your perception of reality by consuming content that will help your health, happiness and productivity.
- Try to get a sense for where your perception of reality comes from and consider if those sources are helping or harming you in the long run.

18

Confronting my shadow in the woods

By Patrick

'You're a disappointment. I never liked you.'

This was the cruelty volleyed upon me by my father, standing proud in a blood red cape, chest thrust forward. I screamed profanities drawn from a void deep within, struggling against the duct tape binding my body, and the half a dozen men holding me back.

Behind me, another version of my father told me he was proud of me.

Well, it wasn't my father per se: it was a man *role-playing a projection of my father*. I was at a masculinity retreat in the woods, confronting what Jung would call my shadow. It was an adventure that would variously see me carrying a stretcher through a midnight forest, losing myself in some wild interpretive dance and brandishing a wooden phallus among a circle of naked men as I confessed my sexual insecurities. In the days beforehand, my wife had written 'Patrick at cult' on our whiteboard planner in the kitchen. It was advertised slightly differently – as a hero's journey.

One thing they don't tell you about taking a hero's journey, though, is that sometimes the hero gets stuck in 90 minutes of traffic on the M5 – as indeed I had on my way to the retreat. Much like Odysseus was waylaid by the Sirens, I had been distracted from my noble quest by a slightly dinged-up BMW. Being stuck like this, I came to learn, was an apt metaphor for my life.

The journey took me five hours in total. I travelled down winding roads deep in the woods, as if I were destined for *The Shining*'s Overlook Hotel. As I stopped to check my route, an owl screamed at me from the darkness. I was a long way from home.

The retreat had heavily encouraged us to carpool. Had I done so, I would have felt even more trapped. (My fear of small talk had saved me.)

I crawled to the front gate, sheepish about my lateness. A man stepped out of the shadows. He wasn't happy, and he let me know.

'What time did you say you'd be here? And what time is it now? You're over an hour late. See that man.'

I made my way to another humourless figure decked in black. This would be a theme for the initiation. Every few feet or so I had to pick up my bags, see another man and put my bags down again. It was a humiliating ritual that stripped me of my autonomy. Little did I know what was to come.

I was eventually directed into an unlit room where I was relieved of my ego entirely. I was no longer Patrick Fagan but rather the number they assigned me: 37. I handed over my smartphone, my car keys, my toiletries, my snacks – everything but the most basic essentials. I was asked to remove anything sacred. My entire identity was dumped into a series of plastic and paper bags.

There were no watches either – or clocks. There was to be no sense of time for the rest of the weekend. The events passed as a sort of formless black hole, a *Twilight Zone* between dawn and dusk. Whenever a staff-member was asked how long an activity would take, the answer was always the same: 'The time is a mystery.'

I was herded into a dark, tiny room, about the size of a bathroom, and instructed to sit on the floor. It was hard to breathe in the room, and hard to sit down too, on account of the 35 other men in there. I tiptoed into the last remaining spot. It was uncomfortable, but it was only a couple of minutes before we were called out into the main room. 'Oh,' I thought. 'That wasn't so bad.'

The other men, like me, had been made to sit in the dark, tiny room upon arrival. The only *slight* difference was that they had been made to stay there until the arrival of the last man (me). I learnt this during a sort of struggle session. We all sat on the floor facing the men decked in black. One of them was carrying a big stick – but he wasn't speaking softly.

'Who was the last man here? Stand up, 37. What do you think the consequences of your actions have been on these men?'

'I have a horrible feeling they were sat in that room waiting for me.'

'And what do you imagine that was like for them?'

'Pretty horrible?'

'Who was the first man here? Stand up 28. Tell 37 what it was like.'

'Yeah, I was there for two hours. It was fucking shit. I have a bad knee, it's killing me. It was really bad,' said 28.

'What do you have to say, 37?'

'I'm sorry. I was stuck in traffic.'

'Sorry doesn't cut it here. How are you going to make it up to 28?'

'Um ... I don't know? I'll help you on one of the activities this weekend?'

'Do you accept this, 28?'

'No. It's not good enough,' he said.

'What else do you have to offer, 37?'

'Uh ... I don't have anything of worth? I don't know ... Uh ... I can give you some psychology insights?'

'What kind of message do you think it gives 28 when you turn up so late?'

'That he's not important?'

'Tell 28.'

'You're ... But I don't believe that?'

'Tell 28.'

'You're not important.'

'No. Tell 28 what the effect on him was.'

'Oh. I made you feel like you're not important.'

'And why would you make people feel that way?'

'Because I feel that way myself?'

'Why is that?'

'Um, because I've never felt truly loved or wanted?'

'Sit down, 37.'

I'm not sure what happened. It wasn't my fault I was stuck in traffic, and the situation with the dark, tiny room had been engineered by the retreat, not me. Besides, every single man there had consented to this. It was not Guantanamo Bay. At any moment anyone could say, 'No, this is not my cup of tea, thank you.'

Coercion rarely happens without your consent.

The ordeal swept away any lingering ego. I was subjugated fully to the process. The entire weekend seemed designed to weaken critical resistance. The only food was an occasional bowl of nuts and roughly chopped fruit, the type of food you might normally see in a bucket, at the zoo. All 36 men slept together in the same room, on the floor. The snoring of one man alone would have been enough to dispel a night's sleep. One night, water dripped on me from the window above. Another night, the fire alarm wailed at 3am. Outside of the activities, attendees were always to 'maintain essential silence' rather than talking to one another. The end result was to be hungry, anxious, lonely and tired – the perfect recipe for breaking down mental barriers.

At the start, the stress position of the dark, tiny room had probably softened up the other attendees even more so. Being late, I had something of an advantage – not to mention I was less hungry than them since, although I *had* been stuck in traffic, I had also stopped for a large Burger King on the way. As the evening's rituals began, I could still taste the pickles percolating in my guilty belly.

That night's events served to break us down further. We had to fill in a quiz that really put the personal in 'personality test'. It probed agreement with statements like 'My mother seduced me physically,' 'My cock is too small' and 'I have killed a human.' There were a lot of questions about my mother – but the joke was on them, since my mother died when I was a child. Psychoanalyse *that*! We were paired with strangers and made to tell them what we thought of their appearance, among other things.

After a sleepless night, we were woken before sunrise and collectively marched outside, naked, for a cold shower. It was November. Consider my ego well and truly stripped. The psychological conditions were perfect to delve into my subconscious and meet my shadow.

The experiences I was part of during the 'hero's journey' are too intimate to recount. Suffice to say at one point I role-played as another attendee's mother, adorned with a purple robe and clutching two plums – his testicles – in my hand, while he screamed at me. He had been asked to pick someone to be his mother and turned without hesitation to me. It was not quite the feeling I had been hoping for from a masculinity retreat.

Watching the other men scream and cry, I thought there was no way I would crumble like that. I did.

There was a lot of trauma in that room. A lot of pain. I learnt much about fatherhood. I hoped that I wouldn't bring the kind of sadness I saw there onto my own son. I vowed to always let him have his voice, and to always let him know he's good enough.

After a long day battling the subconscious, we were told to strip naked again. Well, except for our boots and a blindfold – not strictly naked then, so why not pop on some pants? We held hands in a line. I was pulled out into the November air. My skin was freckled both by rain and by embers from a bonfire. Strange sounds encircled me and fell away into the pounding of drums. Something stirred deep within my heart – an ancestral memory, an ancient spirit kept sedated by a lifetime of office work and Netflix.

We snaked back into the main room, which had been plunged into darkness save for an assembly of candles flickering in the centre. Shadows danced on the grinning faces and naked bodies of my brothers. The drumbeats returned. We danced and yelled and chanted and gurned late into the night.

'Hoo-rah! Rah! Hoo-rah! Rah! Hoo-rah, hoo-rah, hoo-rah, rah! Raaaaaaaaah!'

I had been initiated.

That night I felt the raw, untapped power of masculinity. It was the power of the Spartans, of the Mongols, of William Wallace. I understood why modern culture calls masculinity toxic, why it shows fathers as Homer Simpsons, why it promotes pornography consumption, comfort and estrogenic foods. Men, united by brotherhood and given purpose, with their masculine power unleashed, are a force of nature. No system of control would stand a chance.

The next morning brought a sense of renewal. We crawled into a sweat lodge where, in the steam and the darkness and the frankincense, I saw the eye of God. Naked, I slithered out through the flaps of the tent on my belly, into the cold light. I had been reborn.

At the jovial goodbye feast (no fruit or nuts), I felt relief, ecstasy, and yes, a sense of brotherhood.

It is impossible to put the weekend into words. A rite of passage like this can only be experienced. This is why they tend to come with a symbol or talisman, of which the meaning is inscrutable to the uninitiated. I have mine in my bedside drawer.

Back home, I feel refreshed and clear. I can hear the birds singing; the light seems brighter, the air cleaner. I have a renewed relationship with my wife – 'How much was it again? Worth every penny! Every penny!' I am transformed as a father.

My weekend in the woods undoubtedly used the techniques discussed in this book. I was hungry and tired, I was stripped of my ego and the symbolism was intense. But these are common to rites of passage throughout history, and at the moment I simply feel grateful for the experience. Isn't it good to give your brain a little wash now and then?

19

Stop haunting yourself

When you are manipulated, half of the problem is the messaging itself, but half of the problem is you. Persuaders from pick-up artists to propagandists do their worst by exploiting human weak spots, foibles and insecurities. To defend against brainwashing, you need to understand your own psychological weaknesses and stop haunting yourself.

A state of fear

'When I got home I stripped off in the conservatory because I didn't want to contaminate the house with my clothes. I put my clothes in a plastic bag and I threw my shoes away! I sat in the hottest bath I could, for as long as I could, scrubbing every inch of myself. I looked like a lobster when I got out.'

You might be wondering whether Darren had been exposed to a dangerous radiation leak. Or whether, perhaps, he had fallen into a sewage treatment plant.

No, this dramatic behaviour was prompted by a routine visit to his local hospital to monitor his cancer. The key component in this story was that this was the first time he had left his house after seven weeks' lockdown during the Covid-19 pandemic.[1]

When he finally plucked up the courage to attend an appointment, he chose to drive to the hospital rather than walk the short journey, because he didn't want to risk breathing in the exhalations of passers-by. Upon arriving, the ritualised dispensation of masks and gloves, the spaced-out chairs and the precautionary dots on the ground indicating where to stand all added to the sense of danger. He found himself unusually furious with people who came too close to him.

It's important to caveat that the fear of infection, pandemic and death are normal. Darren's fears were justified, especially given that his cancer made him clinically more vulnerable to Covid-19. However, in order to encourage populations to comply with the non-pharmaceutical interventions to manage the pandemic – such as sheltering at home, lockdowns, social distancing and face coverings – some governments and public health authorities deliberately amplified fears. Even if this was done with the best intentions, people were – in effect – scared into staying at home. Darren's natural fears were put on steroids.

He didn't leave the house for 11 weeks apart from this one terrifying trip to hospital. The fears started with letters, and 'lots of texts' from the NHS and government (not unreasonably, given his health status). Clearly, governments have a responsibility to communicate with citizens to inform them of genuine threats. But, to him, it *felt* like a lot. The ideas conveyed by the government were bellows to Darren's pre-existing fears. The media – which he and his wife gorged on with little else to do while locked down at home – reinforced this messaging:

> There wasn't much to do, so we'd watch TV and we saw programmes about disinfecting your shopping when it arrives, and having a safe zone in the kitchen. The nightly bulletins on the TV about death tolls, the big graphs with huge spikes on them, came at us 'boom, boom, boom!' It was a constant barrage of doom and gloom. My fear of the virus went through the roof.

The bath when he returned home was self-evidently intended to scrub the potential infection from Covid from his body, but it was also a rite of passage, a psychological cleansing. Just as Odysseus bathed on Ithaca to mark the end of his legendary odyssey, so Darren symbolically washed away the fear and exertion of his epic journey.

Self-haunting

Dr Colin Alexander, Senior Lecturer in Political Communications, observed that the media and politicians chose their language carefully in Covid-19 communications, in order to heighten the emotional response.

> The important aspect of fear-mongering propaganda is not the specifics of the content, or the descent into negative terminology. It is that the propagandist understands that the scared person is less likely to have their rational thinking in primacy, they are more likely to accept atrocities in some form or another. The language of the propaganda is only part of the story, the rest of it is 'self-haunting'.

Alexander points out that while self-haunting has not been applied in the context of a pandemic before, it is a term that has been used in several disciplines. In psychology, Hermann Rorschach studied the process through which we internalise meaning from seemingly nondescript objects. For instance, a child might see an object on the bedroom floor through the darkness and imagine it to be a monster. The Roman philosopher Seneca said that 'the things you run from are inside you', and 'we suffer more in imagination than reality'.[2] Indeed, one psychology paper entitled 'Fear in the theater of the mind', by using surveys and skin conductance, found that imagined fears are as scary as real ones.[3]

Glenn Greenwald at The Intercept published influence techniques outlined in a GCHQ document called 'The art of deception: Training for a new generation of online covert operations'.[4] The document has since been shared in full by the American Civil Liberties Union (ACLU), too.[5] One of the techniques it describes is using 'story fragments' to lead people to the conclusion you want them to reach. People have a hardwired tendency towards sense-making, which means they can be relied upon to create stories if you simply leave the ingredients scattered around. The British Navy famously dressed a homeless man's corpse in uniform, strapped a briefcase of misleading documents to his body, and threw him overboard, trusting the Germans would find him, fill in the missing pieces and fall for the ruse.[6] Manipulators rely on the fact that you will invent fictions and haunt yourself: they provide the shadows on the wall and trust you will turn them into the monster under the bed.

Alexander says self-haunting 'reflects what is able to capture the individual's attention. A process encouraged at least in part at the behest of fear-mongering propagandists and their strategists who try to attach whatever their subject matter is to concerns that already exist within the self.'[7] What captures your attention? It could be the fears and insecurities common to us all, such as fear of death, or ostracization fear for your children's futures, insecurity about appearance, loneliness, or monsters in the cupboard. Self-haunting can also arise from experiences that might have been traumatic or imprinting. We are a psychological blueprint born of common human psychology, genetics, our family and upbringing, culture and unique experiences. Our psychological blind spots – emotional landmines – are exploited to gain our attention and command our behaviour. The answer lies in understanding ourselves.

It can be difficult to recognise our own weak spots. When Darren reflected on the pandemic, he was surprised that fear took such a grip of him. He thought of himself as robust. He had served as a police officer for 32 years and not much could throw him. Yet his clinical vulnerabilities, including cancer, meant he was primed when the messaging started. He was part of the cohort of people who needed to take particular care, but his fears escalated beyond the scale of the threat, and became obsessive and long-lasting. Darren's clinical morbidities were an 'emotional landmine' and made him particularly susceptible to the fear messaging.

The role of emotion is known to the advertisers, the propagandists and the self-styled guardians of truth. Hence, fact-checking company Full Fact, in its briefing paper 'Who is most likely to believe and to share misinformation?', concludes that we all tend to share information high in emotion.[8]

The most viral campaigns often use what is known by animal behaviourists as 'trigger stacking' – they layer multiple fears on top of one another.[9] For example, a viral story in April 2022 claimed that Covid-19 was caused by snake venom in the water supply.[10] The story tapped into three fears: that of disease, of snakes and the ancient fear of a traitor poisoning the well.

One social media hoax during the pandemic demonstrated that hope, rather than fear, can spark the sharing of misinformation. In October 2020 a sixth-form student from York created a Twitter account named @UKWoolworths. The bio read: 'Britain's most loved … and missed … retailer, and back on your Twitter'. The account claimed that the high street shop would re-open in 2021. The account was not verified, the website did not work and the tweets contained spelling mistakes. And yet the good people of Twitter fell for it (including one of this book's authors) and multiple media outlets reported it as truth. Why?

The fake account offered to 'save 2020'. This was a time when people were still enduring restrictions, physical shopping had been limited and high street businesses had closed. Hope was the emotion that was manipulated, and the emotional landmines were depression and insecurity induced by the pandemic responses and economic fallout. The student astutely chose Woolworths because of its 'nostalgic appeal'. The resulting disappointment of pic 'n' mix not coming back to the high street really brought alive Nietzsche's words, 'Hope in reality is the worst of all evils because it prolongs the torments of man.'[11]

Big virtue words appeal to hope, and are often used in political advertising and propaganda. When someone talks about what we must do to 'preserve democracy' you will inevitably project your own hopes for democracy onto their words. Donald Trump's 'Make America Great Again' slogan is a prime example. Barack Obama's 'Hope' campaign featured an incredibly simple representation of his face with the word 'hope' underneath, conveying the idea that only he could bring hope to the nation.

No doubt it has ever been thus; advertisers and leaders with the inclination to do so have pillaged our emotions. Back in the 1950s, PR man Mr Miller warned: 'What degree of intensity is proper in seeking to arouse desire, hatred, envy, cupidity, hope, or any of the great gamut of human emotions on which he must play ... One of the fundamental considerations involved here is the right to manipulate human personality.'[12] Such a manipulation, he went on to say, inherently involves a disrespect for the individual personality.

Propaganda and persuasion work when attached to pre-existing passions and preoccupations. It doesn't have to be fear of a virus. As Alexander said:

> Once you are encouraged to be scared it attaches itself to the fears you already have. I am a dad of two boys so I have fears for their future. If you have money fears you may fear for your financial future. This is your nudge moment. You are nudged to self-haunting. So you are more susceptible to self-haunting. The propaganda does half the job, the audience member does the other half.

And let's face it, we all have our problems. From minor character flaws to fully fledged inner demons marauding our mind, we all have psychological predispositions that make us more susceptible to certain types of messaging. As Emily Dickinson wrote:

One need not be a chamber – to be haunted –
One need not be a House –
The Brain – has Corridors surpassing
Material Place.

Your emotional landmines

If propaganda were a garment, it would need a hook inside your brain. Do you know what your hooks are? And what makes some people more susceptible than others? It may depend on the messaging and media, your own perspective and life experience at that time, as well as the environment and community around you. Dominic Cummings, former Chief Advisor to British Prime Minister Boris Johnson, tweeted on 12 May 2022 that 'Social-science-#FBPE-twatter, always the easiest to fool with propaganda, believe what they read in papers, perpetual groupthink & hysteria'. This offers clues to the 'unofficial' views about who is suggestible and why.

In another example of fear-based appeals, firearms advertising in the US likens guns to home protection and burglar alarms. Women, spurred on by fear of crime and being caught unprepared, are the fastest-growing segment of buyers.[13]

The point is, manipulation works best when it is a lightning rod for your own personal foibles. The famous book *The 48 Laws of Power* advised would-be manipulators: 'Always look for passions and obsessions that cannot be controlled.'[14]

In nature, for example, a mousetrap has its tasty bit of cheese, an angler fish has its alluring light and a Venus flytrap has its sweet, red petals. They all exploit their targets' own emotions and desires – their internal 'ghosts' and 'demons'. In the study of scams, it's known as the 'need and greed' principle.[15] Your desires make you vulnerable, and hustlers can easily manipulate you once they know what you want. As in many apocryphal tales throughout history, like the tale of the monkey's paw, you must be careful what you wish for. Romance scams exploit people's lust and loneliness. Fake model agency scams ensnare young women outside of fashion retailers and exploit their wish to be famous. All it takes is one photoshoot, though you do have to pay for it ...

An ex-multi-level marketing member, speaking anonymously, explained a similar principle with pyramid schemes:

> They prey on very vulnerable groups, like young mums with kids struggling with the family finances. They say, 'You don't wanna go to work and leave your kids with a babysitter, do you? That's not being a good mum. If you work with us, you can work from home and see their first steps.' They are playing on guilt. In reality, you end up living your life on the phone. What's the person's pain point? What is the thing you can comfort them with? It's a deliberate strategy. You look for what it is that the person needs. What do they need? Is it financial? Then tell them it's free to join. They home in on the person's weaknesses.

Psychological research has recently identified seven basic motivations that can be exploited: evading physical harm, avoiding disease, making friends, attaining status, acquiring a mate, keeping a mate and caring for family.[16] The passions that manipulators exploit are nothing new: greed, lust, pride and so on. They are used to enslave you. Saint Augustine of Hippo once said that man has 'as many masters as he has vices'.[17] Indeed, another potent tool for self-haunting is envy. The exploitation of body-image insecurity is commonly used in advertising, particularly nowadays on social media, where cosmetics, shape-wear and plastic surgery advertisers abound.

Listerine was once sold only as an antiseptic, but the company saw the opportunity to market it as a mouthwash and toothpaste to exploit the shame of bad breath. 'Halitosis makes you unpopular,' warned an early ad. These fears that brands exploit are not unique to you but identifiably common: being shamed, failure, dependency, conflict, threat, not belonging or being excluded, missing out, peer pressure, illness and, the big one, death.

There is also the fear of being alone. Famous dating expert Matthew Hussey offers courses for women designed to improve their love lives. His website is called howtogettheguy.com – which single lady doesn't want to know how to do that? Among his range of romantic programmes is 'Attraction to commitment'. In a teaser video for the course, Hussey draws an analogy between love and building a castle. Building a castle involves a lot of work, which you and your amour will both undertake together. Some of that work involves taking Hussey's courses. The castle metaphor provides the perfect opportunity to present the image of a couple standing on the ramparts of a fairy-tale castle, arm in arm, gazing yonder into a rosy sunset. This is an image that has been imprinted upon little girls around the world in storybooks and films. The woman is therefore subliminally invited to picture herself as the princess of the fairy-tale castle – after the work, naturally – rather than the 'dysfunctional bubbling quicksand' of 'the dating world' that the voiceover describes. In fact, those are the only two choices Hussey lays out. Option one is to continue fighting the quicksand, unable to see your relationship blind spots. Option two is to take advantage of Hussey's years of insight and walk the easy path to commitment. On cue, as you are invited to take option two, the castle is shown for the fifth time out of seven appearances in the video.

Johnny Cassell, another dating and self-confidence coach, has written an article about the traps of toxic love cycles.[18] Like a lot of blog content, it can be viewed as a sales pitch to entice you to buy one of his courses, but it's also a thoughtful article about repeating negative emotional patterns. He describes a common but toxic love pairing: the 'avoidant' and the 'typical' love addict. This attraction does not guarantee a healthy pairing. Unfortunately, most of us are unaware of our unconscious forces. We can be attracted to trauma bonds as well as love.

And why does this happen? Because many of us are not aware of our emotional landmines. How many people own up to being anxious or avoidant in love? Yet it is a classic coupling of dynamics that leads to unhappiness and failed relationships. As Cassell says, it's 'an absolute powder keg of terrible dynamics'.

Learning your emotional landmines doesn't just protect you from undue influence, it protects you from *you*. As Fyodor Dostoyevsky said, 'If you want to overcome the whole world, overcome yourself.'[19] The key question, though – one the size of a planet – is: how to 'overcome' yourself?

Exorcising your ghosts

Sometimes it takes another person to identify our weaknesses. It was when Darren started picking up his old habits and social contact that a sense of normality returned. His oncologist was concerned about his mental health and suggested he take up golf again, and took him for his first round. An outsider who realised how far his self-haunting had gone was able to persuade him to step outside of his comfort zone. The sky did not fall down and a process of personal inquiry began.

Clinical psychologist Dr Naomi Murphy has spent years devising therapy for prisoners who would once have been known as psychopaths. She recommends honestly assessing which emotions you are most frightened of, or least able to tolerate. 'We all have different landmines,' she says. 'Do you find it hard to tolerate fear? What pushes your buttons? What frightens you the most?'

On a personal level, Murphy has identified that she finds rejection difficult due to a transient childhood and repeatedly having to leave friends. Even as an adult she finds goodbyes or cancellations hard: 'If a friend cancels I can feel annoyed or upset. At times, this is a disproportionate response. Knowing it is my landmine helps to diffuse the vulnerability and look at it differently.'

She recommends schema-focused therapy if you need an expert to help you understand problematic 'landmines' better. During childhood, people develop schemas – broad organising principles – that help to guide them in making sense of their life and experiences. Some schemas can be acquired from toxic or traumatic childhood experiences where the young person's needs were not sufficiently met and are responsible for some mental health problems. Maladaptive schemas are self-defeating core themes or patterns that we keep repeating throughout our lives and can be based on rejection, abandonment, mistrust, social isolation, failure, self-sacrifice, hyper-criticalness, approval-seeking, punishment and abuse, among others. Cognitive behavioural therapy – with a therapist or through specialist self-help books – can help you recognise and defeat the most common repeating thought patterns and behaviour, if that's the route for you.

Named after King Solomon, Solomon's Paradox says that we apply reason more wisely to other people's problems. You can ask people who know you well what makes you self-haunt, or you can follow the advice of psychology professor Igor Grossman and practise 'self-distancing'. If you take a few steps back from a situation and describe the problem to yourself as though you are a fly-on-the-wall observer, or as an older and wiser version of yourself, it helps you to adopt a more reflective attitude.[20] One study showed that writing a diary in the third person resulted in a significant increase in wise reasoning about interpersonal challenges.[21]

The path to your personal enlightenment may literally involve following the path to enlightment. Buddhist monk

Tsering recommends that people try to become more self-aware by practising meditation. He stresses that this does not have to involve becoming a Buddhist or sitting with your legs crossed in the right way. In fact, you can do this with a cup of tea, or at any point of the day.

First, he recommends you practise 'single-pointed meditation'. This involves focusing your gaze steadily on one object for a set period of time to practise finding calm, stabilising the mind, and reducing stress and anxiety. Tsering says Buddhists might focus on a statue of Buddha, but it can be a candle or something in nature. Start with setting a timer for two minutes, and with time and practice you can extend that. Your mind will wander, but the path to enlightenment is not straight.

Once you have practised single-pointed meditation and your mind is more stable, Tsering says you should move to the next stage, 'mindful meditation':

> You can do this at any time and anywhere. Start by considering your feelings. Recognise them: this is a happy feeling, this is a sad feeling. You don't need to do anything. Just recognise it. Now consider your body. How does your body feel? How does the top of your head feel, your forehead, the inside of your nose? What do you feel in your chest. Go through all of your body from your head to your feet.

After practising mindful meditation you are ready for 'analytic meditation'. If your mind is not stable you cannot properly research your mind.

> You learn to recognise your thoughts and 'sub-minds'. If anger comes up in your daily life you should think about why. If you are angry with another person, they are not 100 per cent bad; you must think about the reality of the situation and dilute your anger.

Tsering's advice is in keeping with the Dalai Lama, who also practises it. Pondering the thoughts that influence your behaviour and attitudes can bring about inner change, a more positive state of mind and psychological awareness. If it's good enough for the Dalai Lama and Tsering, it might be worth trying.

Tsering was keen to impart some wise words, which, though too late to help Darren, relate to every human being on earth.

> From the second you are born you start to change. Impermanence is natural. Impermanence is reality. When people resist reality they will have problems. For example, once you are born you must know you will leave this world. It is reality. One has to accept this fact. But we often find that people think they are permanent and will never change and never die. They want things to remain the same. They may know in one sense that they will die but they have less awareness about it. They act as though they are going to live forever.

Propaganda does not have to sell falsehoods. It trades in truth alongside fear. Darren *was* more at risk and he was confronted with the distinct possibility of death, but he feels angry that the risk was exaggerated and that his fears were played upon:

> When I realised I was in a pretty dark place, I started critically analysing what was going on. I now feel anger. I think we were treated with contempt and lied to. Our leaders didn't believe their own propaganda. The media in general failed in its role. The right to express an opinion contrary to the official narrative has become an expression of ignorance, stupidity and marginalisation.
>
> Unfortunately I believe my emotions are still open to nudge and influence, as this in itself is a science. Hopefully I am now better equipped to recognise and deal with it.

Part of your ability to resist undue persuasion lies in you understanding your desires, fears and foibles. But this also invites you to undertake the hardest work of all: can you decode yourself as well as you can learn to decode messaging?

Take Satan's advice in John Milton's *Paradise Lost* when he finds himself in hell after the failed rebellion against God: 'The mind is its own place, and in itself, can make a heaven of hell, a hell of heaven.' It would be false advertising indeed to promise you heaven on earth after reading this book, but you will be more psychologically resilient if you face your own inner demons.

In a capitalist society, companies are going to keep advertising to sell you stuff. Modern marketing exploits your insecurities for profit. Governments will continue to peddle propaganda to soften you up for policies, promote wars and get elected. The easiest emotion to trigger is fear. They want you to self-haunt. Hell, they are probably self-haunting too. The best defence against these dark arts is to develop enough self-awareness of common emotions and your own specific weaknesses.

Professor Alexander said, 'No brain is unwashed. You can't clean a brain either. You can only tidy it up a little bit.' This book has its limits, but it invites you to become aware of your individual weaknesses, quirks and self-haunting. Not only does this help you develop resistance to sales patter, advertising, propaganda and nudging, but it will improve your life. This is the journey of a lifetime, and you might as well take that first step now.

The rules:

- Be aware that your emotions and weaknesses will be deliberately manipulated, and that you are half the problem.
- If self-reflection does not offer enough illumination, maybe you need the perspective of a friend or a therapist.
- Try meditating to become more self-aware.

20

Stand for something or fall for anything

If you don't follow your own map, someone else will direct your journey for you. The solution is to determine your own values and rules for life, which remain set in stone as a bulwark against the chaos of life – else you look for certainty in the arms of a brainwasher.

The Denial of Death

You're going to die. We all are. Our time on this dusty old rock is limited to a measly 80 years on average, if cancer, car crashes or carnivorous coyotes don't get to us first. And one day this dusty old rock itself could get smashed by a meteor, scorched by the sun or crushed by the contractions of the universe.

It is a terrifying realisation. Human life is as brutal as any David Attenborough documentary. At any moment we could be hit by a bus, felled by a virus or drained by a parasite. We could be divorced, fired or shamed without warning. American anthropologist Ernest Becker, in his bestselling book *The Denial of Death*, did not mince his words: 'Mother nature is a brutal bitch, red in tooth and claw, who destroys what she creates.'[1]

The Denial of Death was an important book. It won the Pulitzer Prize and spawned an entire genre of psychological research called 'terror management theory'.[2] Bill Clinton even named it as one of his all-time favourites.

It is a book about how people deal with death, or not. One of its key principles is that human beings have a dual nature: while we are mortal and decaying, we also have the gift of consciousness that allows us, unlike animals, to be both aware that we are dying and able to build psychological defences against that awareness. Whereas animals are connected only to the physical world and respond instinctively to it in a state of dumb unknowing, we humans are connected also to the invisible world of symbols and ideas, which enables us to transcend the physical.

'Man is literally split in two,' wrote Becker:

> he has an awareness of his own splendid uniqueness in that he sticks out of nature with a towering majesty, and yet he goes back into the ground a few feet in order blindly and dumbly to rot and disappear forever ... This is the terror: to have emerged from nothing, to have a name, consciousness of self, deep inner feelings, an excruciating inner yearning for life and self-expression – and with all this yet to die.

Becker wrote that a human being's first awareness that their body putrefies beyond their control is through defecation in infancy, which is thus subconsciously tied up with mortality. The Ernest Becker Foundation suggests that this might be why people stockpiled toilet paper in the early days of the Covid panic. Faced with a brutal reminder of the possibility of death, perhaps they sought to symbolically clean away the stench of their mortality.[3]

The second part of Becker's theory is that human beings seek to escape this awareness of their death. One way or another, many prefer to find refuge in oblivion, since the real world is terrifying. It is infinitely big and chaotic, and reminds us that we will die. Some people escape into drink and drugs, others into Netflix, others into religions, cults or totalitarian regimes. Becker wrote that 'the idea of death, the fear of it, haunts the human animal like nothing else; it is a mainspring of human activity' and that man 'literally drives himself into a blind obliviousness with social games, psychological tricks, [and] personal preoccupations'.

There are ghosts haunting the mind that demand constant distraction.[4] This might be why one study found that some participants chose to give themselves electric shocks rather than sit in silence with their thoughts. French philosopher Blaise Pascal once remarked, 'All of humanity's problems stem from man's inability to sit quietly in a room alone.'[5]

There are swathes of empirical studies to support Becker's point: make a person think about death (by walking them through a graveyard, for example) and they will be more likely to buy high-status goods, among other things.[6] This is perhaps why luxury brands like Gucci make their logos bigger during times of financial crisis.[7]

This is where consciousness comes in. It provides mankind with a link to the symbolic world, and something greater to which we can attach ourselves. Cultural hero systems give people a feeling of cosmic specialness: we build skyscrapers, write stories, buy better homes in the hope that they will last beyond our deaths and give us some kind of meaning. This is the driving force behind religions, revolutions and wars – 'battles between immortality projects', as Becker put it.

If life is a tempestuous sea, most of us would rather be on the safety of a large ship – some group, lifestyle or ideology – than drifting alone in the darkness.

In this way most people, often below the level of conscious awareness, *want* to be brainwashed to some degree – even though consciously we like to think of ourselves as individuals with agency. Finding one's own way is too risky, too frightening. At any rate, the universe is too vast for any of us to know it in its entirety. Every one of us must have some kind of compass inside that gives us direction.

Filling the void

Crucially, nature abhors a vacuum. If people are empty inside, if they do not have some kind of guiding principles, then they risk being filled up by another ideology. As G. K. Chesterton said, 'Those who leave the tradition of truth do not escape into something which we call Freedom. They only escape into something else, which we call Fashion.'[8]

Modern politicians are a case in point: their values are almost identikit, left and right scarcely separated, and they buckle and U-turn at the latest poll or slew of negative headlines. They have weak knees because they don't know what they stand for. Their compass needle wobbles; they have no true north.

When people are empty and fluid, they become reactive, and these are the prime conditions for brainwashing to occur. Loosened from tradition, ideology or community, people become like elements split from a chemical compound – desperate to bind to something new. Cults, for example, seek to foster an insecure attachment style in their followers. When people are insecure, they are more reactive, and more likely to bind to the mass.

Similarly, people are more persuadable when they have a weak sense of self. One study found that teens were less likely to be influenced by their peers if they had high self-esteem.[9] Another found a negative correlation between self-esteem and being influenced by branding.[10] When people know themselves and have a solid sense of self, they tend not to look outside for direction and purpose. Spirituality has a role to play as well: materialism (being connected to physical things rather than having a rich internal world) has been positively correlated with peer influence[11] and advertising susceptibility.[12]

In Philip Zimbardo's famous Stanford prison experiments (where participants quickly acclimatised to their arbitrary roles of prisoner or guard, sometimes to the point of cruelty), one of the subjects, Jerry-4586, noted how 'most of the people in this study derive their sense of identity and well-being from their immediate surroundings rather than from within themselves, and that's why they broke down – just couldn't stand the pressure – they had nothing within them to hold up against all of this'.[13]

Consider the transformation of Chuck, one of the people assigned to be a guard. At the start of the experiment, Chuck referred to himself as anti-establishment and non-conformist with long hair – so much so, he hoped he would be chosen as a prisoner since he thought his life path might at some point diverge into some prison time. On the first day, Chuck worried about how the prisoners would view him. He checked his sunglasses and picked up his club before walking into a cage, since they provided 'a certain power and security'.

By the fifth day, the self-professed anti-establishmentarian Chuck wrote:

> I have singled [a prisoner] out for special abuse both because he begs for it and because I simply don't like him. The real trouble starts at dinner. The new prisoner [416] refuses to eat his sausages. We throw him into the Hole ordering him to hold sausages in each hand. We have a crisis of authority; this rebellious conduct potentially undermines the complete control we have over the others.

It took just five days for Chuck to assume a new identity foisted on him via the external trappings of a uniform and billy club. Perhaps some kind of internal principles might have protected him – though it's hard to know for sure, since not one of the guards refused to participate.

On a lighter note, researchers have found that people are less likely to impulse buy if they plan their shopping trip in advance.[14] In other words, an inner goal or value provides some immunity to external influence. When you go to the casino, for example, having a pre-prepared budget and timeline means you're less likely to blow your life savings at the craps table.

An empty person is the perfect vessel for brainwashing. Psychoanalyst Carl Jung wrote that collective identities, such as memberships of organisations, support of -isms and so on are 'shields for the timid',[15] and that a feeling of meaninglessness puts a man on the road to state slavery.[16]

Drifting in the darkness is lonely. This separateness is the greatest problem of humankind according to Erich Fromm, who wrote in *The Art of Loving* that: 'The deepest need of man, then, is the need to overcome this separateness, to leave the prison of his aloneness.'[17] Just as Becker sees the fear of death as the mainspring of human activity, Fromm similarly sees our need for union as the source of our endeavours. Failure to overcome the emptiness we feel could lead to a drive for orgiastic states, conformity with the herd or, worse, the unhealthy symbiotic unions of sadism or masochism, whether in interpersonal relationships or a relationship with the state.

Philosopher Eric Hoffer was awarded the Presidential Medal of Freedom at least in part due to his book *The True Believer*, which attempted to explain the psychology of mass movements.[18] One of his conclusions was that empty people are at the biggest risk from totalitarian brainwashing: 'The less justified a man is in claiming excellence for his own self, the more ready is he to claim all excellence for his nation, his religion, his race or his holy cause ... [they] crave to dissolve their spoiled, meaningless selves in some soul-stirring spectacular communal undertaking.'

For this reason, mass movements are interchangeable. It is not so much the ideology that appeals to people, but rather the need to belong to some higher cause and find safety in the anonymity of the mass. Hoffer explained how, in Weimar Germany, membership of the communists or the Nazis was often arbitrary; SA leader Ernst Röhm boasted that he could turn the most die-hard communists into nationalists, and on the other side, Karl Radek saw the Nazi Brownshirts as potential communist recruits.

'The current thing'

Today, people searching for meaning, purpose or a temporary crusade shift seamlessly from one 'current thing' to another. You can see it play out on social media accounts, when a European flag emoji gets swapped out for the Black Lives Matter fist, then the face mask emoji, then the Ukrainian flag. Trendy activists campaign for more immigrants from Muslim countries, and then for LGBTQ rights. It doesn't matter that the causes are inconsistent, that the compass needle wobbles wildly; what matters is the feeling of belonging to a powerful mass.

The ultimate emptiness is zero. Zero is a placeholder for a numeral; there is nothing there. As a target for humans to strive towards, it should inspire extreme caution. It's the mathematical equivalent of moral values flatlining. Pol Pot's Year Zero was supposed to signify starting from scratch, a rebirth of Cambodian history. This could only be achieved by purging the old, literally consigning Cambodian society up until that point to history. In essence, it meant destruction and oblivion. To aim for zero is to aim for nothing. We need to beware the emptiness and nihilism of policies that call for zero.

What does it mean that two current popular policies also push for zero? Zero Covid and Net Zero – hotly contested and discussed elsewhere in this book – intriguingly have a nothing at the core of their aims, which risks making history of long-held social, economic and legal values.

Current social conditions point towards our own cultural reset. Hoffer identified several groups of the poignantly frustrated who were most likely to be brainwashed. People who have recently become poor tend to feel a frustration and an emptiness that spurs them towards solidarity in the mass. It was the new poor, the peasants thrown off their fields by landlords, who formed Oliver Cromwell's army and drove the Puritan Revolution. It was the ruined middle classes who formed the foundation of support for Hitler's Germany and Mussolini's Italy.

Hoffer argued that those who belong to a compact group, like a family, religion or tribe, are more immune to proselytising movements; they have a higher revolting point. Mass movements must break down existing group ties in order to convert people – the ideal recruit is isolated, with no group behind which they can hide their meaningless existence. When group cohesion is weak, mass movements move in for the kill; when cohesion is strong, they must first weaken it. Many of these movements are hostile to the family unit for this reason, said Hoffer.

People who feel disenfranchised and alone can also be ripe for mass movements. These are those who have no solid footing in life; they are restless and dissatisfied, finding salvation only in the collective. Similarly, argued Hoffer, while ethnic minorities who preserve their heritage tend to feel a sense of belonging and purpose and are thus sheltered from mass movements, those who try to assimilate into the majority culture are more likely to feel isolated and frustrated and are thus attracted to mass power.

Creative people are less likely to join mass movements too, according to Hoffer. They draw a feeling of potency from their creative efforts and their tangible outputs. 'The decline of handicrafts in modern times is perhaps one of the causes for the rise of frustration and the increased susceptibility of the individual to mass movements,' he wrote. While an interest in knitting and train sets may be unlikely to prevent brainwashing, the point is about having something to fill time and soothe anxieties.

Similarly, Hoffer wrote that the most reliable bellwether for a mass movement is the prevalence of unrelieved boredom. Totalitarianism is often preceded by a period of vast ennui, and its early proponents are often the most bored rather than the most oppressed – they crave meaning and purpose.

If we take Hoffer's analysis at face value, we may be in trouble today. Marriage rates are declining precipitously across the Western world (in the UK they are at a record low), and birth rates are following suit.[19] The National Health Service's pre-natal content talks of 'pregnant people' and 'support partners' in place of mothers and fathers.[20] Activist group Black Lives Matter's manifesto once aspired to 'disrupt the Western-prescribed nuclear family structure'.[21]

Elsewhere, the cultural narrative is dominated by disenfranchised identity groups, so much so that aspirational fashion brand Calvin Klein has replaced supermodels in some of their adverts with 'pregnant men' and the obese. Increasing immigration and accompanying multicultural policies impact on the sense of national solidarity. Various surveys indicate that the proportion of individuals who do not hold religious beliefs in the UK is steadily increasing and perhaps now represents the majority of the UK's population.[22] The 'Culture Wars' are not simply about differences of opinion on contentious topics, but are intertwined with our uncertainty about nationality identity and morality.

Billionaires like Mark Zuckerberg, Elon Musk and Richard Branson have all supported the concept of universal basic income (where everyone is unconditionally guaranteed an income from the government),[23] now being implemented in places like San Francisco.[24] In the future, a person may be completely stripped of their work, their busyness, which gives life structure and meaning. A startling survey conducted by the UK's City and Guilds found that 9 per cent of 18- to 24-year-olds in education or not in work never intend to start working.[25] That's a quarter of a million young people, out of work and potentially bored.

Mass formation

Could these socio-psychological conditions explain some of the emotional fervour exhibited during the pandemic? The NHS, a beloved institution, morphed into a national religion. Brits bashed pots and pans at the sky every Thursday evening in honour of the NHS, while rainbow graffiti and posters graced every city, town and village.

Perhaps so, according to psychoanalyst Professor Mattias Desmet, whose theory of 'mass formation' went viral in 2022:

> People in the grip of mass formation can't take a critical distance from what the group believes in and will radically sacrifice everything that's important to them. They are radically intolerant of dissident voices. In the end they commit atrocities. This is always observed.
>
> The root cause is situated in a kind of loneliness or disconnectedness from their environment. This has increased over the last few centuries due to industrialisation and mechanisation. Due to a more rationalist view of life, and less contact with the eternal music of life, people have become more lonely and more scared of everything related to suffering and death. In the end, it makes people vulnerable to mass formation; the masses wish their leaders would take control and establish a totalitarian state.
>
> Those who are susceptible are disconnected, struggling with meaning-making, suffering with free floating anxiety, and vulnerable to propaganda. They need an object to deal with their anxiety. It creates a collective, heroic battle.

Building on Desmet's theory, the mass hysteria of the last few years was not in response to Covid; rather, Covid was a lightning rod for a societal sickness that pre-dated it. Few would seriously argue that Western society was faultlessly contented before 2020. We live in a state of heightened anxiety about our human vulnerabilities, which is exacerbated and played upon in a culture of fear. It can be read in the blaring daily headlines: fear of viruses, totalitarianism, patriarchy, war, radicals, racism, immigrants, recession, environmental disaster. The Four Horsemen of the Apocalypse run rings around our minds. In a fruitless attempt to put fear at bay, the receding rules and regulations of religions are being replaced by the new rules of health and safety, and diversity, equality and inclusion.

Desmet follows a similar line of thinking to the great thinkers quoted throughout this book, including Jung, who coined the term 'mass formation' in his work *The Undiscovered Self*. Jung worried that industrialised life 'produced an individual who was unstable, insecure, and suggestible' and warned that the atomisation of man creates isolation and mistrust.

This industrialising force is not going away. In fact, it is reaching a bizarre climax, visible in our attitudes towards death and the value of life. Canada, for example, is loosening the law around what it calls 'medical assistance in dying' (euthanasia), so much so that a Canadian woman chose euthanasia because her housing benefits were insufficient.[26] Health experts have calculated that deaths like these will save taxpayers C$139 million dollars a year.[27] In the US, several states have made it legal to dissolve corpses in pressurised vats of potassium hydroxide solution; the remaining sludge can either be flushed down the drain or used to fertilise crops.[28] Plant-food brand Oumph! won a Cannes Lion award for its human-flesh-flavoured vegan burger.[29] Elon Musk is working towards our brains merging with the internet through his Neuralink,[30] while celebrated scholars like Yuval Noah Harari claim that humans are merely hackable animals.[31]

Among these conditions, Covid was something of a godsend to many desperate for solidarity and structure. Consider that a Reddit commenter described how they missed the comradery of getting their Covid vaccine, the thrill of yelling at the bad people who didn't get one and the feeling of fighting the good fight.[32]

Coercing people into taking medical procedures against their will was contrary to informed consent and ignored the multiplicity of objections. It was ethically bereft before Covid, it was ethically bereft during Covid and it will continue to be ethically bereft long into the future. Scapegoating and stigmatising a minority group is universally understood by principled people to be a very bad thing, yet this was done by celebrities, politicians, the media and health authorities. Principles like 'live and let live' and 'love your neighbour' seemed to have been abandoned during the pandemic, yet they are more important during social upheavals, not less. A principle is not a thing to be used and discarded on a whim – it provides purpose, structure and protection against being sucked into the mass movement of the day.

Find your purpose

Songs throughout the ages have provided the answer to our great existential problem – lyrics tell us that love is all there is and love is the answer. According to Fromm, love is the answer to the problem of human existence. It is the key value to nurture. There is the easy kind of falling in love, as well as love for children and family, and brotherly love. But he asserts that none of these are possible in the most desirable and healthy form if you cannot love yourself. This requires self-knowledge and humility. Love is at the centre of world religions. As Paul said in 1 Corinthians, 'Three things will last forever: faith, hope and love – and the greatest of these is love.'

The oldest known musical composition to have survived in its entirety is the 'Seikilos Epitaph' from the first century CE. It was engraved on an ancient marble column used to mark a woman's grave. The lyrics read:

While you live, shine
Have no grief at all
Life exists only for a short while
And time demands its toll.

Face death. You might as well, since it is inevitable and all around us. 'In the midst of life, we are in death,' says the *Book of Common Prayer*. Embrace the discomfort of reality rather than shying away from it. The Roman philosopher Seneca said, 'A person who has learned how to die has unlearned how to be a slave. He is above, or at any rate beyond the reach of, all political powers. What are prisons, warders, bars to him?'[33]

Developing strong individual meaningful values, nurturing love and facing death are intrinsic to the world's religions. Religious value frameworks include the Buddhist Noble Eightfold Path, the Five Pillars of Islam, the Hindu Vedic yamas and niyamas, 'restraints and observances', Christian scripture and the Ten Commandments. Unconditional love is part of the tradition of all major world religions. And humanist non-religious associations describe values, even if they do not codify them as religions do.

For billions of people, religion is one way to live meaningfully according to good principles. In essence, through belief, they have chosen their master.

Father Colin, a monk, explained: 'You discover your freedom through obedience. Jesus submitted to the will of God and died on the cross so that everyone else can have life ... I have the impression that people are wanting answers and wanting spiritual life. The struggle people have is with commitment. You get a sense that people are generally unhappy, stressed and searching for meaning.'

And Carl Jung, in *The Undiscovered Self*, agreed about the importance of faith, too: 'The individual who is not anchored in God can offer no resistance on his own resources to the physical and moral blandishments of the world. For this he needs the evidence of inner, transcendent experience which alone can protect him from the otherwise inevitable submersion in the mass.'

Likewise, in Alcoholics Anonymous, attendees submit their will to a higher power rather than to alcohol. Only by surrendering their freedom can they become truly free.

As Eric Hoffer explained in *The True Believer*, mass movements can be stopped by swapping one movement for another, healthier one. Catholicism is believed to have stopped the spread of communism in Ireland, for example.[34] Similarly, religion can keep prison inmates from falling into gangs,[35] and hobbies and employment also prevent recidivism among alcoholics.[36] Having some kind of busyness and focus protects against brainwashing.

In *Battle for the Mind*, William Sargant explained how Jehovah's Witnesses were reported to be among the best able to resist interrogation in the concentration camps of the Second World War.[37] He wrote that 'a safeguard against conversion is, indeed, a burning and obsessive belief in some other creed or way of life'. (However, it can also be simply focusing on some other non-religious task. Colonel R. H. Stevens, imprisoned by the Gestapo, survived his tortures by reconstructing in his memory his childhood home, down to the most minute detail of books and ornaments.)

The point is to find your own unchanging north star – something to bind to as security against the winds of brainwashing. It is about having what pick-up artists call 'frame', where, 'Let's just be friends', meets, 'With benefits? If you insist.' In other words, if you manage the frame, you're more likely to get your outcome. As influence expert Simon Horton said: 'In terms of protecting yourself, it is often about coming across as strong. The scammer ignores the person who is visibly mentally and physically strong. It's about how you hold yourself, whether it's street swagger, or whether it's just shoulders back, head up, steely stare, the less likely that somebody is going to choose you.'

Without frame, without principles, without something on the inside to keep us solid, we run the risk of being swept up with the winds of the day. If you don't know what you stand for, you can fall for anything.

Our societies have arguably lost meaning, values and purpose. But, first things first. In the event of an aeroplane crash, you attend to your own oxygen mask first. Ascertain your own morals and rules. Indeed, according to Jung, 'Happiness and contentment, equability of soul and meaningfulness of life – these can be experienced only by the individual and not by a State, which, on the one hand, is nothing but a convention of independent individuals and, on the other, continually threatens to paralyze and suppress the individual.'

Ernest Becker argued that nothing could fill that hole quite like God. God, he said, changes shape to fit whatever our own personal vacuum looks like.

Yet, any kind of purpose is better than none – family, work, pastimes. Only you know what works best for you. If you're trying to solve that riddle, you've already taken the first steps on the journey to a purposeful life.

There is meaning in the search for meaning.

The rules:

- Develop a plan and set of principles for any situations where you are liable to be psychologically influenced, whether it's shopping, dating or politics.
- What do you stand for? Determine your principles, morals, beliefs and faith. You must hold them dear and allow them to guide you. If your beliefs are clear it is simply harder for others to foist new beliefs onto you.
- To assist with this, you may need to choose your master; we all have to submit to something, and some masters are healthier than others.

Conclusion

Our minds were changed by writing this book. We hope yours were too.

As a result of our research, we have become more acutely aware of the scale and impact of manipulation. We believe this has made us less susceptible to unwanted influence.

To start with, you might find that you see attempts to influence everywhere. Storylines in soap operas might seem more contrived. You will notice the effort in advertising to make you socially conform. The appeals to ego, fear and hope in propaganda will be more obvious. Awareness is the first stage. Resistance, deflection and some level of immunity follow.

Yet we're not smug. We also realised how easy it is to be manipulated. We recalled the embarrassing number of times we had fallen hook, line and sinker for blatant ads, rushed and clicked the wrong button online, made a terrible buying decision while feeling low, been coerced in our private lives or found ourselves emotionally roused by propaganda.

The more you are aware of manipulation, the more you see it. This presented a pitfall. As Nietzsche said, 'Whoever fights monsters should see to it that in the process he does not become a monster. And if you gaze long enough into an abyss, the abyss will gaze back into you.'[1] The world became alive with symbolism. Conversations rang with attempts to influence. Nudges flowed in cascades online. We accepted we were at war, as the first chapter sets out, but we discovered that we can't live in a permanent state of hyper-vigilance. Life would be exhausting. We also became more aware of our own communications and interactions, and we didn't want to use our new knowledge to bad ends.

As the introduction states, manipulation is not new. But today's confluence of technology, social media and AI, combined with marketing and behavioural science, is new in its sophistication and scale. Propaganda is not the sole preserve of totalitarian regimes; in the West, governments deploy techniques of mass persuasion to soften up populations to comply with policies and to disable dissent. If a government does not use the jackboot, it is more likely to cajole, coax and deploy covert communications.

We would like nudges to be transparent, but often they are not. It is our opinion that governments should consult with the public on the use of behavioural science. We wish companies to put ethics before profit. If only there weren't figures in the darkness always ready to prey upon psychological weaknesses. It all comes down to psychology. There will forever be people willing to manipulate and exploit, and our biases and personal foibles will always leave us vulnerable.

The first element to arming yourself is to identify the external influences that work upon you. You should be aware of bamboozlement – attempts to confuse, tire and scare you, which leave you more susceptible. The manipulator may try to tap into your deepest desires and fears. They will then convey the illusion of autonomy; you will be made to feel as though your decision is your choice. Imagery arouses emotion, and symbols speak to your subconscious. Be aware of pressure to make you conform, or to feel fearful of speaking out, and suspect those who try to exert authority over you. Manipulation is not always obvious in one big dollop, but is delivered in small, repetitive doses.

The second way that this book helps you to free your mind is to encourage you to develop individual agency and resilience. The English poet John Donne famously said, 'No man is an island', since we are all 'involved in mankind'.[2] We cannot be isolated from humanity, nor from our own nature. We cannot free our minds completely, any more than an island can avoid being lapped by the waves.

We should each try to be sovereign of our 'island', while being wise to the continent of humanity. You will be more immune from unwanted influences if you are confident about stepping away from the in-group and speaking up first. A degree of scepticism is healthy. It is prudent to make cool decisions when your emotions are not raised and you do not feel physically challenged. Understanding your own psychological and emotional tendencies, in addition to general human cognitive biases, will leave you less open to exploitation. And, importantly, if you have strong guiding principles and values, you are less likely to be filled with someone else's.

During the course of writing this book we were surprised that we became more open to the idea of being actively influenced, as long as we choose the framework that is right for us. This is not a great, new discovery – it is why people worship every week on the same day, or join clubs with like-minded people. Experiencing positive reinforcing values around you in community offers support and psychological strength.

There are dangers ahead. Technology encourages a hive mind, and smart cities increase atomisation and groupthink, increasing our susceptibility to mass hysteria. We are buffeted by passions, advertisements and manipulators. We live in a post-religious, post-modern age, unsure of our individual and collective values. But there is also hope. We have been contacted by people before and during the writing of this book, who asked us why some people are more likely to be manipulated and how to protect themselves. Digital detox programmes are emerging in response to the saturation of our lives with tech.

Technology and science are developing at a pace that means some of the content of this book will be out of date by the time it's published. That does not negate the advice, but proves the importance of it. Take social media: some of the mechanistic principles, such as setting your timelines to chronological, may be superseded by more sophisticated methods, or even abolished. Who can tell? The important thing is to be aware that social media is an environment that is imbued with personalised and sophisticated manipulation, and awash with bad actors. Forewarned is forearmed. The psychological principle of mindful use will be helpful no matter how technology develops.

In the field of psychology, pre-bunking and accuracy nudging will be used ostensibly to protect you from misinformation. In reality this is likely to also mean softening you up for the 'right' information, because the ends are often thought to justify the means. Governments and big businesses do not conduct behavioural science campaigns according to formal ethical frameworks.

The greatest hope lies within. Humans are vulnerable to the adverse effects of conformity, authority and fear, but they are also founts of creativity, strength and individuality.

We do not believe that humans are mere organic algorithms or social units to be organised. We believe that the human mind is wondrous. Yours should be free.

Notes

Introduction

1. Packard, V. *The Hidden Persuaders*, Penguin Books, 1957.
2. Bernays, Edward L. *Propaganda*, New York, H. Liveright, 1928.
3. Hubert, Antoine. 'Why we need to give insects the role they deserve in our food systems', *World Economic Forum* (12 July 2021); https://www.weforum.org/agenda/2021/07/why-we-need-to-give-insects-the-role-they-deserve-in-our-food-systems/
4. Winchester, Nicole. 'Net zero and behaviour change', House of Lords Library (14 October 2022); https://lordslibrary.parliament.uk/net-zero-and-behaviour-change/
5. Bedard, Paul. 'Out-of-touch media ignore top 10 voting issues to push climate, LGBT, Jan. 6 agenda', *Washington Examiner* (14 September 2022); https://www.washingtonexaminer.com/news/washington-secrets/out-of-touch-media-ignores-top-10-voting-issues-to-push-climate-lgbt-jan-6-agenda
6. Browing, Christopher. *Ordinary Men: Reserve Police Battalion 101 and the Final Solution in Poland*, New York, HarperCollins, 1992.
7. Solzhenitsyn, Alexander. *The Gulag Archipelago, 1918–1956 – Volume 1: An Experiment in Literary Investigation*, Harper Perennial, 2007.
8. Jung, Carl Gustav. *Collected Works of C. G. Jung – Volume 18: The Symbolic Life: Miscellaneous Writings*, Princeton University Press, 2014.

I: Realise your brain is a battleground

1. Brownlie, I. 'Interrogation in depth: The Compton and Parker reports', *The Modern Law Review*, 35(5) (1972), pp. 501–7.
2. Solzhenitsyn, Alexander. *The Gulag Archipelago*, Vol. 2, London, Collins, 1975.
3. Statement from Abu Zubaydah's testimony to the ICRC (the International Committee of the Red Cross), as reported in 'Experimenting with Torture', ACLU (American Civil Liberties Union), 16 October 2009.
4. Dehner, M. M. 'Can the use of enhanced interrogation techniques ever be justified during counter insurgency operations?', *Ad Securitatem*, 84 (2015).
5. Marks, D. F. 'American psychologists, the Central Intelligence Agency, and enhanced interrogation', *Health Psychology Open*, 5(2) (2018).
6. 'MK-Ultra', CBC, 1980.
7. 'Harvard and the Making of the Unabomber', *The Atlantic*, June 2020.
8. Sargant, William. *Battle for the Mind: A Physiology of Conversion and Brainwashing*, Greenwood Press, 1975.
9. Buss, D. M. 'Manipulation in close relationships: Five personality factors in interactional context', *Journal of Personality*, 60(2) (1992), pp. 477–99.
10. 'How to break through content clutter', *Seismic*, October 2015.
11. 'How Many Ads Do You See in One Day?', Red Crow Marketing Inc., 10 September 2015; https://www.redcrowmarketing.com/2015/09/10/many-ads-see-one-day/
12. https://www.thedrum.com/news/2023/05/03/how-many-ads-do-we-really-see-day-spoiler-it-s-not-10000
13. Hilbert, M. 'How much information is there in the "information society"?', *Significance*, 9(4) (2012), pp. 8–12.
14. 'Study reveals we read the equivalent of 174 newspapers a day', Red Drum Marketing, February 2011.
15. Stanovich, K. E. 'Why humans are cognitive misers and what it means for the Great Rationality Debate', *Routledge Handbook of Bounded Rationality*, Routledge, 2021, pp. 196–206.
16. Wilson, T. D. *Strangers to Ourselves*, Harvard University Press, 2004.
17. Hyman Jr, I. E., Boss, S. M., Wise, B. M., McKenzie, K. E. and Caggiano, J. M. 'Did you see the unicycling clown? Inattentional blindness while walking and talking on a cell phone', *Applied Cognitive Psychology*, 24(5) (2010), pp. 597–607.

18. Phillips, D. P. 'The influence of suggestion on suicide: Substantive and theoretical implications of the Werther effect', *American Sociological Review* (1974), pp. 340–54.
19. 'Corona beer sales soared by 40 per cent in 2020 despite Covid association', iNews, December 2020.
20. 'Read Yuval Harari's blistering warning to Davos in full', World Economic Forum, 24 January 2020; https://www.weforum.org/agenda/2020/01/yuval-hararis-warning-davos-speech-future-predications/
21. 'Adults spend almost 10 hours per day with the media, but note only 150 ads', Media Dynamics Incorporated, September 2014.
22. Sharp, B. and Romaniuk, J. *How Brands Grow*, Oxford University Press, 2016.
23. 'Nielsen confirms £164 million government ad spend for 2020', The Media Leader, March 2021.
24. 'A speech by HRH The Prince of Wales at the Opening Ceremony of COP26, Glasgow', 1 November 2021; https://www.google.com/search?client=safari&rls=en&q=www.princeofwales.gov.uk%2Fspeech%2Fspeech-hrh-prince-wales-opening-ceremony-cop26-glasgow&ie=UTF-8&oe=UTF-8#fpstate=ive&vld=cid:66e85d8d,vid:kCSWSpRaXfM
25. Foster, Caitlin. 'The unbelievable story of a Japanese soldier who hid in a jungle cave for 27 years until he was found in 1972', Business Insider, 2 January 2019; https://www.businessinsider.com/the-story-of-a-japanese-soldier-who-hid-in-a-jungle-cave-for-27-years-2019-1
26. Baumeister, R. F., Masicampo, E. J. and Vohs, K. D. 'Do conscious thoughts cause behavior?', *Annual Review of Psychology*, 62 (2011), pp. 331–61.
27. Sun Tzu. *The Art of War*. Translated by Jonathan Clements. Macmillan Collector's Library, 2017.
28. Drake, K. E., Sheffield, D. and Shingler, D. 'The relationship between adult romantic attachment anxiety, negative life events, and compliance', *Personality and Individual Differences*, 50(5) (2011), pp. 742–6.
29. Zuwerink Jacks, J. and Cameron, K. A. 'Strategies for resisting persuasion', *Basic and Applied Social Psychology*, 25(2) (2003), pp. 145–61.
30. Milling, L. S., Miller, D. S., Newsome, D. L. and Necrason, E. S. 'Hypnotic responding and the five factor personality model: Hypnotic analgesia and openness to experience', *Journal of Research in Personality*, 47(1) (2013), pp. 128–31.

31. Liebman, Julie I., McKinley-Pace, Marcia J., Leonard, Anne Marie, Sheesley, Laura A., Gallant, Casey L., Renkey, Mary E. and Lehman, Elyse Brauch. 'Cognitive and psychosocial correlates of adults' eyewitness accuracy and suggestibility', *Personality and Individual Differences*, 33(1) (2002), pp. 49–66.
32. Alexander, D. A. and Klein, S. 'Kidnapping and hostage-taking: A review of effects, coping and resilience', *Journal of the Royal Society of Medicine*, 102(1) (2009), pp. 16–21.
33. Frankl, Viktor. *Man's Search for Meaning*, Simon & Schuster, 1985.

2: Stand your ground

1. Morthland, John. 'A plague of pigs in Texas', *Smithsonian Magazine*, January 2011; https://www.smithsonianmag.com/science-nature/a-plague-of-pigs-in-texas-73769069/
2. Marino, L. and Colvin, C. M. 'Thinking pigs: A comparative review of cognition, emotion, and personality in *Sus domesticus*', *International Journal of Comparative Psychology* (2015).
3. 'Pigs are hard', California Potbellied Pig Association, Inc; http://www.cppa4pigs.org/pigs-are-hard.html
4. 'Capture success matrix', Jager Pro Hog Control Systems, 2 November 2017; https://jagerpro.com/capture-success-matrix/
5. 'WILD HOG CONTROL | JAGER PRO™ TV Show | SOUNDER TRAPPING SUCCESS', YouTube, 20 October 2021; https://www.youtube.com/KDvpXL4iYwU
6. 'HUNGARY: Salami tactics', *TIME*, 2 April 1952; https://content.time.com/time/subscriber/article/0,33009,857130,00.html
7. '102-000 Brief history of income tax', Croner-I Navigate; https://library.croneri.co.uk/cch_uk/btr/102-000
8. Welsh, D. T., Ordóñez, L. D., Snyder, D. G. and Christian, M. S. 'The slippery slope: How small ethical transgressions pave the way for larger future transgressions', *Journal of Applied Psychology*, 100(1) (2015), p. 114.
9. Diver, Tony. 'Coronavirus: Boris Johnson announces three-week UK lockdown', *Telegraph*, 2 March 2020; https://www.telegraph.co.uk/global-health/science-and-disease/coronavirus-latest-lockdown-panic-buying-news-cases-nhs/
10. Johnston, John. 'Eleven times the government has ruled out vaccine passports as they now say they're "considering" them', Politics Home, 2 February 2021; https://www.politicshome.com/news/article/coronavirus-vaccine-passports-government-denial

11. Wood, Poppy. 'Nadhim Zahawi refuses to rule out vaccine passports for pubs later in the year', *City A.M.*, 2 April 2021; https://www.cityam.com/nadhim-zahawi-refuses-to-rule-out-vaccine-passports-for-pubs-later-in-the-year/
12. Barnett, Sophie. 'Vaccine passports for nightclubs and large venues come into force in England', LBC, 2 December 2021; https://www.lbc.co.uk/hot-topics/coronavirus/covid-vaccine-passports-legal-nightclubs-england/
13. Freedman, J. L. and Fraser, S. C. 'Compliance without pressure: The foot-in-the-door technique', *Journal of Personality and Social Psychology*, 4(2) (1966), p. 195.
14. Halpern, D. and Mason, D. 'Radical incrementalism', *Evaluation*, 21(2) (2015), pp. 143–9.
15. The Behavioural Insights Team website, 'Who we are' section.
16. Pandelaere, M., Briers, B., Dewitte, S. and Warlop, L. 'Better think before agreeing twice: Mere agreement – a similarity-based persuasion mechanism', *International Journal of Research in Marketing*, 27(2) (2010), pp. 133–41.
17. Wayne, Corey. 'Seduction: 2 Steps Forward, 1 Step Back', UnderstandingRelationships.com, 20 April 2022; https://understandingrelationships.com/seduction-2-steps-forward-1-step-back/72760
18. Cialdini, R. B., Vincent, J. E., Lewis, S. K., Catalan, J., Wheeler, D. and Darby, B. L. 'Reciprocal concessions procedure for inducing compliance: The door-in-the-face technique', *Journal of Personality and Social Psychology*, 31(2) (1975), p. 206.
19. Grow, Cory. 'Motley Crue on "Girls, Girls, Girls" at 30: "It Was Like 'Caligula'"', *Rolling Stone*, 2 August 2017; https://www.rollingstone.com/music/music-features/motley-crue-on-girls-girls-girls-at-30-it-was-like-caligula-121895/
20. Mayer, Milton. *They Thought They Were Free: The Germans, 1933–45*, University of Chicago Press, 1955.
21. Milgram, S. 'The dilemma of obedience', *The Phi Delta Kappan*, 55(9) (1974), pp. 603–6.
22. Liebling, Alison. 'The abuse lurking in our institutions', British Psychological Society, 2 August 2016; https://www.bps.org.uk/psychologist/abuse-lurking-our-institutions
23. Fransen, M. L., Smit, E. G. and Verlegh, P. W. 'Strategies and motives for resistance to persuasion: An integrative framework', *Frontiers in Psychology*, 6 (2015), p. 1201.
24. Street, C. N. and Masip, J. 'The source of the truth bias: Heuristic processing?', *Scandinavian Journal of Psychology*, 56(3) (2015), pp. 254–63.

25. Wegner, D. M. 'Ironic processes of mental control', *Psychological Review*, 101(1) (1994), p. 34.
26. Zajonc, R. B. 'Attitudinal effects of mere exposure', *Journal of Personality and Social Psychology*, 9(2; Part 2) (1968), p. 1.
27. Hassan, A. and Barber, S. J. 'The effects of repetition frequency on the illusory truth effect', *Cognitive Research: Principles and Implications*, 6(1) (2021), pp. 1–12.
28. Havel, Václav. *The Power of the Powerless*, M. E. Sharpe, 1985.
29. de La Boétie, Étienne. *The Discourse on Voluntary Servitude*, 1577. Translated by H. Kurz. New York, Columbia University Press, 1942.
30. Sargant, William. *Battle for the Mind: A Physiology of Conversion and Brainwashing*, Greenwood Press, 1975.
31. Duane, James. *You Have the Right to Remain Innocent*, Little A, 2016.

3: Get immunity

1. Andrews, James. 'Pickpocket hotspots', Money.co.uk, 2 July 2022; https://www.money.co.uk/travel/pickpocket-hotspots
2. Jackson, Katie. 'Don't Let It Happen to You! How to Avoid My $4,000 Mistake', Fodor's Travel, 2 March 2022; https://www.fodors.com/world/europe/france/experiences/news/dont-let-it-happen-to-you-how-to-avoid-my-4000-mistake
3. Durney, Ellen. '2 People Have Finally Been Charged In Connection With Kim Kardashian's 2016 Paris Robbery, Which Entirely Changed How She Navigates Her Public Image', Buzzfeed News, 2 November 2021; https://www.buzzfeednews.com/article/ellendurney/12-people-charged-after-kim-kardashian-paris-robbery
4. Asch, Solomon E. *Social Psychology*, New York, Prentice-Hall, 1952.
5. Friestad, M. and Wright, P. 'The persuasion knowledge model: How people cope with persuasion attempts', *Journal of Consumer Research*, 21(1) (1994), pp. 1–31.
6. Fransen, M. L., Verlegh, P. W., Kirmani, A. and Smit, E. G. 'A typology of consumer strategies for resisting advertising, and a review of mechanisms for countering them', *International Journal of Advertising*, 34(1) (2015), pp. 6–16.
7. 'Redesigning online banking environments to reduce fraud', The Behaviouralist; https://thebehaviouralist.com/portfolio-item/open-banking/

8. Jefferson, Thomas. Letter to Du Pont de Nemours, 2 April 1816.
9. Etcheverry, J. (ed.). *Ideas Magicas: Principio de Cobertura*, Madrid, Ediciones Paginas, 2000. Translated by G. Kuhn et al., 2014.
10. Svalebjørg, M., Øhrn, H. and Ekroll, V. 'The illusion of absence in magic tricks', *i-Perception*, 11(3) (2020).
11. Chabris, C. and Simons, D. *The Invisible Gorilla: How Our Intuitions Deceive Us*, Harmony, 2011.
12. Drew, T., Võ, M. L. H. and Wolfe, J. M. 'The invisible gorilla strikes again: Sustained inattentional blindness in expert observers', *Psychological Science*, 24(9) (2013), pp. 1848–53.
13. Drake, K. E., Sheffield, D. and Shingler, D. 'The relationship between adult romantic attachment anxiety, negative life events, and compliance', *Personality and Individual Differences*, 50(5) (2011), pp. 742–6.
14. Cialdini, Robert. *Influence: The Psychology of Persuasion*, revised edition, New York, William Morrow, 2006.
15. 'Watch: Diners flee restaurant as runners get mistaken for robbers', *Indian Express*, 2 September 2022; https://indianexpress.com/article/trending/trending-globally/diners-flee-restaurant-as-runners-get-mistaken-for-robbers-8174489/
16. Milgram, S., Bickman, L. and Berkowitz, L. 'Note on the drawing power of crowds of different size', *Journal of Personality and Social Psychology*, 13(2) (1969), p. 79.
17. Morton, R. B., Muller, D., Page, L. and Torgler, B. 'Exit polls, turnout, and bandwagon voting: Evidence from a natural experiment', *European Economic Review*, 77 (2015), pp. 65–81.
18. Ionescu, R. and Radulescu, I. 'Behavioral finance and the fast evolving world of fintech', *Economic Insights – Trends and Challenges*, VIII(LXXI) (2019).
19. Worchel, S., Lee, J. and Adewole, A. 'Effects of supply and demand on ratings of object value', *Journal of Personality and Social Psychology*, 32(5) (1975), p. 906.
20. Free, C. J., Hoile, E., Knight, R., Robertson, S. and Devries, K. M. 'Do messages of scarcity increase trial recruitment?', *Contemporary Clinical Trials*, 32(1) (2011), pp. 36–9.
21. Simmonds, Ellie. '99.5% of Black Friday "deals" cheaper or the same price at other times of the year', *Which?*, 2 November 2021.
22. Evans, Natalie. 'Serious shopping: Black Friday deaths and disasters show how far some people will go for a bargain', *Mirror*, 2 November 2021; https://www.mirror.co.uk/news/weird-news/black-friday-deaths-and-disasters-show-1452562

23. Mazzella, R. and Feingold, A. 'The effects of physical attractiveness, race, socioeconomic status, and gender of defendants and victims on judgments of mock jurors: A meta-analysis 1', *Journal of Applied Social Psychology*, 24(15) (1994), pp. 1315–38.
24. Hamermesh, D. S. and Biddle, J. 'Beauty and the labor market', NBER Working Paper Series 4518 (1993).
25. Casserly, Meghan. 'Beyoncé's $50 million Pepsi deal takes creative cues from Jay Z', *Forbes*, 10 December 2012; https://www.forbes.com/sites/meghancasserly/2012/12/10/beyonce-knowles-50-million-pepsi-deal-takes-creative-cues-from-jay-z/
26. Tanner, R. J. and Maeng, A. 'A tiger and a president: Imperceptible celebrity facial cues influence trust and preference', *Journal of Consumer Research*, 39(4) (2012), pp. 769–83.
27. Kelly, Jack. 'Thousand-dollar cash payments and a TikTok "influencer army" are part of the campaign to get people vaccinated', *Forbes*, 2 August 2021; https://www.forbes.com/sites/jackkelly/2021/08/04/thousand-dollar-cash-payments-and-tiktok-influencer-army-are-part-of-the-campaign-to-get-people-vaccinated/?sh=2c76059f4684
28. Schino, G. and Aureli, F. 'The relative roles of kinship and reciprocity in explaining primate altruism', *Ecology Letters*, 13(1) (2010), pp. 45–50.
29. LeBas, N. R., Hockham, L. R. and Ritchie, M. G. 'Sexual selection in the gift-giving dance fly, *Rhamphomyia sulcata*, favors small males carrying small gifts', *Evolution*, 58(8) (2004), pp. 1763–72.
30. Nazir, Sahar. 'Valentine's Day spend set to disappoint, new research finds', *Retail Gazette*, 12 February 2020; https://www.retailgazette.co.uk/blog/2020/02/valentines-day-spend-set-disappoint-new-research-finds/
31. Cracknell, R., Uberoi, E. and Burton, M. 'UK election statistics: 1918–2022 – A century of elections', House of Commons Library, 5 December 2022; https://commonslibrary.parliament.uk/research-briefings/cbp-7529/
32. Nunes, J. C. and Drèze, X. 'The endowed progress effect: How artificial advancement increases effort', *Journal of Consumer Research*, 32(4) (2006), pp. 504–12.
33. Milgram, S. 'The dilemma of obedience', *The Phi Delta Kappan*, 55(9) (1974), pp. 603–6.
34. Levine, B. A., Moss, K. C., Ramsey, P. H. and Fleishman, R. A. 'Patient compliance with advice as a function of communicator

expertise', *The Journal of Social Psychology*, 104(2) (1978), pp. 309–10.

35. Thaler, Richard and Sunstein, Cass. *Nudge: Improving Decisions about Health, Wealth and Happiness*, Penguin, 2009.
36. 'Online choice architecture: How digital design can harm competition and consumers', Competition and Markets Authority, 2 April 2022; https://www.gov.uk/government/publications/online-choice-architecture-how-digital-design-can-harm-competition-and-consumers
37. Filou, Emilie and Hawkins, Amy. 'Edible insects and lab-grown meat are on the menu', *The Economist*, 2 November 2020; https://www.economist.com/the-world-ahead/2020/11/17/edible-insects-and-lab-grown-meat-are-on-the-menu
38. Van Huis, A., Halloran, A., Van Itterbeeck, J., Klunder, H. and Vantomme, P. 'How many people on our planet eat insects: 2 billion?', *Journal of Insects as Food and Feed*, 8(1) (2022), pp. 1–4.
39. Engström, Anders. 'The top 5 list of celebrities endorsing edible insects', Bug Burger, 2 February 2021; https://www.bugburger.se/attityder/the-top-5-list-of-celebrities-endorsing-edible-insects/
40. Wentworth, India. 'Great British Bake Off: East Sussex baker uses insects in Halloween special', *Sussex World*, 2 October 2022; https://www.sussexexpress.co.uk/arts-and-culture/film-and-tv/great-british-bake-off-east-sussex-baker-uses-insects-in-halloween-special-3885297
41. Beans, C. 'How to convince people to eat insects', *Proceedings of the National Academy of Sciences*, 119(46) (2022), e2217537119.
42. Hassan, A. and Barber, S. J. 'The effects of repetition frequency on the illusory truth effect', *Cognitive Research: Principles and Implications*, 6(1) (2021), pp. 1–12.
43. 'Edible insects and plant-based proteins to be the subject of classroom debates', Cardiff University, 2 May 2022; https://www.cardiff.ac.uk/news/view/2627488-edible-insects-and-plant-based-proteins-to-be-the-subject-of-classroom-debates
44. 'Net Zero: Principles for successful behaviour change initiatives – key principles from past government-led behaviour change and public engagement initiatives', BEIS Research Paper Number 2021/063, October 2021.
45. Dolan, P., Hallsworth, M., Halpern, D., King, D. and Vlaev, I. 'MINDSPACE Influencing behaviour through public policy', Cabinet Office, Institute for Government (2010).

46. 'Optimising Vaccination roll out – dos and don'ts for all messaging, documents and "communications" in the widest sense', NHS England and Improvement Unit, December 2020. http://www.doctoryourself.com/NHS%20Propaganda%20Vax.pdf
47. Alford, Justine. 'Star-studded video campaign launched to address COVID-19 vaccine concerns', Imperial College London, 2 May 2021; https://www.imperial.ac.uk/news/220433/star-studded-video-campaign-launched-address-covid-19/
48. Dodsworth, L. *A State of Fear: How the UK Government Weaponised Fear During the Covid-19 Pandemic*, London, Pinter & Martin, 2021.
49. 'HOW SLOVAKIA TESTED ITS WHOLE POPULATION FOR COVID-19', Behavioural Insights Team, 2 November 2020; https://www.bi.team/wp-content/uploads/2020/11/Slovakia-COVID-19-Population-Testing-Report.pdf
50. Toffler, A. and Toffler, H. *War and Anti-war: Survival at the Dawn of the 21st Century*, Boston, Little, Brown, 1993.
51. Freud, Sigmund. *The Penguin Freud Library, Vol. 12: Civilization, Society and Religion: Group Psychology, Civilization and Its Discontents and Other Works*, Penguin, 1991.
52. Hitchens, Christopher. 'The narcissism of the small difference', Slate, 2 June 2010; https://slate.com/news-and-politics/2010/06/in-ethno-national-conflicts-it-really-is-the-little-things-that-tick-people-off.html
53. 'SICK & TWISTED: Russia accused of bombing NURSERY as pictures show it "surrounded by bodies" in strikes that killed child & four others', *Sun*, 2 February 2020; https://www.thesun.co.uk/news/17772443/russia-bombed-nursery-kindergarten-bodies/
54. Don, Gav. 'Nursery school bombing photographs look like a false flag attack – by Ukraine', bne IntelliNews, 2 February 2022; https://intellinews.com/nursery-school-bombing-photographs-look-like-a-false-flag-attack-by-ukraine-235517/
55. Zitser, Joshua. 'Hillary Clinton likened Donald Trump's Ohio rally to Adolf Hitler speeches, report says', Business Insider, 2 September 2022; https://www.businessinsider.com/hillary-clinton-compares-trumps-ohio-rally-hitler-events-fox-news-2022-9?r=US&IR=T
56. 'Pelosi says Trump will be "fumigated out" if he refuses to leave after White House loss', Reuters, 20 July 2020; https://www.reuters.com/article/us-usa-election-pelosi-idUSKCN24L2DP
57. English, Rebecca and Pickles, Kate. '"Think about others rather than yourselves": The Queen makes plea over vaccine take-up as

she says jab "didn't hurt at all" when she had it and suggests those refusing it are selfish', *Daily Mail*, 2 February 2021; https://www.dailymail.co.uk/news/article-9301373/Queen-intervenes-vaccine-rollout-encourage-Britons-jabbed.html
58. William, Helen. 'Getting Covid-19 jab is a moral issue, Archbishop of Canterbury says', *Independent*, 2 December 2021; https://www.independent.co.uk/news/health/justin-welby-archbishop-canterbury-vaccine-moral-b1980400.html
59. Gragg, D. 'A multi-level defense against social engineering', *SANS Reading Room*, 13 (2003), pp. 1–21.
60. Dewey, John. *How We Think*, Dover Publications Inc., 2003.
61. Brunt, B. A. 'Models, measurement, and strategies in developing critical-thinking skills', *The Journal of Continuing Education in Nursing*, 36(6) (2005), pp. 255–62.
62. Janssen, L., Fennis, B. M. and Pruyn, A. T. H. 'Forewarned is forearmed: Conserving self-control strength to resist social influence', *Journal of Experimental Social Psychology*, 46(6) (2010), pp. 911–21.
63. McGuire W. J. 'The effectiveness of supportive and refutational defenses in immunizing and restoring beliefs against persuasion', *Sociometry*, 24(2) (1961), pp. 184–97.
64. Traberg, C. S., Roozenbeek, J. and van der Linden, S. 'Psychological inoculation against misinformation: Current evidence and future directions', *The Annals of the American Academy of Political and Social Science*, 700(1) (2022), pp. 136–51.
65. Ravan, S., De Groeve, T., Mani, L., Bjorgo, E., Moissl, R., Roncero, J. M. and Kofler, R. 'When It strikes, are we ready? Lessons identified at the 7th Planetary Defense Conference in preparing for a near-Earth object impact scenario', *International Journal of Disaster Risk Science*, 13(1) (2022), pp. 151–9.
66. Van der Linden, S., Leiserowitz, A., Rosenthal, S. and Maibach, E. 'Inoculating the public against misinformation about climate change', *Global Challenges*, 1(2) (2017), 1600008.
67. Neimeyer, G. J., Taylor, J. M. and Rozensky, R. H. 'The diminishing durability of knowledge in professional psychology: A Delphi poll of specialties and proficiencies', *Professional Psychology: Research and Practice*, 43(4) (2012), p. 364.
68. Duarte, J. L., Crawford, J. T., Stern, C., Haidt, J., Jussim, L. and Tetlock, P. E. 'Political diversity will improve social psychological science', *Behavioral and Brain Sciences*, 38 (2015).

69. Rathje, S., He, J. K., Roozenbeek, J., Van Bavel, J. J. and van der Linden, S. 'Social media behavior is associated with vaccine hesitancy', *PNAS Nexus*, 1(4) (2022), pgac207.
70. Roozenbeek, J., Van Der Linden, S., Goldberg, B., Rathje, S. and Lewandowsky, S. 'Psychological inoculation improves resilience against misinformation on social media', *Science Advances*, 8(34) (2022), eabo6254.
71. Kumaraguru, P., Sheng, S., Acquisti, A., Cranor, L. F. and Hong, J. 'Teaching Johnny not to fall for phish', *ACM Transactions on Internet Technology (TOIT)*, 10(2) (2010), pp. 1–31.
72. Sellier, A. L., Scopelliti, I. and Morewedge, C. K. 'Debiasing training improves decision making in the field', *Psychological Science*, 30(9) (2019), pp. 1371–9.

4: Don't overthink it

1. Fegan, Thomas. *The Baby Killers: German Air Raids on Britain in the First World War*, London, Leo Coop, 2002.
2. Doyle, Arthur Conan. *The Coming of the Fairies*, University of Nebraska Press, 2006.
3. Hyman, Ray. In *Why Smart People Can Be So Stupid*, ed. Sternberg, R., New Haven, Yale University Press, 2002, pp. 18–19.
4. Basterfield, C., Lilienfeld, S. O., Bowes, S. M. and Costello, T. H. 'The Nobel disease: When intelligence fails to protect against irrationality', *Skeptical Inquirer*, 44(3) (2020), pp. 32–7.
5. Isaacson, Walter. *Steve Jobs by Walter Isaacson: The Exclusive Biography*, Abacus, 2015.
6. As quoted in *Dictionary of Foreign Quotations* (1980) by Mary Collison and Robert L. Collison, p. 98.
7. Proctor, Robert N. *Racial Hygiene: Medicine Under the Nazis*, Harvard University Press, 1998.
8. Haque, O. S., De Freitas, J., Viani, I., Niederschulte, B. and Bursztajn, H. J. 'Why did so many German doctors join the Nazi Party early?', *International Journal of Law and Psychiatry*, 35(5–6) (2012), pp. 473–9.
9. Scopelliti, I., Morewedge, C. K., McCormick, E., Min, H. L., Lebrecht, S. and Kassam, K. S. 'Bias blind spot: Structure, measurement, and consequences', *Management Science*, 61(10) (2015), pp. 2468–86.
10. Stanovich, K. E., West, R. F. and Toplak, M. E. 'Myside bias, rational thinking, and intelligence', *Current Directions in Psychological Science*, 22(4) (2013), pp. 259–64.

11. Schmechel, L. L. K. *The Relationship of Children's Belief in Santa Claus to Causal Reasoning and Fantasy Predisposition*, The University of Texas at Austin, 1975.
12. Stanovich, K. E. 'Dysrationalia: A new specific learning disability', *Journal of Learning Disabilities*, 26(3) (1993), pp. 501–15.
13. West, R. F., Meserve, R. J. and Stanovich, K. E. 'Cognitive sophistication does not attenuate the bias blind spot', *Journal of Personality and Social Psychology*, 103(3) (2012), p. 506.
14. Eby, Margaret. 'Hocus Pocus', *Paris Review*, 2 March 2012; https://www.theparisreview.org/blog/2012/03/21/hocus-pocus
15. Bechtel, S. and Stains, L. R. *Through a Glass Darkly: Sir Arthur Conan Doyle and the Quest to Solve the Greatest Mystery of All*, New York, St. Martin's Press, 2017, p. 147.
16. Tarran, Brian. 'Questioning the nature of research', *Research Live*, 2 August 2011; https://www.research-live.com/article/features/questioning-the-nature-of-research/id/4005918
17. Hall, L., Johansson, P. and Strandberg, T. 'Lifting the veil of morality: Choice blindness and attitude reversals on a self-transforming survey', *PLOS One*, 7(9) (2012), e45457.
18. Meerloo, Joost. *Delusion and Mass-delusion* (No. 79), Johnson Reprint Corporation, 1968.
19. Kunda, Z. 'The case for motivated reasoning', *Psychological Bulletin*, 108(3) (1990), p. 480.
20. Kaplan, J. T., Gimbel, S. I. and Harris, S. 'Neural correlates of maintaining one's political beliefs in the face of counterevidence', *Scientific Reports*, 6(1) (2016), pp. 1–11.
21. Nickerson, R. S. 'Confirmation bias: A ubiquitous phenomenon in many guises', *Review of General Psychology*, 2(2) (1998), pp. 175–220.
22. Festinger, Leon, Riecken, Henry and Schachter, Stanley. *When Prophecy Fails: A Social and Psychological Study of a Modern Group that Predicted the Destruction of the World*, Lulu Press, Inc., 2017.
23. Miller, J. M., Saunders, K. L. and Farhart, C. E. 'Conspiracy endorsement as motivated reasoning: The moderating roles of political knowledge and trust', *American Journal of Political Science*, 60(4) (2016), pp. 824–44.
24. Kahan, D. M., Peters, E., Wittlin, M., Slovic, P., Ouellette, L. L., Braman, D. and Mandel, G. 'The polarizing impact of science literacy and numeracy on perceived climate change risks', *Nature Climate Change*, 2(10) (2012), pp. 732–5.

25. Kahan, D. M., Peters, E., Dawson, E. C. and Slovic, P. 'Motivated numeracy and enlightened self-government', *Behavioural Public Policy*, 1 (2017), pp. 54–86.
26. Turpin, M. H., Kara-Yakoubian, M., Walker, A. C., Walker, H. E., Fugelsang, J. A. and Stolz, J. A. 'Bullshit ability as an honest signal of intelligence', *Evolutionary Psychology*, 19(2) (2021), 14747049211000317.
27. Pauls, C. A. and Crost, N. W. 'Cognitive ability and self-reported efficacy of self-presentation predict faking on personality measures', *Journal of Individual Differences*, 26(4) (2005), p. 194.
28. Gino, F. and Ariely, D. 'The dark side of creativity: Original thinkers can be more dishonest', *Journal of Personality and Social Psychology*, 102(3) (2012), p. 445.
29. 'The danger of intellectuals', Hannah Arendt Center for Politics and Humanities, 2 July 2013; https://hac.bard.edu/amor-mundi/the-danger-of-intellectuals-2013-07-22
30. Orwell, George. *Notes on Nationalism*, Penguin Classics, 2018. ('One has to belong to the intelligentsia to believe things like that: no ordinary man could be such a fool.')
31. 'The General Social Survey', NORC at the University of Chicago; https://gss.norc.org/Documents/codebook/GSS%202021%20Codebook%20R1.pdf
32. Jones, Jeffrey M. 'Belief in God in U.S. dips to 81%, a new low', Gallup, 2 June 2022; https://news.gallup.com/poll/393737/belief-god-dips-new-low.aspx
33. Harari, Yuval Noah. 'Yuval Noah Harari on big data, Google and the end of free will', *Financial Times*, 2 August 2016; https://www.ft.com/content/50bb4830-6a4c-11e6-ae5b-a7cc5dd5a28c
34. Jung, Carl Gustav. *The Undiscovered Self*, Routledge, 2002.
35. Weaver, Richard M. *Ideas Have Consequences: Expanded Edition*, University of Chicago Press, 2013.
36. Fromm, Erich. *The Fear of Freedom*, Routledge, 2021.
37. Woodley, M. A. 'Are high-IQ individuals deficient in common sense? A critical examination of the "clever sillies" hypothesis', *Intelligence*, 38(5) (2010), pp. 471–80.
38. Brooks, David. 'How we are ruining America', *New York Times*, 2 July 2017; https://www.nytimes.com/2017/07/11/opinion/how-we-are-ruining-america.html
39. Dunning, D. 'The Dunning–Kruger effect: On being ignorant of one's own ignorance', *Advances in Experimental Social Psychology*, 44 (2011), pp. 247–96.

40. Rowe, Christopher. *The Last Days of Socrates*, London, Penguin, 2010.
41. Duttle, K. 'Cognitive skills and confidence: Interrelations with overestimation, overplacement and overprecision', *Bulletin of Economic Research*, 68(S1) (2016), pp. 42–55.
42. Sonm, L. K. and Kornell, N. 'The virtues of ignorance', *Behavioural Processes*, 83(2) (2010), pp. 207–12.
43. Ottati, V., Price, E., Wilson, C. and Sumaktoyo, N. 'When self-perceptions of expertise increase closed-minded cognition: The earned dogmatism effect', *Journal of Experimental Social Psychology*, 61 (2015), pp. 131–8.
44. Charlton, B. G. 'Clever sillies: Why high IQ people tend to be deficient in common sense', *Medical Hypotheses*, 73(6) (2009), pp. 867–70.
45. 'RationalWiki', Wikipedia, no date; https://en.wikipedia.org/wiki/RationalWiki
46. Robson, David. *The Intelligence Trap: Why Smart People Make Dumb Mistakes*, W. W. Norton & Company, 2020.
47. Langer, E. J., Blank, A. and Chanowitz, B. 'The mindlessness of ostensibly thoughtful action: The role of "placebic" information in interpersonal interaction', *Journal of Personality and Social Psychology*, 36(6) (1978), p. 635.
48. Damasio, Antonio. *Descartes' Error*, Random House, 2006.
49. Seo, M. G. and Barrett, L. F. 'Being emotional during decision making – good or bad? An empirical investigation', *Academy of Management Journal*, 50(4) (2007), pp. 923–40.
50. Hafenbrack, A. C., Kinias, Z. and Barsade, S. G., 'Debiasing the mind through meditation: Mindfulness and the sunk-cost bias', *Psychological Science*, 25(2) (2014), pp. 369–76.
51. See Mamede, S. and Schmidt, H. G., 'Reflection in medical diagnosis: A literature review', *Health Professions Education*, 3(1) (2017), pp. 15–25.
52. Brienza, J. P., Kung, F. Y., Santos, H. C., Bobocel, R. and Grossman, I. 'Situated wise reasoning scale', *Journal of Personality and Social Psychology*, 2018.
53. Franklin, Benjamin. *The Autobiography of Benjamin Franklin*, Dover Publications, 2016.
54. 'From Benjamin Franklin to John Lining, 18 March 1755', Founders Online; https://founders.archives.gov/documents/Franklin/01-05-02-0149
55. Mahajan, J. 'The overconfidence effect in marketing management predictions', *Journal of Marketing Research*, 29(3) (1992), pp. 329–42.

56. Sun, Q., Zhang, H., Sai, L. and Hu, F. 'Self-distancing reduces probability-weighting biases', *Frontiers in Psychology*, 9 (2018), p. 611.

5: Be aware of your sensations

1. Hopkin, M. 'Link proved between senses and memory', *Nature*, 31 May 2004.
2. 'How to control emotion and influence behavior', Dawn Goldworm, TEDxEAST, 25 July 2016.
3. Scent Australia website.
4. Spangenberg, E. R., Grohmann, B. and Sprott, D. E. 'It's beginning to smell (and sound) a lot like Christmas: The interactive effects of ambient scent and music in a retail setting', *Journal of Business Research*, 58(11) (2005), pp. 1583–9.
5. Huang, X., Zhang, M., Hui, M. K. and Wyer, R. S. 'Warmth and conformity: The effects of ambient temperature on product preferences and financial decisions', *Journal of Consumer Psychology*, 24(2) (2014), pp. 241–50.
6. Areni, C. S. and Kim, D. 'The influence of background music on shopping behavior: Classical versus top-forty music in a wine store', *ACR North American Advances* (1993).
7. Plato. *Laws*. Translated by Griffith, T. Edited by Schofield, M. Cambridge Texts in the History of Political Thought, 8 September 2016.
8. Plato. *The Republic*. Translated by Griffith, T. Edited by Ferrari, G. R. F. Cambridge Texts in the History of Political Thought, 12 October 2000.
9. Rauscher, F. H. and Shaw, G. L. 'Key components of the Mozart effect', *Perceptual and Motor Skills*, 86(3) (1998), pp. 835–41.
10. Hallam, S., Price, J. and Katsarou, G. 'The effects of background music on primary school pupils' task performance', *Educational Studies*, 28(2) (2002), pp. 111–22.
11. Kennaway, J. 'Musical hypnosis: Sound and selfhood from mesmerism to brainwashing', *Social History of Medicine*, 25(2) (2012), pp. 271–89.
12. Sargant, William. *Battle for the Mind: A Physiology of Conversion and Brainwashing*, Greenwood Press, 1975.
13. Beaman, C. P. and Williams, T. I. 'Earworms (stuck song syndrome): Towards a natural history of intrusive thoughts', *British Journal of Psychology*, 101(4) (2010), pp. 637–53.

14. Hassan, A. and Barber, S. J. 'The effects of repetition frequency on the illusory truth effect', *Cognitive Research: Principles and Implications*, 6(1) (2021), pp. 1–12.
15. Lamoureux, Mack. '"Neo-Nazi weird Al" gets 10 years for far-right parody raps', *Vice*, 2 April 2022; https://www.vice.com/en/article/z3n78x/neo-nazi-rapper-mr-bond
16. 'Wayhome, Coachella and the sensory overload machine', Unaffiliated Press, April 2017.
17. 'Inside the long-standing relationship between Coachella and American Express', *Forbes*, April 2022.
18. Chen, J. L., Zatorre, R. J. and Penhune, V. B. 'Interactions between auditory and dorsal premotor cortex during synchronization to musical rhythms', *Neuroimage*, 32(4) (2006), pp. 1771–81.
19. Leow, L. A., Waclawik, K. and Grahn, J. A. 'The role of attention and intention in synchronization to music: Effects on gait', *Experimental Brain Research*, 236(1) (2018), pp. 99–115.
20. Lewis, M. B. and Bowler, P. J. 'Botulinum toxin cosmetic therapy correlates with a more positive mood', *Journal of Cosmetic Dermatology*, 8(1) (2009), pp. 24–6.
21. 'Vision and breathing may be the secrets to surviving 2020', *Scientific American*, November 2020.
22. Ibid.
23. Goldsby, T. L., Goldsby, M. E., McWalters, M. and Mills, P. J. 'Effects of singing bowl sound meditation on mood, tension, and well-being: An observational study', *Journal of Evidence-Based Complementary Alternative Medicine* (2017), pp. 401–6.
24. Baldassi, S., Megna, N. and Burr, D. C. 'Visual clutter causes high-magnitude errors', *PLOS Biology* (2006).

6: Practise social media distancing

1. Statista, November 2022.
2. 'Thanks a billion!' Tiktok Community blog, 27 September 2021.
3. Statista, July 2022.
4. Harari, Y. N. *Homo Deus*, Vintage Digital, 2016.
5. Mayim Bialik and Yuval Noah Harari in conversation, SXSW Online 2021, 27 May 2021.
6. Frey, C. B. and Osborne, M. 'The Future of Employment', Oxford Martin Programme on Technology and Employment (2013).
7. Holbrook, C., Izuma, K., Deblieck, C., Fessler, D. M. and Iacoboni, M. 'Neuromodulation of group prejudice and religious belief', *Social Cognitive and Affective Neuroscience*, 11(3) (2016), pp. 387–94.

8. Capoot, Ashley. 'Elon Musk shows off updates to his brain chips and says he's going to install one in himself when they are ready', CNBC, 2 December 2022; https://www.cnbc.com/2022/12/01/elon-musks-neuralink-makes-big-claims-but-experts-are-skeptical-.html
9. Statt, Nick. 'Facebook acquires neural interface startup CTRL-Labs for its mind-reading wristband', The Verge, 2 September 2019; https://www.theverge.com/2019/9/23/20881032/facebook-ctrl-labs-acquisition-neural-interface-armband-ar-vr-deal
10. Krugman, P. 'Why most economists' predictions are wrong', *Red Herring*, 10 June 1998.
11. McLaughlin, Kelly. 'Sextremism: People are more likely to engage in kinky sex if they have anti-establishment political views (with right-wingers enjoying spanking and left-wingers into threesomes)', Mail Online, 20 April 2017; https://www.dailymail.co.uk/news/article-4428394/Extremist-voters-likely-engage-kinky-sex.html
12. Shi, F., Shi, Y., Dokshin, F. A., Evans, J. A. and Macy, M. W. 'Millions of online book co-purchases reveal partisan differences in the consumption of science', *Nature Human Behaviour*, 1(4) (2017), pp. 1–9.
13. Rentfrow, P. J. and Gosling, S. D. 'The do re mi's of everyday life: The structure and personality correlates of music preferences', *Journal of Personality and Social Psychology*, 84(6) (2003), p. 1236.
14. Ambady, N. and Rosenthal, R. 'Thin slices of expressive behavior as predictors of interpersonal consequences: A meta-analysis', *Psychological Bulletin*, 111(2) (1992), p. 256.
15. Voiskounsky, A., Fedunina, N., Evdokimenko, A. and Smyslova, O. 'Attitudes towards alternative identities in social networking sites', *Digital Transformation and Global Society* (2019), pp. 622–34.
16. Anderson, I., Gil, S., Gibson, C., Wolf, S., Shapiro, W., Semerci, O. and Greenberg, D. M. '"Just the Way You Are": Linking music listening on Spotify and personality', *Social Psychological and Personality Science*, 12(4) (2021), pp. 561–72.
17. Kosinski, M., Stillwell, D. and Graepel, T. 'Private traits and attributes are predictable from digital records of human behavior', *Proceedings of the National Academy of Sciences USA* (2013).
18. Segalin, C., Lepri, B., Cristani, M., Celli, F., Polonio, L., Kosinski, M., Stillwell, D. and Sebe, N. 'What your Facebook profile picture reveals about your personality', Association for Computing Machinery (2017), pp. 460–8.

19. Wang, Y. and Kosinski, M. 'Deep neural networks are more accurate than humans at detecting sexual orientation from facial images', *Journal of Personality and Social Psychology*, 114(2) (2018), pp. 246–57.
20. 'Technology at MindGeek', MindGeek; https://www.mindgeek.com/tech/
21. Sylwester, K. and Purver, M. 'Twitter language use reflects psychological differences between Democrats and Republicans', *PLOS One* (2015).
22. Matz, S. C., Kosinski, M., Nave, G. and Stillwell, D. J. 'Psychological targeting as an effective approach to digital mass persuasion', *Proceedings of the National Academy of Sciences*, 114(48) (2017), pp. 12714–19.
23. Bond, R. M., Fariss, C. J., Jones, J. J., Kramer, A. D. I., Marlow, C., Settle, J. E. and Fowler, J. H. 'A 61-million-person experiment in social influence and political mobilization', *Nature* (2012), pp. 295–8.
24. Tappin, B. M., Wittenberg, C., Hewitt, L., Berinsky, A. and Rand, D. G. 'Quantifying the persuasive returns to political microtargeting', PsyArXiv Preprints (2022).
25. Jones, Rhett. 'Your credit score should be based on your web history, IMF says', Gizmodo, 2 December 2020; https://gizmodo.com/your-credit-score-should-be-based-on-your-web-history-1845912592
26. Youyou, W., Kosinski, M. and Stillwell, D. 'Computer-based personality judgments are more accurate than those made by humans', *Proceedings of the National Academy of Sciences* (2015).
27. Thomas Jefferson to Charles Yancey, 2 January 1816.
28. 'News use across social media platforms in 2020', Pew Research Centre 2021.
29. 'News consumption in the UK', Ofcom, 2019.
30. Huxley, Aldous. *Brave New World Revisited*, Vintage Classics, 2004.
31. 'HIDDEN CAMERA: Twitter engineers to "ban a way of talking" through "shadow banning"', published by Project Veritas on YouTube, 11 January 2018.
32. 'Going global: The UK government's "CVE" agenda, counter-radicalisation and covert propaganda', openDemocracy, 4 May 2016.
33. Epstein, R. and Robertson, R. E. 'The search engine manipulation effect (SEME) and its possible impact on the outcomes of elections', *Proceedings of the National Academy of Sciences*, 112(33) (2015).

34. 'How internet platforms are combatting disinformation and misinformation in the age of Covid-19', New America.
35. 'An update on our work to keep people informed and limit misinformation about COVID-19', Meta, first published April 2020.
36. Stepanov, A., Director, Product Management, 'Sharing our content distribution guidelines', Meta blog post, 23 September 2021.
37. 'The online information environment', The Royal Society, 19 January 2022.
38. Varol, O., Ferrara, E., Davis, C. A., Menczer, F. and Flammini, A. 'Online human–bot interactions: detection, estimation, and characterization', The Association for the Advancement of Artificial Intelligence, 2017.
39. King, G., Pan, J. and Roberts, M. E. 'How the Chinese government fabricates social media posts for strategic distraction, not engaged argument', *Cambridge Core*, 111(3) (2017), Cambridge University Press.
40. 'How China built a twitter propaganda machine then let it loose on coronavirus', ProPublica, 26 March 2020.
41. Cresci, S., Di Pietro, R., Petrocchi, M., Spognardi, A. and Tesconi, M. 'The paradigm-shift of social spambots: Evidence, theories, and tools for the arms race', arXiv (2017).
42. Caldarelli, G., De Nicola, R., Del Vigna, F., Petrocchi, M. and Saracco, F. 'The role of bot squads in the political propaganda on Twitter', *Communications Physics*, 3(81) (2020).
43. 'Going global: The UK government's "CVE" agenda, counter-radicalisation and covert propaganda', openDemocracy, 4 May 2016.
44. Whitford, T., 'Practices and possibilities: A review of instructional intelligence and counterintelligence literature informing right-wing extremist groups', *Journal of the Australian Institute of Professional Intelligence Officers*, 28 (2020), pp. 3–15.
45. Wells, G., Horwitz, J., Seetharaman, D. 'Facebook knows Instagram is toxic for teen girls, company documents show', *Wall Street Journal*, 14 September 2021.
46. Duffy, B. and Thain, M. 'Do we have your attention? How people focus and live in the modern information environment', Kings College London, February 2022.
47. Ibid.
48. Mark, G., Gudith, D. and Klocke, U. 'The cost of interrupted work: more speed and stress', Association for Computing Machinery (2008), pp. 107–10.

49. Duffy, B. and Thain, M. 'Do we have your attention? How people focus and live in the modern information environment', Kings College London, February 2022.
50. Ward, A. F., Duke, K., Gneezy, A., and Bos, M. W. 'Brain drain: The mere presence of one's own smartphone reduces available cognitive capacity', *Journal of the Association for Consumer Research* (2017), pp. 140–54.
51. Barr, N., Pennycook, G., Stolz, J. A. and Fugelsang, J. A. 'The brain in your pocket: Evidence that Smartphones are used to supplant thinking', *Computers in Human Behavior*, 48 (2015), pp. 473–80.
52. Henkel, L. A. 'Point-and-shoot memories: The influence of taking photos on memory for a museum tour', *Psychological Science*, 25(2) (2014), pp. 396–402.
53. Duffy, B. and Thain, M. 'Do we have your attention? How people focus and live in the modern information environment', Kings College London, February 2022.
54. Uhls, Y. T., Michikyan, M., Morris, J., Garcia, D., Small, G. W., Zgourou, E. and Greenfield, P. M. 'Five days at outdoor education camp without screens improves preteen skills with nonverbal emotion cues', *Computers in Human Behavior*, 39 (2014), pp. 387–92.
55. Kushlev, K., Proulx, J. and Dunn, E. W. '"Silence your phones": Smartphone notifications increase inattention and hyperactivity symptoms', in *Proceedings of the 2016 CHI Conference on Human Factors in Computing Systems*, 2016, pp. 1011–20.
56. Allcott, H., Braghieri,L., Eichmeye, S. and Gentzkow, M. 'The welfare effects of social media', NBER, 20190.
57. Amsalem, Eran and Zoizner, Alon, 'Do people learn about politics on social media? A meta-analysis of 76 studies', *Journal of Communication* (2022).
58. Miller, Matt. 'Artificial intelligence, our final invention?', *The Washington Post*, 2 December 2013; https://www.washingtonpost.com/opinions/matt-miller-artificial-intelligence-our-final-invention/2013/12/18/26ed6be8-67e6-11e3-8b5b-a77187b716a3_story.html

8: Turn off your TV

1. Schwitzgebel, E. 'Do people still report dreaming in black and white? An attempt to replicate a questionnaire from 1942', *Perceptual and Motor Skills*, 96 (2003), pp. 25–9.

2. Yang, Maya. 'Having a go: US parents say Peppa Pig is giving their kids British accents', *Guardian*, 2 July 2021; https://www.theguardian.com/tv-and-radio/2021/jul/19/peppa-pig-american-kids-british-accents
3. Creative Diversity Network. 'The fifth cut: Diamond at 5'; https://creativediversitynetwork.com/diamond/diamond-reports/the-fifth-cut-diamond-at-5/
4. YouGov poll, commissioned by the Campaign for Common Sense, June 2022.
5. 'Which of the following hobbies and interests do you do in your spare time at home?', *Statista*, November 2019 to May 2020.
6. Sussman, S. and Moran, M. B. 'Hidden addiction: Television', *Journal of Behavioral Addictions* 2(3) (2013), pp. 125–32.
7. Horvath, C. W. 'Measuring television addiction', *Journal of Broadcasting & Electronic Media*, 48(3) (2004), pp. 378–98.
8. Botta, R. A. 'Television images and adolescent girls' body image disturbance', *Journal of Communication*, 49(2) (1999), pp. 22–41.
9. Werneck, A. O., Vancampfort, D., Oyeyemi, A. L., Stubbs, B. and Silva, D. R. 'Associations between TV viewing, sitting time, physical activity and insomnia among 100,839 Brazilian adolescents', *Psychiatry Research*, 269 (2018), pp. 700–6.
10. Zimmerman, F. J. and Christakis, D. A. 'Associations between content types of early media exposure and subsequent attentional problems', *Pediatrics*, 120(5) (2007), pp. 986–92.
11. Jago, R., Baranowski, T., Baranowski, J. C., Thompson, D. and Greaves, K. A. 'BMI from 3–6 y of age is predicted by TV viewing and physical activity, not diet', *International Journal of Obesity*, 29(6) (2005), pp. 557–64.
12. Sussman, S. and Moran, M. B. 'Television and growing up: The impact of televised violence', Report to the Surgeon General, United States Public Health Service, US Department of Justice (1972).
13. Bandura, A. 'Social cognitive theory of mass communication', *Media Psychology*, 3 (2001), pp. 265–99.
14. Dougherty, R. J., Hoang, T. D., Launer, J. L., Jacobs, D. R., Sidney, S. and Yaffe, K. 'Long-term television viewing patterns and gray matter brain volume in midlife', *Brain Imaging Behaviour* (2022), pp. 637–44.
15. 'How giving up TV for a month changed my brain and my life', *Fast Company*, June 2016.
16. 'BBC ON THIS DAY | 1957: BBC fools the nation', BBC; http://news.bbc.co.uk/onthisday/hi/dates/stories/april/1/newsid_2819000/2819261.stm

17. 'Banned BBC show "Ghostwatch" left traumatised viewers in tears and "unable to sleep for MONTHS"', *Manchester Evening News*, 30 October 2022; https://www.manchestereveningnews.co.uk/news/tv/banned-bbc-show-ghostwatch-left-25351016
18. Huxley, Aldous. *Brave New World Revisited*, Vintage Classics, 2004.
19. 'News consumption in the UK: 2022', OFCOM, 2 July 2022; https://www.ofcom.org.uk/__data/assets/pdf_file/0027/241947/News-Consumption-in-the-UK-2022-report.pdf
20. Xia, S. 'Amusing ourselves to loyalty? Entertainment, propaganda, and regime resilience in China', *Political Research Quarterly* (2022), pp. 1096–112.
21. Pomerantsev, P. 'The Hidden Author of Putinism', *The Atlantic*, November 2014.
22. Jowett, Garth S. and O'Donnell, Victoria. *Propaganda and Persuasion*, SAGE Publications, Inc., 7th edition (2018).
23. '"Weave in key talking points" – Pentagon contract for *Top Gun: Maverick*', Spy Culture, 2 June 2019; https://www.spyculture.com/weave-in-key-talking-points-pentagon-contract-for-top-gun-maverick/
24. 'Top Gun for Hire: Why Hollywood is the US military's best wingman', *Guardian*, 27 May 2022; https://www.theguardian.com/film/2022/may/26/top-gun-for-hire-why-hollywood-is-the-us-militarys-best-wingman
25. 'The power of TV: Nudging viewers to decarbonize their lifestyles', The Behavioural Insights Team, November 2021.
26. Lowery, S. A. and DeFleur, M. L. *Milestones in Mass Communication Research*, New York, Longman (1988).
27. Chiricos, T., Eschholz, S. and Getz, M. 'Crime, news and fear of crime: Toward an identification of audience effects', 44(3) (1997), pp. 342–57.
28. 'Sky defends new chief's private jet commute', *Telegraph*, 30 October 2021.
29. Waterson, J. and Clinton, J. 'Sky calls for climate action from TV firms, despite CEO's private jet use', *Guardian*, 31 October 2021.
30. Corley, T. C. *Rich Habits: The Daily Success Habits of Wealthy Individuals*, Hillcrest Publishing Group, 2010.
31. Crawford, M. 'The back-alley abortion that almost didn't make it into *Dirty Dancing*', *Vice*, August 2017.
32. Jowett, Garth S. and O'Donnell, Victoria. *Propaganda and Persuasion*, SAGE Publications, Inc., 7th edition (2018).
33. Orwell, George. *1984*, Secker & Warburg, 1949.

34. Bush, K. 'Communication technology use and well-being: Does less screen time lead to greater happiness?', Eastern Washington University EWU Digital Commons, autumn 2018.
35. 'Turn off, tune out … er, then?', *The Times*, May 2007.
36. 'Mass media, behaviour change & peacebuilding', The Behavioural Insights Team, January 2022.

9: Get it in writing

1. 'Photos: A hit tip to the presidents', CNN Politics, 2 February 2016; https://edition.cnn.com/2013/04/12/politics/gallery/presidents-hats/index.html
2. King, Josh. 'Dukakis and the Tank', *Politico Magazine*, 2 November 2013; https://www.politico.com/magazine/story/2013/11/dukakis-and-the-tank-099119/
3. McCandless, James. 'How a bacon sandwich derailed Ed Miliband's UK political career', HuffPost, 2 October 2018.
4. Ernst, Douglas. 'Scott Adams of "Dilbert" says women will elect Hillary Clinton, own "everything that goes wrong"', *Washington Times*, 2 October 2016; https://www.washingtontimes.com/news/2016/oct/14/scott-adams-of-dilbert-says-women-will-elect-hilla/
5. Fahmy, S., Cho, S., Wanta, W. and Song, Y. 'Visual agenda-setting after 9/11: Individuals' emotions, image recall, and concern with terrorism', *Visual Communication Quarterly*, 13(1) (2006), pp. 4–15.
6. Shepard, R. N. 'Recognition memory for words, sentences, and pictures', *Journal of Verbal Learning and Verbal Behavior*, 6(1) (1967), pp. 156–63.
7. Graber, D. A. 'Say it with pictures', *The Annals of the American Academy of Political and Social Science*, 546(1) (1996), pp. 85–96.
8. Malik, Tariq. 'Scientist admits "space telescope" photo is actually chorizo in tasty Twitter prank', Space.com, 2 August 2022; https://www.space.com/james-webb-space-telescope-scientist-chorizo-prank
9. Stanley-Becker, Isaac and Nix, Naomi. 'Fake images of Trump arrest show "giant step" for AI's disruptive power', *The Washington Post*, 22 March 2023; https://www.washingtonpost.com/politics/2023/03/22/trump-arrest-deepfakes/
10. Mowlana, H., Gerbner, G. and Schiller, H. I. *Triumph of the Image: The Media's War in the Gulf – a Global Perspective*, Boulder, Westview Press, 1992.

11. Wittenberg, C., Tappin, B. M., Berinsky, A. J. and Rand, D. G. 'The (minimal) persuasive advantage of political video over text', *Proceedings of the National Academy of Sciences*, 118(47) (2021), e2114388118.
12. Petty, R. E. and Cacioppo, J. T. 'The elaboration likelihood model of persuasion', in *Communication and Persuasion*, New York, Springer, 1986, pp. 1–24.
13. Grabe, M. E. and Bucy, E. P. *Image Bite Politics: News and the Visual Framing of Elections*, Oxford University Press, 2009.
14. Pfau, M., Haigh, M., Fifrick, A., Holl, D., Tedesco, A., Cope, J. and Martin, M. 'The effects of print news photographs of the casualties of war', *Journalism & Mass Communication Quarterly*, 83(1) (2006), pp. 150–68.
15. Garcia, M. R. and Stark, P. *Eyes on the News*, St. Petersburg, FL: The Poynter Institute for Media Studies, 1991.
16. Matthews, W. J., Benjamin, C. and Osborne, C. 'Memory for moving and static images', *Psychonomic Bulletin & Review*, 14(5) (2007), pp. 989–93.
17. Kaye, H. and Pearce, J. M. 'The strength of the orienting response during Pavlovian conditioning', *Journal of Experimental Psychology: Animal Behavior Processes*, 10(1) (1984), p. 90.
18. Sokolov, E. N. 'The orienting response, and future directions of its development', *The Pavlovian Journal of Biological Science*, 25(3) (1990), pp. 142–50.
19. Paivio, A. 'Dual coding theory: Retrospect and current status', *Canadian Journal of Psychology*, 45(3) (1991), p. 255.
20. Neuman, W. R., Just, M. R. and Crigler, A. N. *Common Knowledge: News and the Construction of Political Meaning*, University of Chicago Press, 1992.
21. Bergen, L., Grimes, T. and Potter, D. 'How attention partitions itself during simultaneous message presentations', *Human Communication Research*, 31(3) (2005), pp. 311–36.
22. McLuhan, Marshall. *Understanding Media: The Extensions of Man*, MIT Press, 1994.
23. Postman, Neil. *Amusing Ourselves to Death: Public Discourse in the Age of Showbusiness*, Penguin Books, 1985.
24. Sigman, A. 'Visual voodoo: The biological impact of watching TV', *Biologist*, 54(1) (2007), pp. 12–17.
25. Barnhurst, K. G. and Steele, C. A. 'Image-bite news: The visual coverage of elections on US television, 1968–1992', *Harvard International Journal of Press/Politics*, 2(1) (1997), pp. 40–58.
26. Conway III, L. G. and Zubrod, A. 'Are US presidents becoming less rhetorically complex? Evaluating the integrative complexity

of Joe Biden and Donald Trump in historical context', *Journal of Language and Social Psychology* (2022), 0261927X221081126.
27. 'Full text: 2017 Donald Trump inauguration speech transcript', Politico, 20 January 2017; https://www.politico.com/story/2017/01/full-text-donald-trump-inauguration-speech-transcript-233907
28. Tobar, Hector. 'American adults have low (and declining) reading proficiency', *LA Times*, 2 October 2013; https://www.latimes.com/books/jacketcopy/la-et-jc-american-adults-have-low-and-declining-reading-proficiency-20131008-story.html
29. Huxley, Aldous. *Brave New World Revisited*, Vintage Classics, 2004.
30. Lillard, A. S. and Peterson, J. 'The immediate impact of different types of television on young children's executive function', *Pediatrics*, 128(4) (2011), pp. 644–9.
31. Kamarudin, S. S. and Dannaee, M. 'Media screen time and speech delay: Comparison study in children with and without speech delay', *International Studies*, 3(4) (2018), p. 5.
32. Christakis, D. A., Ramirez, J. S. and Ramirez, J. M. 'Overstimulation of newborn mice leads to behavioral differences and deficits in cognitive performance', *Scientific Reports*, 2(1) (2012), pp. 1–6.
33. Mayer, Beth Ann. 'Some think "CoComelon" is too stimulating for their kids, so we asked an expert to weigh in', Parents, 2 August 2022; https://www.parents.com/news/some-think-cocomelon-is-too-stimulating-for-their-kids-we-asked-an-expert-to-weigh-insome-think-cocomelon-is-too-stimulating-for-their-kids-we-asked-an-expert-to-weigh-in/
34. Sha, P. and Dong, X. 'Research on adolescents regarding the indirect effect of depression, anxiety, and stress between TikTok use disorder and memory loss', *International Journal of Environmental Research and Public Health*, 18(16) (2021), p. 8820.
35. Mendelsohn, M. 'The media's persuasive effects: The priming of leadership in the 1988 Canadian election', *Canadian Journal of Political Science/Revue canadienne de science politique*, 27(1) (1994), pp. 81–97.
36. Chaiken, S. and Eagly, A. H. 'Communication modality as a determinant of persuasion: The role of communicator salience', *Journal of Personality and Social Psychology*, 45(2) (1983), pp. 241.
37. Wright, P. L. 'Analyzing media effects on advertising responses', *Public Opinion Quarterly*, 38(2) (1974), pp. 192–205.

38. Irving, Z. C., McGrath, C., Flynn, L., Glasser, A. and Mills, C. 'The shower effect: Mind wandering facilitates creative incubation during moderately engaging activities', *Psychology of Aesthetics, Creativity, and the Arts* (2022).
39. Knightley, Phillip. 'The disinformation campaign', *Guardian*, 2 October 2001; https://www.theguardian.com/education/2001/oct/04/socialsciences.highereducation
40. 'CIA's final report: No WMD found in Iraq', NBC News, 2 April 2005; https://www.nbcnews.com/id/wbna7634313

10: Watch out for the blip

1. Myre, Greg. 'How the U.S. military used Guns N' Roses to make a dictator give up', NPR, 30 May 2017; https://www.npr.org/sections/thetwo-way/2017/05/30/530723028/how-the-u-s-military-used-guns-n-roses-to-make-a-dictator-giv
2. Tweedale, Douglas. 'Analysis UPI World Focus Vatican envoy won psychological battle with Noriega', UPI, 2 January 1990; https://www.upi.com/Archives/1990/01/04/Analysis-UPI-World-Focus-Vatican-envoy-won-psychological-battle-with-Noriega/5813631429200/
3. Planas, Antonio. 'Inmates at Oklahoma jail subjected to "torture" by hearing "Baby Shark" on loop, lawsuit says', NBC News, 2 November 2021; https://www.nbcnews.com/news/us-news/inmates-oklahoma-jail-subjected-torture-hearing-baby-shark-loop-lawsuit-n1283385
4. Klein, Naomi. *The Shock Doctrine: The Rise of Disaster Capitalism*, Picador USA, 2008.
5. 'Kubark counterintelligence interrogation', Central Intelligence Agency, July 1963; https://nsarchive2.gwu.edu/NSAEBB/NSAEBB122/CIA%20Kubark%201-60.pdf
6. Orwell, George. *1984*, Secker & Warburg, 1949.
7. Meerloo, Joost. *The Rape of the Mind: The Psychology of Thought Control, Menticide, and Brainwashing* (Vol. 118), World Publishing Company, 1956.
8. Hunter, Edward. *Brainwashing: The Story of Men Who Defied It*, Pickle Partners Publishing, 2016.
9. Swift, Stephen. *The Cardinal's Story: The Life and Work of Joseph Cardinal Mindszenty*, Kessinger Publishing, 2007.
10. Stein, Alexandra. *Terror, Love and Brainwashing: Attachment in Cults and Totalitarian Systems*, Routledge, 2021.
11. Koestler, Arthur. *Arrow in the Blue*, Random House, 2011.
12. Huxley, Aldous. *The Devils of Loudun*, Random House, 2005.

13. Deren, Maya. *Divine Horsemen: Living Gods of Haiti*, McPherson & Co. Publishers, 1985.
14. Schein, Edgar H. *Coercive Persuasion: A Socio-Psychological Analysis of the 'Brainwashing' of American Civilian Prisoners by the Chinese Communists*, New York, W.W. Norton, 1961.
15. Dolinski, D. and Nawrat, R. '"Fear-then-relief" procedure for producing compliance: Beware when the danger is over', *Journal of Experimental Social Psychology*, 34(1) (1998), pp. 27–50.
16. Wheeler, S. C., Briñol, P. and Hermann, A. D. 'Resistance to persuasion as self-regulation: Ego-depletion and its effects on attitude change processes', *Journal of Experimental Social Psychology*, 43(1) (2007), pp. 150–6.
17. Yoon, C., Lee, M. P. and Danziger, S. 'The effects of optimal time of day on persuasion processes in older adults', *Psychology & Marketing*, 24(5) (2007), pp. 475–95.
18. Hitler, Adolf. *Mein Kampf* (Vol. 1), Motilal Banarsidass, 2014.
19. Davis, B. P. and Knowles, E. S. 'A disrupt-then-reframe technique of social influence', *Journal of Personality and Social Psychology*, 76(2) (1999), p. 192.
20. Stajano, F. and Wilson, P. 'Understanding scam victims: Seven principles for systems security', *Communications of the ACM*, 54(3) (2011), pp. 70–5.
21. 'Risk of radicalisation', Action Counters Terrorism; https://actearly.uk/radicalisation/reduce-the-risk/
22. Singer, Margaret Thaler. *Cults in Our Midst: The Continuing Fight Against Their Hidden Menace*, Jossey-Bass, 2003.
23. Hunt, Tom. 'Former Jehovah's Witness admits: We targeted grief-stricken as "ripe fruit"', *Stuff*, 2 June 2016; https://www.stuff.co.nz/dominion-post/news/80708572/former-jehovahs-witness-admits-we-targeted-griefstricken-as-ripe-fruit
24. King Jr, Neil and Dreazen, Yochi J. 'Amid chaos in Iraq, tiny security firm found opportunity', *Wall Street Journal*, 2 August 2004; https://www.wsj.com/articles/SB109234861785890362
25. Abroshan, H., Devos, J., Poels, G. and Laermans, E. 'COVID-19 and phishing: Effects of human emotions, behavior, and demographics on the success of phishing attempts during the pandemic', *IEEE Access*, Vol. 9 (2021), 121916–29.
26. Pavlov, I. P. 'Relation between excitation and inhibition and their delimitations; Experimental neuroses in dogs', in I. P. Pavlov and W. H. Gantt (trans.), *Lectures on Conditioned Reflexes: Twenty-five Years of Objective Study of the Higher Nervous Activity (Behaviour) of Animals*, Liverwright Publishing Corporation, 1928, pp. 339–49.

27. Strauss, William and Howe, Neil. *The Fourth Turning: What the Cycles of History Tell Us About America's Next Rendezvous with Destiny*, Crown, 2009.
28. 'Edelman Trust Barometer 2021', Edelman, 2 February 2021; https://www.edelman.co.uk/sites/g/files/aatuss301/files/2021-02/2021%20Edelman%20Trust%20Barometer%20-%20UK%20Media%20Deck.pdf
29. Kirk, Isabelle. 'One in eight Britons feel tired all the time', YouGov, 2 January 2022; https://yougov.co.uk/topics/society/articles-reports/2022/01/11/one-eight-britons-feel-tired-all-time
30. Reed, Susanne. 'How using the HALT concept prevents alcohol relapse', Alcoholics Anonymous, 2 March 2022; https://alcoholicsanonymous.com/how-using-the-halt-concept-prevents-alcohol-relapse/
31. Gosnell, E., Berman, K., Juarez, L. and Mathera, R. 'How behavioral science reduced the spread of misinformation on TikTok', Irrational Labs; https://irrationallabs.com/content/uploads/2021/03/IL-TikTok-Whitepaper2.pdf

II: Be sceptical of Big Brother

1. Bernays, Edward L. *Propaganda*, New York, H. Liveright, 1928.
2. 'This unsettling Army recruitment video is a master class in psychological warfare', Task & Purpose, May 2022.
3. Orwell, George. *1984*, Secker & Warburg, 1949.
4. 'How Ukraine's "Ghost of Kyiv" legendary pilot was born', BBC News website, May 2022.
5. Paul, C. and Matthews, M. 'The Russian "Firehose of Falsehood" propaganda model', The Rand Corporation, 2016.
6. Smart, B., Watt, J., Benedetti, S., Mitchell, L. and Roughan, M. '#IStandWithPutin versus #IStandWithUkraine: The interaction of bots and humans in discussion of the Russia/Ukraine war', arXiv (2022).
7. 'Pentagon opens sweeping review of clandestine psychological operations', *The Washington Post*, September 2022.
8. 'Going global: The UK government's "CVE" agenda, counter-radicalisation and covert propaganda', openDemocracy, May 2016.
9. '"Controlled spontaneity": The secret UK government blueprints shaping post-terror planning', Middle East Eye, May 2019.
10. Easthope, L. 'I'm an emergency planner. Manchester shows we need new ways to heal', *Guardian*, 24 May 2017.

11. Halpern, D. 'Personal responsibility and changing behaviour: The state of knowledge and its implications for public policy: February 2004', The Cabinet Office.
12. Bakir, V., Herring, E., Miller, D. and Robinson, P. 'Organized persuasive communication: A new conceptual framework for research on public relations, propaganda and promotional culture', *Critical Sociology*, 45(3) (2019), pp. 311–28.
13. Thaler, R. and Sunstein, C. *Nudge*, Penguin, 1st edition (2009).
14. Rolnick, Matthew. 'Beware of the "Cobra Effect" in business', *Forbes*, 2 August 2020; https://www.forbes.com/sites/forbesbusinessdevelopmentcouncil/2020/08/26/beware-of-the-cobra-effect-in-business/?sh=62339e775f6f
15. Earp, B. D., Dill, B., Harris, J., Ackerman, J. and Bargh, J. A. 'Incidental exposure to no-smoking signs primes craving for cigarettes: An ironic effect of unconscious semantic processing', *Yale Review of Undergraduate Research in Psychology*, 2(1) (2011), pp. 12–23.
16. Pinola, Melanie. 'Be wary of pickpocket warning signs (and other tips to avoid getting pickpocketed)', Lifehacker, 2 November 2012; https://lifehacker.com/be-wary-of-pickpocket-warning-signs-and-other-tips-to-5960156
17. 'Behaviour change', House of Lords Science and Technology Select Committee report, 2010.
18. Dolan, P., Hallsworth, M., Halpern, D., King, D. and Vlaev, I. 'MINDSPACE influencing behaviour through public policy', Cabinet Office, Institute for Government (2010).
19. 'Bringing dark patterns to light', Federal Trade Commission, September 2022.
20. 'Online choice architecture: How digital design can harm competition and consumers', Competition and Markets Authority, 2 April 2022; https://www.gov.uk/government/publications/online-choice-architecture-how-digital-design-can-harm-competition-and-consumers
21. 'Influence government: Exploring practices, ethics, and power in the use of targeted advertising by the UK state', The Scottish Centre for Crime and Justice Research, September 2021.
22. 'Loan Charge All-Party Parliamentary Group Report on the Morse Review into the Loan Charge, March 2020', Loan Charge APPG, March 2020.
23. 'Science and Technology Select Committee Behaviour Change', Science and Technology Select Committee, 2010.
24. Popper, K. *The Open Society and Its Enemies*, Routledge Classics, 2002.

25. Sunstein, C. and Vermuele, A. 'Conspiracy theories', *John M. Olin Program in Law and Economics Working Paper*, 387 (2008).
26. Coady, D. 'Cass Sunstein and Adrian Vermeule on conspiracy theories', *Argumenta* (2018).
27. Barnet, A. 'Millions were in germ war tests', *Guardian*, 21 April 2002.
28. Thiessen, Marc A. 'The suppression of Hunter Biden's laptop is a huge scandal', *The Washington Post*, 2 December 2022; https://www.washingtonpost.com/opinions/2022/12/09/hunter-biden-laptop-suppression-twitter-fbi-social-media/
29. Trump, Donald Jr. 'What's the difference between a conspiracy theory and the truth??? About 6 Months! Imaging all the "conspiracy theories" that all came true right after it no longer mattered and the leftist got what they wanted', Instagram, 2 May 2022; https://www.instagram.com/p/CdV1mq_urXm
30. Coady, D. 'Cass Sunstein and Adrian Vermeule on conspiracy theories', *Argumenta*.
31. A more accurate translation of Voltaire's famous and widely quoted saying is: 'It is dangerous to be right in matters where established men are wrong.' Originally published in *Le Siècle de Louis XIV* (1752).
32. 'Emmanuel Macron promises ban on fake news during elections', *Guardian*, January 2018.
33. 'Breastfeeding after Covid-19 vaccine is recommended as safe', Full Fact website, August 2021.
34. Hanna, N., Heffes-Doon, A., Lin, X., De Mejia, C. M., Botros, B., Gurzenda, E. and Nayak, A. 'Detection of Messenger RNA COVID-19 vaccines in human breast milk', *JAMA Pediatrics* (December 2022).
35. 'Scientists believed Covid leaked from Wuhan lab – but feared debate could hurt international harmony', *Telegraph*, January 2022.
36. Knapton, Sarah. 'UK experts helped shut down Covid lab leak theory – weeks after being told it might be true', *Telegraph*, 23 November 2022; https://www.telegraph.co.uk/news/2022/11/23/uk-experts-helped-shut-covid-lab-leak-theory-weeks-told-might/
37. 'Ministry of Truth: The secretive government units spying on your speech', Big Brother Watch, January 2023.
38. Fraser, B. C., Sharman, R. and Nunn, P. D. 'Associations of locus of control, information processing style and anti-reflexivity with climate change scepticism in an Australian sample', *Public Understanding of Science* (2022), p. 4.

12: Consider your options

1. Lewis, C. S. *The Problem of Pain*, The Centenary Press, 1940.
2. Presson, P. K. and Benassi, V. A. 'Illusion of control: A meta-analytic review', *Journal of Social Behavior and Personality*, 11(3) (1996), p. 493.
3. Seligman, M. E. 'Learned helplessness', *Annual Review of Medicine*, 23(1) (1972), pp. 407–12.
4. Kammeyer-Mueller, J. D., Judge, T. A. and Piccolo, R. F. 'Self-esteem and extrinsic career success: Test of a dynamic model', *Applied Psychology*, 57(2) (2008), pp. 204–24.
5. Gale, C. R., Batty, G. D. and Deary, I. J. 'Locus of control at age 10 years and health outcomes and behaviors at age 30 years: The 1970 British Cohort Study', *Psychosomatic Medicine*, 70(4) (2008), pp. 397–403.
6. Libet, B. 'Do we have free will?', *Journal of Consciousness Studies*, 6(8–9) (1999), pp. 47–57.
7. Rosenberg, B. D. and Siegel, J. T. 'A 50-year review of psychological reactance theory: Do not read this article', *Motivation Science*, 4(4) (2018), pp. 281–300.
8. Wehbe, M. S., Basil, M. and Basil, D. 'Reactance and coping responses to tobacco counter-advertisements', *Journal of Health Communication*, 22(7) (2017), pp. 576–83.
9. Shoenberger, H., Kim, E. and Sun, Y. 'Advertising during COVID-19: Exploring perceived brand message authenticity and potential psychological reactance', *Journal of Advertising*, 50(3) (2021), pp. 253–61.
10. Carpenter, C. J. 'A meta-analysis of the effectiveness of the "but you are free" compliance-gaining technique', *Communication Studies*, 64(1) (2013), pp. 6–17.
11. Roberts, Monty. *Horse Sense for People: The Man Who Listens to Horses Talks to People*, Anchor Canada, 2002.
12. Trinkaus, J. 'Preconditioning an audience for mental magic: An informal look', *Perceptual and Motor Skills* 51(1) (1980), p. 262.
13. Pailhes, A., Rensink, R. A. and Kuhn, G. 'A psychologically based taxonomy of magicians' forcing techniques: How magicians influence our choices, and how to use this to study psychological mechanisms', *Consciousness and Cognition*, 86 (2020), 103038.
14. French, C. C. 'Population stereotypes and belief in the paranormal: Is there a relationship?', *Australian Psychologist*, 27(1) (1992), pp. 57–8.

15. Olson, J. A., Amlani, A. A., Raz, A. and Rensink, R. A. 'Influencing choice without awareness', *Consciousness and Cognition*, 37 (2015), pp. 225–36.
16. Saal, Marco. 'Burger King Austria erklärt fleischlose Whopper zur neuen Normalität', Horizont, 2 July 2022; https://www.horizont.net/marketing/nachrichten/normal-oder-mit-fleisch-burger-king-austria-erklaert-fleischlose-whopper-zur-neuen-normalitaet-201354?crefresh=1#:~:text=%22Normal%2C%20oder%20mit%20Fleisch%3F%22%2C%20lautet%20entsprechend%20der,pflanzliches%20Sortiment%20aufmerksam%20machen%20will
17. Houston, Amy. 'Quorn's "food porn" ad encourages deli meat lovers to go plant-based', The Drum, 2 September 2022; https://www.thedrum.com/news/2022/09/21/quorn-s-food-porn-ad-encourages-deli-meat-lovers-go-plant-based
18. Jachimowicz, J. M., Duncan, S., Weber, E. U. and Johnson, E. J. 'When and why defaults influence decisions: A meta-analysis of default effects', *Behavioural Public Policy*, 3(2) (2019), pp. 159–86.
19. Garman, M. B. and Kamien, M. I. 'The paradox of voting: Probability calculations', *Behavioral Science*, 13(4) (1968), pp. 306–16.
20. Frazer, James George. *The Golden Bough: A Study in Comparative Religion*, Macmillan and Co., 1890.
21. Pailhès, A., Rensink, R. A. and Kuhn, G. 'A psychologically based taxonomy of magicians' forcing techniques: How magicians influence our choices, and how to use this to study psychological mechanisms', *Consciousness and Cognition*, 86 (2020), 103038.
22. Lifton, Robert Jay. *Thought Reform and the Psychology of Totalism: A Study of 'Brainwashing' in China*, New York, Norton, 1961.
23. Orwell, George. *1984*, Secker & Warburg, 1949.
24. Hunter, Edward. *Brainwashing: The Story of Men Who Defied It*, Pickle Partners Publishing, 2016.
25. Bruns, H. and Perino, G. 'Point at, nudge, or push private provision of a public good?', *Economic Inquiry*, 59(3) (2021), pp. 996–1007.
26. Debnam, J. and Just, D. R. 'Endogenous responses to paternalism: Examining psychological reactance in the lab and the field', unpublished working paper, 2017.
27. Morris, Chris. 'An updated list of free stuff you can get for showing your COVID-19 vaccine card', *Fortune*, 2 March 2021;

https://fortune.com/2021/03/23/covid-vaccine-freebies-card-cdc-krispy-kreme-donuts-free-weed-marijuana-cannabis-food-uber-lyft-rides-running-list-discounts/

28. Thaler, Richard H. 'More than nudges are needed to end the pandemic', *New York Times*, 2 August 2021; https://www.nytimes.com/2021/08/05/business/vaccine-pandemic-nudge-passport.html
29. Nail, P. R. and Thompson, P. L. 'An analysis and empirical demonstration of the concept of self-anticonformity', *Journal of Social Behavior and Personality*, 5(3) (1990), p. 151.
30. Pailhès, A. and Kuhn, G. 'Don't read this paper! Reverse psychology, contrast and position effects in a magician forcing technique', Psychology Department, Goldsmiths, University of London, UK.
31. Hoffman, Michael. *Secret Societies and Psychological Warfare*, Independent History and Research, 2001.
32. Eigenberg, H., Garland, T. and Moriarty, L. J. 'Victim blaming', in Laura Moriarty, *Controversies in Victimology*, Routledge, 2008, pp. 21–36.
33. Juhila, K. and Raitakari, S. 'Responsibilisation in governmentality literature', in *Responsibilisation at the Margins of Welfare Services*, Routledge, 2016, pp. 19–42.

13: Learn the language of symbols

1. Lorenz, Konrad. *The Foundations of Ethology*, Springer, 1981.
2. McHenry, R. E. and Shouksmith, G. A. 'Creativity, visual imagination and suggestibility: Their relationship in a group of 10-year-old children', *British Journal of Educational Psychology*, 40(2) (1970), pp. 154–60.
3. Williamson, Judith. *Decoding Advertisements* (Vol. 4), London, Marion Boyars, 1978.
4. Bey, Hakim. *Taz: The Temporary Autonomous Zone, Ontological Anarchy, Poetic Terrorism*, Autonomedia, 2003.
5. Cheong, Charissa. 'A white influencer who spent $250,000 on surgery to resemble a K-pop star said they want to "look more Korean" despite facing backlash and death threats', Insider, 2 February 2022; https://www.insider.com/oli-london-korean-trolls-hate-death-threats-surgery-2022-2
6. In the course of writing this book, London subsequently identified as a woman, and then a detransitioned Christian.
7. Karlson-Weimann, C. 'The Baphomet: A discourse analysis of the symbol in three contexts', Uppsala University, 2013.

8. Spencer, Paul. 'Trump's occult online supporters believe "meme magic" got him elected', *Vice*, 2 November 2016.
9. Palau, Adria Salvador and Roozenbeek, J. 'How an ancient Egyptian god spurred the rise of Trump', The Conversation, 2 March 2017; https://theconversation.com/how-an-ancient-egyptian-god-spurred-the-rise-of-trump-72598
10. Pageau, Jonathan. 'The metaphysics of Clown World', YouTube, 2 April 2019; https://www.youtube.com/watch?v=MzEwaUCw9Bo
11. Zadrozny, Brandy and Collins, Ben. 'QAnon looms behind nationwide rallies and viral #SavetheChildren hashtags', NBC News, 2 August 2020; https://www.nbcnews.com/tech/tech-news/qanon-looms-behind-nationwide-rallies-viral-hashtags-n1237722
12. Kalbitzer, J., Mell, T., Bermpohl, F., Rapp, M. A. and Heinz, A. 'Twitter psychosis: A rare variation or a distinct syndrome?', *The Journal of Nervous and Mental Disease*, 202(8) (2014), p. 623.
13. DiTrollio, Megan. 'This is how real-life resistance witches say they're taking down the patriarchy', *Marie Claire*, 2 August 2021; https://www.marieclaire.com/culture/a24440291/witches-2018-midterms/
14. Ellis, Emma Grey. 'Trump's presidency has spawned a new generation of witches', *Wired*, 20 October 2019; https://www.wired.com/story/trump-witches/
15. Huxley, Aldous. *Brave New World Revisited*, Vintage Classics, 2004.
16. Hall, Manly P. *Secret Teachings of All Ages: An Encyclopedic Outline of Masonic, Hermetic, Qabbalistic and Rosicrucian Symbolical Philosophy*, Jeremy P. Tarcher, 2004.
17. Stevens, Dana. 'On every box of cake mix, evidence of Freud's theories', *New York Times*, 2 August 2005; https://www.nytimes.com/2005/08/12/movies/on-every-box-of-cake-mix-evidence-of-freuds-theories.html
18. Bernays, Edward L. *Propaganda*, New York, H. Liveright, 1928.
19. Oakeshott, Isabel. 'The truth about Matt Hancock', *The Spectator*, 10 December 2022.
20. Liles, Jordan. 'Do McDonald's golden arches symbolize a mother's breasts?', Snopes, 2 November 2021; https://www.snopes.com/fact-check/mcdonalds-golden-arches-breasts/
21. Jung, Carl Gustav. *The Archetypes and the Collective Unconscious*, Routledge, 1991.
22. Erdman, Stephan. 'Attractive MALE ARCHETYPES That WOMEN get OBSESSED With!', YouTube, 2 January 2021; https://www.youtube.com/watch?v=PpUD92R2O_M

23. Da Silva, S. G. and Tehrani, J. J. 'Comparative phylogenetic analyses uncover the ancient roots of Indo-European folktales', *Royal Society Open Science*, 3(1) (2016), 150645.
24. Elgendi, M., Kumar, P., Barbic, S., Howard, N., Abbott, D. and Cichocki, A. 'Subliminal priming – state of the art and future perspectives', *Behavioral Sciences*, 8(6) (2018), p. 54.
25. Gillath, O., Mikulincer, M., Birnbaum, G. E. and Shaver, P. R. 'When sex primes love: Subliminal sexual priming motivates relationship goal pursuit', *Personality and Social Psychology Bulletin*, 34(8) (2008), pp. 1057–69.
26. Gillath, O. and Canterberry, M. 'Neural correlates of exposure to subliminal and supraliminal sexual cues', *Social Cognitive and Affective Neuroscience*, 7(8) (2012), pp. 924–36.
27. Holcomb, S. M. 'Symbolism and ritual as used by the National Socialists', Marshall University, 2002.
28. Kertzer, David I. *Ritual, Politics, and Power*, New Haven, Yale University Press, 1988.
29. Bryant, Kenzie. 'The most lavish high-society parties of the last half-century', *Vanity Fair*, 2 November 2016; https://www.vanityfair.com/style/photos/2016/11/most-lavish-parties-black-and-white-surrealist-proust-ball
30. Flock, Elizabeth. 'Bohemian Grove: Where the rich and powerful go to misbehave', *The Washington Post*, 2 June 2011; https://www.washingtonpost.com/blogs/blogpost/post/bohemian-grove-where-the-rich-and-powerful-go-to-misbehave/2011/06/15/AGPV1sVH_blog.html
31. 'Marina Abramovic's Spirit Cooking', MIT Press, 2 June 2017; https://mitpress.mit.edu/blog/marina-abramovics-spirit-cooking/
32. Levitz, Eric. 'Spirit Cooking explained: Satanic ritual or fun dinner?', *New York Magazine*, 2 November 2016; https://nymag.com/intelligencer/2016/11/spirit-cooking-explained-satanic-ritual-or-fun-dinner.html
33. Sanderson, David. 'Microsoft drops Marina Abramovic ad after claims of satanism', *The Times*, 2 April 2020; https://www.thetimes.co.uk/article/microsoft-drops-marina-abramovic-ad-after-claims-of-satanism-pnfn98wvc
34. Twitter, 2 August 2013; https://twitter.com/ladygaga/status/368597529786466306?lang=en
35. Harris, Taylor. 'Lady Gaga artpops in at watermill benefit', *Women's Wear Daily*, 2 July 2013; https://wwd.com/eye/parties/lady-gaga-artpops-in-at-watermill-benefit-7069511/

36. Burrichter, Felix. 'Naked ambition: Marina Abramovic's museum gala', *New York Times*, 2 November 2011; https://archive.nytimes.com/tmagazine.blogs.nytimes.com/2011/11/15/naked-ambition-marina-abramovics-moca-gala/
37. Weiner, Jonah. 'Is Lady Gaga a satanist Illuminati slave?', Slate, 2 November 2011; https://slate.com/culture/2011/11/lady-gaga-kanye-west-jay-z-the-conspiracy-theories-that-say-pop-stars-are-illuminati-pawns.html
38. 'Television Advertising Standards Code', Advertising Standards Authority; https://www.asa.org.uk/static/uploaded/3760a9e4-5136-4b4a-85aec3bcc6a3321c.pdf
39. Madani, Doha. 'Nike denies involvement with Lil Nas X "Satan Shoes" containing human blood', NBC News, 2 March 2021; https://www.nbcnews.com/pop-culture/pop-culture-news/nike-denies-involvement-lil-nas-x-satan-shoes-containing-human-n1262280
40. Franklin-Wallis, Oliver. 'Tom Holland is in the center of the web', *GQ*, 2 November 2021; https://www.gq.com/story/tom-holland-superhero-of-the-year-2021
41. Nees, M. A. and Phillips, C. 'Auditory pareidolia: Effects of contextual priming on perceptions of purportedly paranormal and ambiguous auditory stimuli', *Applied Cognitive Psychology*, 29(1) (2015), pp. 129–34.
42. Morrison, Grant. 'Pop magic!', in Metzger, Richard (ed.), *Book of Lies: The Disinformation Guide to Magick and the Occult*, Red Wheel Weiser, 2003.
43. Moore, Alan. *The Mindscape of Alan Moore*, DVD, directed by Dez Vylenz and Moritz Winkler, The Disinformation Company, 2008.
44. Moore, Alan. *Promethea TP Book 05*, DC Comics, 2006.
45. 'Is the Oscar statuette inspired by an Ancient Egyptian god?', The African History, 30 March 2022; https://theafricanhistory.com/2529
46. Meta. 'The Tiger & the Buffalo', YouTube, 2 November 2021; https://www.youtube.com/watch?v=G2W9YVkkn9U
47. 'Paintings for the Temple', Guggenheim; https://www.guggenheim.org/teaching-materials/hilma-af-klint-paintings-for-the-future/paintings-for-the-temple

14: Brainworms and love bombs on transgender subreddits

1. Herman, J. L., Flores, A. R. and O'Neill, K. K. 'How many adults and youth identify as transgender in the United States?', UCLA: The Williams Institute (2022).
2. 'The 2022 year in review', Pornhub; https://www.pornhub.com/insights/2022-year-in-review#top-20-countries
3. Littman, L. 'Parent reports of adolescents and young adults perceived to show signs of a rapid onset of gender dysphoria', *PLOS One*, 13(8) (2018).
4. 'What are brainworms?', Reddit, 3 August 2022; https://www.reddit.com/r/4tranSelfieTrain/comments/wewghc/what_are_brainworms/

15: Be the first to speak up

1. Sargant, William. *Battle for the Mind: A Physiology of Conversion and Brainwashing*, Greenwood Press, 1975.
2. Zimbardo, Philip. 'The psychology of evil', TED; https://www.ted.com/talks/philip_zimbardo_the_psychology_of_evil?language=en
3. Sunstein, C. *Conformity: The Power of Social Influences*, NYU Press (2019).
4. Asch, S. E. 'Effects of group pressure upon the modification and distortion of judgments', *Organizational Influence Processes*, 58 (1951), pp. 295–303.
5. Bond, R. and Smith, P. B. 'Culture and conformity: A meta-analysis of studies using Asch's (1952b, 1956) line judgment task', *Psychological Bulletin*, 119(1) (1996), p. 111.
6. Drury, J., Novelli, D. and Stott, C. 'Managing to avert disaster: Explaining collective resilience at an outdoor music event', *European Journal of Social Psychology* (May 2015), p. 2.
7. Huxley, Aldous. *Brave New World Revisited*, Vintage Classics, 2004.
8. Jung, Carl Gustav. *The Undiscovered Self*, Routledge, 2002.
9. Avenanti, A., Sirigu, A. and Aglioti, S. M. 'Racial bias reduces empathic sensorimotor resonance with other-race pain', *Current Biology*, 20(11) (2010), pp. 1018–22.
10. Kuklinski, J. H. and Hurley, N. L. 'On hearing and interpreting political messages: A cautionary tale of citizen cue-taking', *The Journal of Politics*, 56(3) (1994), pp. 729–51.
11. Leman, P. J. and Cinnirella, M. 'Beliefs in conspiracy theories and the need for cognitive closure', *Frontiers in Psychology*, 4 (2013), p. 378.

12. Jung, Carl Gustav. *The Structure and Dynamics of the Psyche* (Collected Works of C. G. Jung), Routledge, 1970.
13. 'How to build a Net Zero society', Behavioural Insights Team, 25 January 2023.
14. 'Fix the Planet', *New Scientist* newsletter, April 2022.
15. 'Education Secretary puts climate change at the heart of education', gov.uk, November 2021.
16. Two metres of sea level rise (SLR) by the end of the century is far outside any plausible projection offered by the scientific consensus, as represented by the Intergovernmental Panel on Climate Change (IPCC). IPCC projections based on different economic and policy scenarios vary between about 30 mm and 1.1 metres SLR by 2100. However, belying these projections is a scientific debate about the rate at which seas are rising based on observations. Some estimates suggest a lower rate of around 1.4 mm per year, and some are higher at 3.6 mm/year. That is to say that the observed rate suggests an SLR of between 109 mm and 280 mm by 2100 – a much smaller range.
17. Lynas, M., Houlton, B. Z. and Perry, S. 'Greater than 99 per cent consensus on human-caused climate change in the peer-reviewed scientific literature', IOP Science *Environmental Research Letters*, 16 (October 2021).
18. 'More than 99.9% of studies agree: humans caused climate change', *Cornell Chronicle*, October 2021.
19. 'How mobilisation by climate-sceptic actors on Facebook during COP26 undermined the summit', Institute for Strategic Dialogue, November 2021.
20. 'Written evidence, Carnegie UK (CCE0010)', DCMS Select Committee, September 2021.
21. 'Covering scientific consensus: What to avoid and how to get it right', The Journalist's Resource, Harvard Kennedy School's Shorenstein Center on Media, Politics and Public Policy, November 2021.
22. 'BBC freezes out climate sceptics', *The Times*, September 2018.
23. Marks, E., Hickman, C., Pihkala, P., Clayton, S., Lewandowski, E. R., Mayall, E. E., Wray, B., Mellor, C. and van Susteren, L. 'Climate anxiety in children and young people and their beliefs about government responses to climate change: A global survey', *The Lancet Planetary Health*, December 2021.
24. Fraser, B. C., Sharman, R. and Nunn, P. D. 'Associations of locus of control, information processing style and anti-reflexivity with climate change scepticism in an Australian sample', *Public Understanding of Science* (2022), pp. 1–18.

25. 'Heroes of the environment 2008', *Time*.
26. Michael Shellenberger testimony to the House Committee on Oversight & Reform for a hearing on: 'Fueling the climate crisis: examining big oil's prices, profits, and pledges', 15 September 2022.
27. Alimonti, G., Mariani, L., Prodi, F. and Ricci, R. A. 'A critical assessment of extreme events trends in times of global warming', *The European Physical Journal Plus* (2021), p. 112.
28. 'World Climate Declaration. There is no climate emergency', Global Climate Intelligence Group, October 2022.
29. Centola, D., Becker, J., Brackbill, D. and Baronchelli, A. 'Experimental evidence for tipping points in social convention', *Science* (2018), pp. 1116–19.
30. Theory developed by Erica Chenoweth Professor of Public Policy at Harvard Kennedy School.
31. Quote by Steve Jobs from Apple's 'Think Different' TV commercial, 1997.
32. 'The revised psychology of human misjudgement', a talk given by Charlie Munger at Harvard Kennedy Business School in 1995.
33. Meerloo, Joost. *The Rape of the Mind: The Psychology of Thought Control, Menticide, and Brainwashing* (Vol. 118), World Publishing Company, 1956.
34. Zajenkowski, M., Jonason, P. K., Leniarska, M., and Kozakiewicz, Z. 'Who complies with the restrictions to reduce the spread of COVID-19?: Personality and perceptions of the COVID-19 situation', *Personality and Individual Differences*, 166 (2020), 110199.
35. Dear, K., Dutton, K. and Fox, E. 'Do "watching eyes" influence antisocial behavior? A systematic review & meta-analysis', *Evolution and Human Behavior*, 40(3) (2019), pp. 269–80.
36. 'Kubark counterintelligence interrogation', Central Intelligence Agency, July 1963; https://nsarchive2.gwu.edu/NSAEBB/NSAEBB122/CIA%20Kubark%201-60.pdf
37. Whelan, Zara. 'Two women fined £200 each for driving five miles to go for a walk in the park', *Manchester Evening News*, 2 January 2021; https://www.manchestereveningnews.co.uk/news/uk-news/two-women-fined-200-each-19591839
38. Sansome, Jessica. 'Police warn people to stay away from the Lake District during lockdown', *Manchester Evening News*, 2 March 2020; https://www.manchestereveningnews.co.uk/news/uk-news/police-warn-people-stay-away-17992135
39. Yeatman, Dominic. 'Police helicopter orders sunbathers in Australia to clear off beach during lockdown', *Metro*, 2 August

2021; https://metro.co.uk/2021/08/02/police-helicopter-orders-sunbathers-in-australia-to-clear-off-beach-15022501/

40. '95% of UK burglaries and robberies not solved, data suggests', *Guardian*, 2 June 2018; https://www.theguardian.com/uk-news/2018/jun/17/figures-less-than-5-of-burglaries-and-robberies-in-uk-solved
41. 'D-Day's parachuting dummies and inflatable tanks', Imperial War Museum; https://www.iwm.org.uk/history/d-days-parachuting-dummies-and-inflatable-tanks
42. 'The inner child and the nude politician', by Ursula K. Le Guin, published on ursulakleguin.com, October 2014.

16: Don't be a slave to sex

1. 'Operation Defensive Shield', *IDF*, 30 October 2017; https://www.idf.il/en/mini-sites/wars-and-operations/operation-defensive-shield/
2. 'Porn run on seized TV channels, say residents', *Sydney Morning Herald*, 2 April 2002; https://www.smh.com.au/world/middle-east/porn-run-on-seized-tv-channels-say-residents-20020401-gdf5uw.html
3. Bennet, James. 'Mideast turmoil: The fighting; As Israeli troops tighten grip, Bush says Arafat must do more to avert new terror attacks', *New York Times*, 2 March 2002; https://www.nytimes.com/2002/03/31/world/mideast-turmoil-fighting-israeli-troops-tighten-grip-bush-says-arafat-must-more.html
4. Friedman, Herbart. 'Looking back: Sex in psychological warfare', *British Psychological Society*, 20 January 2009; https://www.bps.org.uk/psychologist/looking-back-sex-psychological-warfare
5. Ibid.
6. Gottschall, J. 'Explaining wartime rape', *Journal of Sex Research*, 41(2) (2004), pp. 129–36.
7. 'Everything is about sex except sex. Sex is about power', *Quote Investigator*, 5 June 2018; https://quoteinvestigator.com/2018/06/05/sex-power/
8. Delgado, Kasia. 'This is what happens when a feminist spends the night in a hardcore fetish club', *Stylist*, 2 December 2016; https://www.stylist.co.uk/life/sex-spanking-suspenders-british-fetish-club-torture-garden-feminism-london/68004
9. Pitagora, D. 'No pain, no gain? Therapeutic and relational benefits of subspace in BDSM contexts', *Journal of Positive Sexuality*, 3(3) (2017), pp. 44–54.

10. Réage, Pauline. *Story of O*, Jean-Jacques Pauvert, 1954.
11. Fromm, Erich. *The Fear of Freedom*, Routledge, 2021.
12. Kranc, Lauren. 'How NXIVM seduced Hollywood stars and America's most powerful elite into a barbaric "sex cult"', *Esquire*, 2 October 2022; https://www.esquire.com/entertainment/tv/a33658764/what-is-nxivm-sex-cult-celebrities-stars-the-vow-hbo-true-story/
13. Carter, C. S. 'Oxytocin and sexual behavior', *Neuroscience & Biobehavioral Reviews*, 16(2) (1992), pp. 131–44.
14. Sukel, Kayt. 'Sex on the brain: Orgasms unlock altered consciousness', *New Scientist*, 2 May 2011; https://www.newscientist.com/article/mg21028124-600-sex-on-the-brain-orgasms-unlock-altered-consciousness
15. Huxley, Aldous. *Brave New World* (1932), Vintage Classics, 2007.
16. Orwell, George. *1984*, Secker & Warburg, 1949.
17. Reich, Wilhelm. *The Mass Psychology of Fascism*, Farrar, Straus and Giroux, 1946.
18. Kinzer, Stephen. *Poisoner in Chief: Sidney Gottlieb and the CIA Search for Mind Control*, New York, Henry Holt and Co., 2019.
19. Fleischman, D. S. 'An evolutionary behaviorist perspective on orgasm', *Socioaffective Neuroscience & Psychology*, 6(1) (2016), 32130.
20. MacKinnon, Catharine. *Only Words*, Harvard University Press, 1993.
21. Pfaus, J. G., Quintana, G. R., Mac Cionnaith, C. E., Gerson, C. A., Dubé, S. and Coria-Avila, G. A. 'Conditioning of sexual interests and paraphilias in humans is difficult to see, virtually impossible to test, and probably exactly how it happens: A comment on Hsu and Bailey (2020)', *Archives of Sexual Behavior*, 49(5) (2020), pp. 1403–7.
22. Rachman, S. 'Sexual fetishism: An experimental analogue', *Psychological Record*, 16 (1966), pp. 293–6.
23. Parent, N., Bond, T. A. and Shapka, J. D. 'Smartphones as attachment targets: An attachment theory framework for understanding problematic smartphone use', *Current Psychology* (2021), pp. 1–12.
24. Dodsworth, L. *Manhood: The Bare Reality*, Pinter & Martin, 2017.
25. Dodsworth, L. *Womanhood: The Bare Reality*, Pinter & Martin, 2019.
26. MacKinnon, Catharine, *Only Words*, Harvard University Press, 1993.

27. Wagemans, F., Brandt, M. J. and Zeelenberg, M. 'Disgust sensitivity is primarily associated with purity-based moral judgments', *Emotion*, 18(2) (2018), p. 277.
28. Long, X., Tian, F., Zhou, Y., Cheng, B., Yi, S. and Jia, Z. 'The neural correlates of sexual arousal and sexual disgust' (2019), Available at SSRN 3458493.
29. Similarweb, October 2022.
30. 'Can porn cause people to have gender dysphoria? (r/Pornfree)', in *Your Brain on Porn*; https://www.yourbrainonporn.com/rebooting-accounts/rebooting-accounts-page-3/do-you-guys-think-porn-can-cause-people-to-have-gender-dysphoria/
31. Chu, A. L. 'Did sissy porn make me trans?', *Queer Disruptions*, 2 (2018), pp. 1–12.
32. Park, B. Y., Wilson, G., Berger, J., Christman, M., Reina, B., Bishop, F., Klam, W. P. and Doan, A. P. 'Is internet pornography causing sexual dysfunctions? A review with clinical reports', *Behavioral Sciences*, 8(6) (2018), pp. 55.
33. Daspe, M. È., Vaillancourt-Morel, M. P., Lussier, Y., Sabourin, S. and Ferron, A. 'When pornography use feels out of control: The moderation effect of relationship and sexual satisfaction', *Journal of Sex & Marital Therapy*, 44(4) (2018), pp. 343–53.
34. Unwin, Joseph Daniel. *Sex and Culture*, Oxford University Press, 1934.
35. Cartner-Morley, Jess. 'Balenciaga apologises for ads featuring bondage bears and child abuse papers', *Guardian*, 2 November 2022; https://www.theguardian.com/fashion/2022/nov/29/balenciaga-apologises-for-ads-featuring-bondage-bears-and-child-abuse-papers
36. Milton, Josh. 'Who is Giorgia Meloni – the far right candidate set to be Italy's first female PM?', *Metro*, 2 September 2022; https://metro.co.uk/2022/09/26/who-is-giorgia-meloni-the-far-right-candidate-set-to-be-italys-pm-17449122/
37. 'Putin signs law expanding Russia's rules against "LGBT propaganda"', Reuters, 2 December 2022; https://www.reuters.com/world/europe/putin-signs-law-expanding-russias-rules-against-lgbt-propaganda-2022-12-05/

17: Choose your illusion

1. Hergovich, A., Schott, R. and Burger, C. 'Biased evaluation of abstracts depending on topic and conclusion: Further evidence of a confirmation bias within scientific psychology', *Current Psychology*, 29(3) (2010), pp. 188–209.

2. Gal, D. and Rucker, D. D. 'Experimental validation bias limits the scope and ambition of applied behavioural science', *Nature Reviews Psychology*, 1(1) (2022), pp. 5–6.
3. Griffin, Louise. 'Good Morning Britain hit with 145 Ofcom complaints over Richard Madeley's "misogynistic" interview', *Metro*, 2 July 2021; https://metro.co.uk/2021/07/07/good-morning-britain-hit-with-complaints-over-richard-madeley-interview-14888216/
4. Duarte, J. L., Crawford, J. T., Stern, C., Haidt, J., Jussim, L. and Tetlock, P. E. 'Political diversity will improve social psychological science', *Behavioral and Brain Sciences*, 38 (2015), pp. 1–58.
5. Huxley, Aldous. *Brave New World Revisited*, Vintage Classics, 2004.
6. Kozinets, R. V. 'Can consumers escape the market? Emancipatory illuminations from Burning Man', *Journal of Consumer Research*, 29(1) (2002), pp. 20–38.
7. Baudrillard, J. and Lancelin, A. 'The Matrix decoded: Le Nouvel Observateur interview with Jean Baudrillard', *International Journal of Baudrillard Studies*, 1(2) (2004).
8. Ross, L. and Ward, A. 'Naive realism in everyday life: Implications for social conflict and misunderstanding', *Values and Knowledge* (1996), pp. 103–35.
9. Kahan, D. M., Hoffman, D. A., Braman, D. and Evans, D. 'They saw a protest: Cognitive illiberalism and the speech–conduct distinction', *Stanford Law Review*, 64 (2012), p. 851.
10. Frankovic, Kathy. 'More Americans think Kyle Rittenhouse should be convicted than say he will be', YouGov America, 2 November 2021; https://today.yougov.com/topics/politics/articles-reports/2021/11/18/kyle-rittenhouse-perception-guilt-poll
11. Smith, Matthew. 'Is BBC News pro-Brexit or anti-Brexit?', YouGov, 2 February 2018; https://yougov.co.uk/topics/politics/articles-reports/2018/02/22/bbc-news-pro-brexit-or-anti-brexit
12. Nickerson, R. S. 'Confirmation bias: A ubiquitous phenomenon in many guises', *Review of General Psychology*, 2(2) (1998), pp. 175–220.
13. Karlsson, N., Loewenstein, G. and Seppi, D. 'The ostrich effect: Selective attention to information', *Journal of Risk and Uncertainty*, 38(2) (2009), pp. 95–115.
14. Törnberg, P. 'How digital media drive affective polarization through partisan sorting', *Proceedings of the National Academy of Sciences*, 119(42) (2022), e2207159119.

15. Tokita, C. K., Guess, A. M. and Tarnita, C. E. 'Polarized information ecosystems can reorganize social networks via information cascades', *Proceedings of the National Academy of Sciences*, 118(50) (2021), e2102147118.
16. Sanders, Linley. 'Americans are less likely to have friends of very different political opinions compared to 2016', YouGov America, 2 October 2020; https://today.yougov.com/topics/politics/articles-reports/2020/10/06/friends-different-politics-poll
17. Rothschild, Neal. 'Young Dems more likely to despise the other party', Axios, 2 December 2021; https://www.axios.com/2021/12/08/poll-political-polarization-students
18. Raab, M. H., Ortlieb, S. A., Auer, N., Guthmann, K. and Carbon, C. C. 'Thirty shades of truth: Conspiracy theories as stories of individuation, not of pathological delusion', *Frontiers in Psychology*, 4 (2013), pp. 406.
19. van Prooijen, J. W. 'Psychological benefits of believing conspiracy theories', *Current Opinion in Psychology* (2022), 101352.
20. Rayner, K. 'The gaze-contingent moving window in reading: Development and review', *Visual Cognition*, 22(3–4) (2014), pp. 242–58.
21. Felin, T., Koenderink, J. and Krueger, J. I. 'Rationality, perception, and the all-seeing eye', *Psychonomic Bulletin & Review*, 24(4) (2017), pp. 1040–59.
22. Loftus, E. F. and Palmer, J. C. 'Reconstruction of automobile destruction: An example of the interaction between language and memory', *Journal of Verbal Learning and Verbal Behavior*, 13(5) (1974), pp. 585–9.
23. Epictetus and Lebell, Sharon. *Art of Living: The Classical Manual on Virtue, Happiness, and Effectiveness (Plus)*, HarperOne, 2007.
24. Braghieri, L., Levy, R. E. and Makarin, A. 'Social media and mental health', *American Economic Review*, 112(11) (2022), pp. 3660–93.
25. Boukes, M. and Vliegenthart, R. 'News consumption and its unpleasant side effect: Studying the effect of hard and soft news exposure on mental well-being over time', *Journal of Media Psychology: Theories, Methods, and Applications*, 29(3) (2017), p. 137.
26. Sirgy, M. J., Gurel-Atay, E., Webb, D., Cicic, M., Husic, M., Ekici, A. and Johar, J. S. 'Linking advertising, materialism, and life satisfaction', *Social Indicators Research*, 107(1) (2012), pp. 79–101.
27. Marks, E., Hickman, C., Pihkala, P., Clayton, S., Lewandowski, E. R., Mayall, E. E. and van Susteren, L. 'Young people's voices

on climate anxiety, government betrayal and moral injury: A global phenomenon', working paper (2021).
28. Lomborg, Bjorn. 'Believe it or not, the world is getting better. We just don't hear about it', *The Herald*, 2 October 2022; https://www.heraldscotland.com/opinion/23039603.believe-not-world-getting-better-just-dont-hear/
29. Peterkin, A. and Grewal, S. 'Bibliotherapy: The therapeutic use of fiction and poetry in mental health', *International Journal of Person Centered Medicine*, 7(3) (2018), p. 175.
30. Epton, T., Harris, P. R., Kane, R., van Koningsbruggen, G. M. and Sheeran, P. 'The impact of self-affirmation on health-behavior change: A meta-analysis', *Health Psychology*, 34(3) (2015), p. 187.

19: Stop haunting yourself

1. Dodsworth, Laura. *A State of Fear: How the UK Weaponised Fear During the Covid-19 Pandemic*, Pinter & Martin (2021); interview with Darren, pp. 14–16.
2. Seneca. *Letters from a Stoic: Epistulae Morales ad Lucilium*, Penguin Classics, 2004.
3. Burleigh, L., Jiang, X. and Greening, S. G. 'Fear in the theater of the mind: Differential fear conditioning with imagined stimuli', *Psychological Science*, 33(9) (2022), pp. 1423–39.
4. 'How covert agents infiltrate the internet to manipulate, deceive, and destroy reputations', The Intercept, 24 February 2014; https://theintercept.com/2014/02/24/jtrig-manipulation/
5. 'The art of deception', ACLU, no date; https://www.aclu.org/sites/default/files/assets/the_art_of_deception_training_for_online_covert_operations_0.pdf
6. Smyth, Denis. *'Brief Encounter', Deathly Deception: The Real Story of Operation Mincemeat*, Oxford Academic, 2011.
7. Alexander, C. 'Coronavirus propaganda – reflections on an episode of mass self-haunting', essay on blog.
8. Vicol, D-O. 'Who is most likely to believe and to share misinformation?', Dr Dora-Olivia Vicol, Full Fact, February 2020.
9. Edwards, P. T., Smith, B. P., McArthur, M. L. and Hazel, S. J., 'Fearful fido: Investigating dog experience in the veterinary context in an effort to reduce distress', *Applied Animal Behaviour Science*, 213 (2019), pp. 14–25.
10. Frank, Brieanna, J. 'Fact check: COVID-19 caused by a virus, not snake venom', *USA Today*, 2 May 2022; https://eu.usatoday.com/

story/news/factcheck/2022/05/15/fact-check-covid-19-caused-virus-not-snake-venom/9590087002/
11. Nietzsche, F. *Human, All Too Human – A Book for Free Spirits.* Translated by M. Faber, with S. Lehmann, University of Nebraska Press, 1985.
12. Packard, V. *The Hidden Persuaders*, Ig Publishing, 2007.
13. 'Gun sellers' message to Americans: Man up', *New York Times*, June 2022.
14. Greene, Robert. *The 48 Laws of Power*, Penguin, 2000.
15. Stajano, F. and Wilson, P. 'Understanding scam victims: Seven principles for systems security', *Communications of the ACM*, 54(3) (2011), pp. 70–5.
16. Griskevicius, V. and Kenrick, D. T. 'Fundamental motives: How evolutionary needs influence consumer behavior', *Journal of Consumer Psychology*, 23(3) (2013), pp. 372–86.
17. St Augustine of Hippo. *The City of God*, Hendrickson, 2009.
18. 'Typical and avoidant love addicts: How to break the toxic cycle of love addiction', Johnny Cassell blog, February 2022.
19. Dostoyevsky, F. *The Possessed* or *The Devils*, first published in the journal *The Russian Messenger* in 1871–72.
20. Grossmann, I., Dorfman, A., Oakes, H., Santos, H. C., Vohs, K. D. and Scholer, A. A. 'Training for wisdom: The distanced-self-reflection diary method', *Psychological Science*, 32(3) (2021), pp. 381–94.
21. Ibid.

20: Stand for something or fall for anything

1. Becker, Ernest. *The Denial of Death*, Free Press, 1973.
2. 'Understanding terror management theory', Psych Central; https://psychcentral.com/health/terror-management-theory#sub-theories
3. 'What's with all the toilet paper hoarding?', Ernest Becker Foundation; https://ernestbecker.org/this-mortal-life/covid-19/in-the-news/
4. Wilson, T. D., Reinhard, D. A., Westgate, E. C., Gilbert, D. T., Ellerbeck, N., Hahn, C. and Shaked, A. 'Just think: The challenges of the disengaged mind', *Science*, 345(6192) (2014), pp. 75–7.
5. Pascal, Blaise. *Pensées* (1670), Penguin Classics, 1995.
6. Arndt, J., Solomon, S., Kasser, T. and Sheldon, K. M. 'The urge to splurge: A terror management account of materialism and consumer behavior', *Journal of Consumer Psychology*, 14(3) (2004), pp. 198–212.

7. Nunes, J. C., Drèze, X. and Han, Y. J. 'Conspicuous consumption in a recession: Toning it down or turning it up?', *Journal of Consumer Psychology*, 21(2) (2011), pp. 199–205.
8. Chesterton, Gilbert Keith. *The Well and the Shallows* (1935), Ignatius Press, 2007.
9. Zawadzka, A. M., Borchet, J., Iwanowska, M. and Lewandowska-Walter, A. 'Can self-esteem help teens resist unhealthy influence of materialistic goals promoted by role models?', *Frontiers in Psychology* (2022), p. 5724.
10. Koller, M., Floh, A., Zauner, A. and Rusch, T. 'Persuasibility and the self – Investigating heterogeneity among consumers', *Australasian Marketing Journal (AMJ)*, 21(2) (2013), pp. 94–104.
11. Achenreiner, G. B. 'Materialistic values and susceptibility to influence in children', *ACR North American Advances* (1997).
12. Cartwright, R. F., Opree, S. J. and van Reijmersdal, E. A. '"Fool's gold": Linking materialism to persuasion knowledge activation and susceptibility to embedded advertising', *Advances in Advertising Research IX* (2018), pp. 17–28.
13. Zimbardo, Philip. *The Lucifer Effect: How Good People Turn Evil*, Random House, 2011.
14. Upadhye, B., Sivakumaran, B., Pradhan, D. and Lyngdoh, T. 'Can planning prompt be a boon for impulsive customers? Moderating roles of product category and decisional procrastination', *Psychology & Marketing*, 38(8) (2021), pp. 1197–1219.
15. Jung, Carl Gustav. *Memories, Dreams, Reflections*, Random House, 1973.
16. Jung, Carl Gustav. *The Undiscovered Self*, Routledge, 2002.
17. Fromm, Erich. *The Art of Loving: The Centennial Edition*, A. & C. Black, 2000.
18. Hoffer, Eric. *The True Believer: Thoughts on the Nature of Mass Movements*, HarperCollins, 2011.
19. 'What declining birth rates mean for our future', *The Week*, 2 October 2022; https://www.theweek.co.uk/news/society/958081/what-declining-birth-rates-mean-for-our-future
20. 'Lateral flow tests for pregnant people and support partners', East Lancashire Hospitals Trust; https://elht.nhs.uk/about-us/coronavirus-covid-19-guidance/maternity/lateral-flow
21. Bernstein, Brittany. 'Black Lives Matter removes language about disrupting the nuclear family from website', Yahoo! News, 2 September 2020; https://news.yahoo.com/black-lives-matter-removes-language-185621063.html

22. Booth, William. 'England and Wales no longer majority Christian nations, census reveals', *The Washington Post*, 2 November 2022; https://www.washingtonpost.com/world/2022/11/29/uk-religion-census-christian/
23. Chapman, Ben. 'Richard Branson backs universal basic income joining Mark Zuckerberg and Elon Musk', *Independent*, 2 August 2017; https://www.independent.co.uk/news/business/news/richard-branson-universal-basic-income-mark-zuckerberg-elon-musk-virgin-ceo-a7911866.html
24. 'San Francisco launches new guaranteed income program for trans community', SF.gov, 2 November 2022; https://sf.gov/news/san-francisco-launches-new-guaranteed-income-program-trans-community
25. 'Youth misspent: Uncovering the harsh realities for Britain's young people in today's job market', City and Guilds, December 2022.
26. Kilander, Gustaf. 'Canadian woman, 31, who applied for assisted suicide pauses request after well-wishers donate $65k to her', *Independent*, 2 June 2022; https://www.independent.co.uk/news/world/americas/assisted-suicide-canada-toronto-gofundme-b2091802.html
27. Trachtenberg, A. J. and Manns, B. 'Cost analysis of medical assistance in dying in Canada', *Canadian Medical Association Journal*, 189(3) (2017), E101–E105.
28. Campbell, Hayley. 'In the future, your body won't be buried … you'll dissolve', *Wired*, 2 August 2017; https://www.wired.co.uk/article/alkaline-hydrolysis-biocremation-resomation-water-cremation-dissolving-bodies
29. Getahun, Hannah. 'Cannibals with a conscience rejoice: Fake human meat burgers are here', Insider, 2 July 2022; https://www.insider.com/oumph-fake-human-meat-burger-winning-awards-cannes-lions-festival-2022-7
30. Capoot, Ashley. 'Elon Musk shows off updates to his brain chips and says he's going to install one in himself when they are ready', CNBC, 2 December 2022; https://www.cnbc.com/2022/12/01/elon-musks-neuralink-makes-big-claims-but-experts-are-skeptical-.html
31. 'Yuval Noah Harari: Humans are now hackable animals', CNN, 2 November 2019; https://www.cnn.com/videos/world/2019/11/26/yuval-noah-harari-interview-anderson-vpx.cnn
32. Twitter, 8 October 2022; https://twitter.com/reddit_lies/status/1578745278622232578
33. Seneca. *Letters from a Stoic: Epistulae Morales ad Lucilium*, Penguin Classics, 2004.

34. Zách, L. 'Catholicism and anti-communism: The reactions of Irish intellectuals to revolutionary changes in Hungary (1918–1939)', *Diacronie. Studi di Storia Contemporanea*, 33(1) (2018), pp. 1–23.
35. Johnson, A. and Densley, J. 'Rio's new social order: How religion signals disengagement from prison gangs', *Qualitative Sociology*, 41(2) (2018), pp. 243–62.
36. Wiseman, J. P. 'Sober time: The neglected variable in the recidivism of alcoholic persons', in *Proceedings of the 2nd Annual Alcoholism Conference*, NIAAA (1973), pp. 165–84.
37. Sargant, William. *Battle for the Mind: A Physiology of Conversion and Brainwashing*, Greenwood Press, 1975.

Conclusion

1. Nietzsche, F. *Jenseits von Gut und Böse* (1886), ch. 4, p. 146.
2. 'Devotions Upon Emergent Occasions, and severall steps in my Sicknes', a sermon by John Donne, 1624.

Acknowledgements

Writing a book is not a solitary endeavour. In this case, it was not even a two-person endeavour. We would like to thank a myriad of kind people who helped us in various ways.

We would like to extend our gratitude to Joel Simons and the publishing team at HarperCollins for believing in this book.

We can't say enough about Laura's patient, dedicated and creative agent, Rory Scarfe at The Blair Partnership. You saved our minds.

We are indebted to our families for their unwavering support. Our heartfelt thanks go to Dominic and Jasmine, our patient partners.

To the many people we interviewed: thank you. You are either named within the book or anonymous, but you know who you are. Your expertise and generosity were vital to the book.

Finally, we would like to thank our readers for giving us the opportunity to share our ideas with you. Your minds are wondrous. Let them be free.